THE LITTLE ALIEN WHO MIGHT

Bibix calmed himself. He reached for the small bomb on his desk. Grasping it with two hands, he lowered his head and bent his eyestalks to examine it closely. A wicked thought filled his mind.

He stood up and went to the south wall of his office. Laying a hand on a row of prefabricated panels, he closed his eyes just for a moment. Veknar might still be in its office. It was a creature of habit that disliked leaving its office for trivial matters. It would still be in there, sitting behind its desk, being arrogant.

"There's nothing in here I'm going to miss," he mumbled.

Bibix pulled the arming tape off the device and flipped the trigger tab into its upright, locked position. Giving it a full turn, he pressed the activator button and laid the charge on the floor with its rounded top facing the wall. Then he left his office at a quick walk.

OTHER FICTION BY JUSTIN OLDHAM

Novels

Haven's Legacy

Search for Haven

Crisis at the Kodiak Starport

Showdown at the Kodiak Starport

Anthologies

Before the Collapse

During the Collapse

After the Collapse

Tales from the Kodiak Starport

Bibix

Justin Oldham

**Shadow Fusion LLC
Anchorage**

Copyright © 2011 Justin Oldham.

All rights reserved under International and Pan American copyright laws.

Published in the United States of America by Shadow Fusion LLC.

Visit us at http://www.shadowfusionbooks.com.

Cover photo: NASA

This is a work of fiction. Names, characters, places, and situations are either the product of the author's imagination or used fictitiously. Any similarity to any person (living or dead), entity, location, or event is entirely coincidental.

ISBN 978-1-935964-75-9

Chapter 1

"You've got to be kidding." Carl tossed the partially assembled weapon from one hand to the other as he regarded his bulbous benefactor. The unhealthy pallor of his skin, along with his sunken eyes, hinted at malnutrition and exposure to extreme weather conditions. The air in the dilapidated house smelled of rotten wood.

"I rescued you. You've got to help me." Bibix looked up at the human, grimacing as he forced both of his eyestalks together. His large, green eyes moved closer to each other as he made an effort to form a stern gaze. At a mere four feet six inches in height,

2 | Bibix

his gray, hairless body couldn't possibly adopt any pose that would be threatening to the six foot tall human, and he knew it. His eyes, and the displeasure they conveyed, were all he had to work with.

The surly man shifted slowly in his chair. "These weapons were old before I went into cryo. Where did you get these things from, a museum?"

The Lapropod tried not to show his frustration. "Yes, Captain Tippet. It's where I work, so that's where I got them."

Carl grunted and sighed. His dirty camouflage uniform hung in rags. He scraped his muddy boots across the splintered floor. "I'm good, but I'm not that good. No way."

Bibix started to shake with anger. He gestured with all four spindly arms as he talked. "I read your service record. You're the best we had in storage. I've seen you on video. You used these weapons all the time."

Tippet remained unmoved. "I'm grateful for being thawed out. I really am. It's quite the brave new world you've got here. But, hey, I'm just one man. Do you know what my ten years of military service got me? A lungful of genetically engineered cancer, which your scientists deliberately used as a weapon. That, and my fabulous war record, is why they put me in the freezer, you know."

Bibix tried to reason with the smelly man. "The decision to use bioweapons is still being talked about by my people. I'm sorry my ancestors invaded your world. I know you don't believe me, but it really was an accident. I wasn't even born when it happened.

4 | Bibix

"Your own people are in this, too," he continued. "Even if you don't want to help my kind, help your own. Those troops you saw in the city? Ha! You don't know the half of it! Those aren't just police, or peacekeepers, or whatever you'd like to call them. They're meat inspectors."

Tippet's recollection was fuzzy. He put the broken gun on the table and shook his unkempt head. "I get it. Okay? I get it. I've heard every word, you little freak."

Bibix cringed. "There's no need for that."

Carl scratched at the grit in his beard as fading light from the afternoon sun fell on his scarred face and neck. "I've paid close attention to everything you gave me to read. I get it. Even if I did want to help you – which I don't – it wouldn't make a whit of difference. I saw their weapons and that armor.

Those guys have their act together. And they're friggin' huge, in case you didn't notice."

"The NorCons aren't anything like us," Bibix replied. "They kill for fun. They eat anything with red blood, including us. They think my people taste terrible, but it doesn't seem to slow them down very much."

He pressed on when the agitated human didn't respond. "Your technology almost defeated us, Captain. I've read more than a hundred accounts of our arrival. We weren't prepared for your exceptional tool use or your creativity under adverse conditions. It's been sixty years since you were frozen. Our people never have absorbed the lessons that period should have taught us. That's why the NorCons have done so well against us. They showed up fifteen years ago. We held out for less than three months. That's nothing compared to the amount of time your

6 | Bibix

people fought back against us. You and your skills can help me beat them."

Tippet held up his emaciated wrist to indicate the translator band. "You guys didn't have any problems coming up with this. If you can make a language translator, you can make your own weapons. You can learn how to use them, too." He paused. "You said you had the cure for my cancer. Give it to me or put me back in the tube. Being on display in somebody's history annex is better than getting involved in this."

Bibix waggled a trio of fingers. "They've got to know you're out by now. If I take you back, they'll just eat you, the same way your kind used to devour aged cheese and wine. 'Mm, Twenty-First Century human warrior.' They'll think you're yummy."

Carl bent over in the semidarkness to rest his arms on the rickety table. "Give me the cure, then. I'll take my chances in the wilderness. We lost to you. Now it's you're turn. If your people hadn't been so quick to pounce, we might be in this as allies."

"Can't you and I be friends and allies now?" Bibix asked hopefully.

The question made the ailing soldier laugh. "On the way out here, you kept going on about how the invasion wasn't really an invasion. Honestly, I don't care. Call yourselves refugees from a dying world if you like, but the facts speak for themselves. No warnings. No effort to communicate. All ten billion of you fell out of the sky one day and—"

"I told you a dozen times, we had no way of knowing how small this world was! Our telescopes still aren't as good as yours were. Our sun was failing. We had

8 | Bibix

to leave while we still could. Finding your planet was just too good to be true. It was our only chance, and we took it. Our ships and FTL drives were built in great haste. There simply wasn't time to build for anything beyond a one-way trip." He paused. "Look, if you won't help fight, then show me how to use these…things."

Tippet snorted. Looking down at the Lapropod, he tried to imagine the squishy little fellow decked out in combat gear. "Thirteen years, Bibix. That's how long we held out against you guys before I went into cryo. I don't know exact figures, but I do know we capped a lot of you little buggers."

"Three billion," Bibix retorted, hiding his disappointment. The old wives' tale that said you couldn't bargain with humans appeared to be true.

Carl remained unfazed. "My father used to tell me what life was like before the invasion. I was ten when it started, so I don't remember much before that. Finding and killing you guys is all I know how to do. I've never done anything else. Even the cancer couldn't keep me off the battlefield. Not at first, anyway. Then one day I started coughing up blood, and…here I am. No, Bibs, it's your turn. Live and die by your own hand, you little freak. We did. Now, give me the cure or I'll wring your scrawny neck."

"We don't have fragile necks," Bibix pronounced, as if advertising his typical Lapropodian neck, short and thick, as being an advantage.

Sitting forward, Tippet's chair groaned under his weight. "You're stubborn."

10 | Bibix

"I'm in a difficult position, Captain. Violence comes naturally to your people and the NorCons. I can't relate to it, so I need somebody to teach me."

Carl swore. "Every instinct I have is telling me to kill you and move on. I wouldn't expect a turd like you to understand. You're just one. One! You don't speak for the rest of your kind. Everything you've said could be a lie. I'm not going to take you seriously until I've seen what's out there for myself."

Bibix clasped all four of his hands in grim perseverance. "Show me how to use these guns and I'll do the rest myself."

The man shook his head fiercely. "It's just not that simple. Weapons are only part of what you need to have any hope of winning."

Bibix thought he understood. "Bullets? Power packs? We've got all that back at the museum. I've spent most of my adult life taking care of those exhibits. We have enough in long-term storage to fight a dozen battles."

Tippet coughed, scrunching his shoulders in pain. He licked a drop of blood from his lower lip. "Weapons and supplies don't mean a thing without tactics and the understanding that what you're doing is taking life, pure and simple."

The observation sobered Bibix. "I've watched nearly two thousand hours of video – stuff your news crews and biographers left behind. I think I understand the taking of life. Tell me about tactics."

A gust of wind shook the old house. Carl brushed falling plaster from his thick, matted hair and looked down at his faded uniform. The pain in his chest faded.

"Books," he mumbled.

Shuffling on all four pods, Bibix tried to coax more details from the human. "Yes. Most of the libraries have been kept intact. There's a popular theory going around that each of your nations hid or destroyed the really good stuff, before…you know. I suppose that explains the saying, 'Small world, small brain.' Ha."

Tippet let the unintended insult pass. He was in over his head, and he knew it. "First you, and now the new conquerors. It seems like everybody's way ahead of us puny humans. Nah, my dad was right. We had our chance and we didn't make the cut. Look, Bibs, give me something to write with. I'm gonna clue you into a few authors who can tell you all about tactics."

The Lapropod laid one hand over his translator band. "In some of your languages, my name translates to something that relates to computers. In my tongue, it means grateful, gratitude, or a good gesture. 'Bibs,' as my translator band conveys it, sounds like 'dangerous.' Are you mocking me?"

Carl flicked some dust off his sleeve. "This translator thing is no fun for me, either. I get just enough of what you say to stay in the loop. I wasn't mocking you before, but I will now. Trust me, Bibs, the last thing you are is dangerous."

Rummaging through his day sack, Bibix gave the cagey man a writing box and a stylus. "I'll never understand why my own people never had the good sense to form our own army. If we had—"

Tippet smirked. "You might be where I am now."

14 | Bibix

"Point taken." Bibix waited quietly while the human wrote.

Out in the overgrown yard, birds chirped and flitted from tree to tree. Carl tried not to think about how the wind reminded him of a faraway, crying woman. "Before I give you this, I want the cure. If I'm gonna be on the lam, I should at least be healthy."

"We have a deal, then? The cure in exchange for showing me how to use these weapons, and your notes?"

"Agreed." Tippet handed over the writing box with a smile.

"My pen? I'm always lending pens and never getting them back."

"Sure." The tired man erupted into a series of long, painful coughs and handed the stylus over.

Bibix went back to his day sack and returned with a pair of large injectors. "I got this from a friend who works at one of the NorCon processing centers. I told him it was for one of my bosses, who was buying humans off the black market. It's an updated formula, based on something we brought with us from the home world. It must be good. They use it on fifty thousand humans a day."

Carl didn't ask about the black market or the processing plant. The prospect of relieving the pain in his chest was powerful enough to drive away his fear of gulags. In his misery, the idea of being somebody else's food wasn't quite real.

Bibix read the instructions on the syringes. "Use the whole thing. You should only need one, but I brought two just to be sure. Here." Giving Tippet both injectors, he explained their use and moved out of the way.

"So, where exactly are we?" Carl asked as he rolled up his sleeve.

"Polar region. This town used to be called Anchorage."

The man looked up. "Sounds like we're still in Alaska. What city did we come from?"

Bibix waited for Tippet to inject himself. "As I said, it was called Anchorage. The NorCons built a new settlement near here, using forced labor gangs. That's where I live and work. When the NorCons came fifteen years ago—"

"Right. How long does this medicine take to work?" Tippet grimaced as the drug set fire to his veins.

Bibix shrugged. "For us, about ten minutes. For you, an hour, or maybe two. It's common for humans to be sleepless for a day or two after the drug kicks in. It's doctor stuff."

Carl struggled to cope with the rising pain that crept into every part of his body. "How is it you work in a museum when the NorCons banned all things human?"

The Lapropod snickered. "They like their trophies. After they rounded up the humans, they put most of us to work building their settlements. We're not good laborers, so they didn't make us go underground. We gathered up all the human things we could find and they divided them up amongst their invasion force commanders. Trophies. That's what they call all the stuff they keep in their museums."

Tippet examined the empty syringe and set it on the table. "Anyone know you're out here? I know you must have thought this through, but I have to ask."

Bibix raised and lowered his eyes in a gesture signifying sneakiness. "I'm on vacation. I haven't taken a day off in five years. My boss practically ordered me to go after I made a few 'mistakes' that weren't really mistakes. I snuck in after hours and rolled you right out the back door when the night guard wasn't looking. Getting your cryo tube into the back of my lev was harder but, as you say, here we are."

Carl laughed. "I've never been stolen property before."

Bibix smiled widely. "Naturally, I'll be shocked when I go back to work. All for show, of course. The NorCons believe in private property. We have a more community-based outlook on such things."

Absorbing what he had been told, Tippet's mind raced with new questions as his muscles ached. "You did say fifteen years, right? What are the NorCons like without their armor?"

Bibix folded all of his hands over his smooth chest. "Nobody knows. Bipedal, like you. Their hands have three fingers and opposable thumbs. They remind me of claws. Seven feet tall, on the average. They seem to be both sexes in the same body, or possibly they are genderless. They can't breathe this planet's air without adjusting the pressure. Nitrogen seems to be their preferred gas to breathe. We've never seen children or young adults. Inside their administrative facilities, offices, and homes, our kind has to wear life support gear. Even then, the NorCons don't take the armor off. Popular gossip says they could be from a heavier gravity world. We speculate that this is a very hostile environment for them."

"Good observations," Carl nodded.

"We may have surrendered sooner than your kind did, but we're still observant."

"How very French of you." Tippet leaned on one elbow, playing with the second syringe.

Bibix glanced at the translator band on one of his own wrists. "That's a nationality. I'm not sure I understand the reference."

Carl snorted. "Never mind. None of that matters now. It probably never will again."

He spent the next two hours going over the oddball collection of guns that Bibix had plundered from the back rooms of his trophy hall.

As a people, Lapropods had no concept of weaponry. Their tool use was confined to entirely non-offensive endeavors. When threatened, they would fight, using sheer numbers and determination to overwhelm the foe. This was a fact Carl knew all too well.

He rearranged Bibix's arms to cradle a patched-together gauss repeater. "No, like this. Hold it up so you can look all the way down the barrel. The most important thing about this weapon, for you, is the lack of recoil. Check your battery pack, then point and shoot. Once you learn how to use the sights, you'll do just fine. Take it out some place remote and plink around."

22 | Bibix

Bibix looked from the gun to his teacher. "Excuse me? 'Plink?' I'm not sure the translators are interpreting that word correctly. Did you just say p-l-i-n-k, plink?"

Carl glared at the device on his wrist. "Did I say something that actually offended you?"

Bibix laughed when he realized Carl didn't understand what the translator had said. "Yes. Very rude."

The man tapped the black device. "What does it mean, when you hear it?"

The Lapropod pulled himself together. "Roughly translated, it means that you have sex with your mother."

Carl smirked, and then shrugged. "Sorry. It's my first alien swear word. Look, you need to take this stuff out where nobody can see or hear you and practice with it. Shoot stuff. Get used to it. Then read those books I told you about. I mean, if you can."

Bibix put his weapon on safety and shuffled over to the table, where he set it down. "As a museum curator, I read English, Spanish, and German without electronic help. The hard part will be getting the books." He thought for a moment. "If I can tie them into a few of the exhibits, I should be able to read them on the job, right in front of my bosses."

Tippet sat down and took a long drink from a water bottle. "All right, you little freak, don't get cocky. I don't care what that word means to you, just don't do it. Don't do anything out of the ordinary in front of the NorCons. Don't give them any reason to suspect you. If these guys are predators, they'll be looking for any sign of disloyalty."

24 | Bibix

Bibix thought about that. "Deception. Hmm. Yes."

Carl gestured at the gloomy interior of the house. "Do you own this place?"

The Lapropod glanced at long cobwebs hanging from the ceiling. "No. It's abandoned. The structures are still here, but anything worth taking is gone."

Tipped emptied his water bottle. "Sounds good. Don't take any of this gear home with you. Bury it. Make multiple caches. If you take more loot from the museum, be sure to make it look like a robbery or a mistake in bookkeeping."

Bibix liked that idea. "An error in bookkeeping? That's dangerous. The brutes who own these trophy halls fight over them. I'm told it's a common practice on their home world. They steal from each other all the time. It shames me to admit that my own people carry out some of these thefts. It'll be better to make it look like that has happened. I won't have any trouble covering my tracks."

Carl looked out the nearest window at the setting sun. "If this is Alaska, it must be summer. Do they fight over their loot up here?"

Bibix had to think about that. "There was a fight three years ago. Some place called Fairbanks. I forget the NorCon name for the town. I didn't pay attention at the time. Now that you mention it, I think they were having it out over a trophy hall."

Tippet unwrapped a sandwich and started eating. He gagged. "What is this?"

Bibix shrugged. "It's what they feed humans. The bread was my idea. How is it?"

26 | Bibix

"If you have to ask, you don't want to know." Tippet grunted and forced the food down.

The Lapropod watched with interest. "If it's that bad, why are you eating it?"

Carl finished wolfing down the sandwich and reached for a fresh water bottle. "My last meal before they put me in cryo was peanut butter on a stick. Food was pretty scarce in my day, thanks to you guys. I learned to eat anything I could get past my tongue."

Bibix shuddered, feeling bad about his own extravagant eating habits. "I'm sorry. I didn't think. When we crowded you out, we really messed things up, even if there are some Earth foods that we can't eat. For what it's worth, my grandfather tells me that the food on Earth is much better than where we came from."

Carl burped. "Great. We taste good and we can cook. What a deal. I need air."

Tippet got to his feet, taking one of the plasma rifles with him. Bibix scooped up his gauss repeater and followed. The two went through the wrecked home, out into the back yard.

Chapter 2

Kicking loose gravel with the toes of his ruined combat boots, the troubled soldier squinted at the setting sun. Spying an apple tree, he slung his weapon and walked over to it.

Bibix sat on a small, marble bench nearby. "That fruit is poisonous to Lapropods."

"It has always been thus." Tippet picked a small red apple. Raising it in a mock toast, he bit it in half. He chewed slowly, relishing the taste.

Bibix approved. "That's a biblical reference. I didn't know you were so well-read."

"That's why they made me an officer. I read. I write. If the NorCons catch me, they'll sell me by the slice." He finished his apple and reached for another.

"Just one more reason why you should help me."

Tippet shook his head as he ate the second apple. "Nope. Come over here. Let me show you how to change clips on that thing and we'll do some target practice."

Bibix cradled the stubby black weapon in two of his hands. "I'm glad you're seeing this my way. To be honest, I wasn't sure if I'd done the right thing. You scare me."

Carl cradled the battered plasma rifle as if it were an extension of his own body. "These things are tools. They can gather dust if you leave them hanging on the wall, or they can be used. Tell me, Bibs, what made a little guy like you decide to get militant?"

The question was unsettling to the Lapropod. He shuffled further into the yard. The orange glow from the setting sun made his eyes water. "My people had no natural predators before they came to Earth. What you think of as passivity is our way of life. It may sound silly to you, but we thought of ourselves as the only intelligent life in the universe."

Tippet followed Bibix, swinging his gun on its shoulder strap. "My parents and teachers said the same thing. I can't tell you much about it, but I know that several countries had thriving space programs before the invasion. I've seen a book about the efforts to explore Mars. I think we may have even sent people there, though I'm not sure. You turds fought pretty hard."

The shorter being stopped walking. "Do you always have to be so rude?" Shrugging, he continued. "We had numbers on our side. Your governments and armies didn't have enough time to mobilize for a proper defense. Look, I know where this is going, and I want to avoid the arguments. Humans were, and still are, the scariest things I've ever seen. If anyone can show me how to fight the NorCons, it would be you."

Carl stepped in close to flip the safety selector on Bibix's weapon to the 'off' position. "See that green light? If that little switch is flipped up, the weapon will fire when you pull the trigger. Point and shoot."

The timid curator regarded his weapon with concern. "Huh. That isn't so hard."

The soldier stepped away from Bibix. Turning, he raised his gun and fired a white-hot bolt of accelerated plasma into the sky. "Just like that. Safety off, point, and shoot."

"Point and shoot." Bibix repeated the command. Spreading his pods, he steadied himself in the tall grass, raised his gun, and pulled the trigger. The gauss made a rapid <u>thwip-thwip-hwup</u> as a trio of metal slugs ripped through the sound barrier and fled into the darkening sky.

Carl put his rifle on safe and slung it over one shoulder. "The gauss is probably your best bet until we can get some more plasma weapons. It has no recoil to speak of, and it's durable. As long as you have bullets and batteries, you'll be good to go. Do you have any specs on the NorCon armor?"

The Lapropod shook his head. "We know very little about them. They don't allow us to study their language, and we don't get to see them in private.

'NorCon' is what they've told us to call them. I think it's a term they use among themselves that might translate to 'master' or some such slave-related appellation."

Carl grunted. He was starting to like Bibix, and that bothered him. "That could easily be so. The armor they wear looks like it can take some punishment. Are these guys all military, all the time?"

Bibix put his weapon on safety and hung it around his ample neck. "I believe so. Their caste structure is very much like your chain of command. They don't seem to have what you'd call private sector jobs. They use us for that."

Tippet spat in disgust. "That sounds about right."

Bibix nodded. "Yes, and we're good at it, thanks to all the stuff your people left behind."

34 | Bibix

"We're a helpful species," Carl muttered.

Bibix rubbed his translator band. "Was that sarcasm?"

Carl changed the subject. "The NorCons walk around in power-assisted suits. What about vehicles and aircraft? What kind and how many do they have?"

The nervous Lapropod cringed at the thought. "They seem to prefer one-on-one combat. The armor they wear can support a variety of weapons packages. The more I read about human weapons, the more I can relate to theirs. They use what you'd call troop carriers and trucks, but they don't seem to like tanks."

"How would you know that?" Tippet growled, turning away from the setting sun.

Bibix ignored the human's contempt. "They collect human war machines, but they don't keep them indoors in a climate-controlled environment like they do so many other things that were left behind by your species. More importantly, I've never seen the NorCon equivalent of tanks, artillery, or airplanes."

"No airplanes?" Carl turned, his surprise obvious on his face.

The smaller being shook his head. "Nothing that relates to flight at all, other than cargo barges that can reach their ships in orbit. They're big, noisy things. You can hear them coming long before you see them. Before you ask, I don't know anything about their spacecraft. That information is off-limits."

Tipped pointed to a large stump. "Pretend that's me and shoot it."

36 | Bibix

Bibix grabbed his gun, activated it as he turned, and held the trigger down as he aimed. The short-range attack destroyed the rotting wood in a spectacular spray of chunks and splinters. He screamed as they rained down on his broad head.

Carl watched his pupil empty the clip into the stump. When the little fellow stopped his screeching, the human bent over to pick up a long, thin strip of shredded bark. "If you can do that to a tree, you can do it to a NorCon."

The panicked curator released his grip on the smoking gun. When it flopped onto his chest, swinging from the lanyard, he squirmed. "Gagh! It's hot!"

The veteran snickered. "That's because it's not hooked up to a cooling system. Lots of our guns need coolers. That reminds me… Those magnets in the front aren't shielded. Don't let that thing get too close to whatever you have for private parts."

Bibix held the weapon with great care. "Are you saying this thing can make me sterile?"

"Yep." Tippet made a show of picking his teeth with the bark splinter.

The Lapropod removed the gun from his person and dropped it to the ground. "What kind of maniac uses a weapon like this? Wait. Don't answer that. I forgot that I'm talking to a…uh."

Carl tossed away the splinter. "Say it."

Bibix fidgeted with all four hands. "It's not like that."

Tippet moved closer and laid the barrel of his rifle on the Lapropod's chest. "Sure it is. You want to be angry. I can see it on your face. Your eyestalks

38 | Bibix

twitch when you get cranky. It's not enough to be morally outraged. You've gotta be really mad when you pull that trigger."

Bibix shook his head. "I don't think I want—"

The human stepped in fast, striking Bibix – two quick jabs with a balled fist followed by three savage blows with the butt of the plasma rife. "It's not about what you want! It's about what you've got to do! You hear me, you little freak?"

The Lapropod was bowled over. He'd seen this kind of physical attack many times while watching pre-Collapse video recordings. In an effort to toughen up, he'd watched the most violent images he could find, over and over again, until they no longer scared him. In spite of that conditioning, Carl's attack hurt in ways that he'd never thought possible.

The soldier loomed over him. "If you don't fight back, I'm gonna hit you again!"

Bibix felt his mouth fill with blood. He stood on all four pods and raised his fists.

Years of hate and frustration overwhelmed Carl. He didn't pull his next punch, or the kick that followed. "Right idea, wrong move. Your eyes. I can pull those stalks out real easy, right by the roots. Then you'll be blind!"

Bibix rolled with the kick that knocked the wind out of him. He'd seen video of Carl in action. He knew the experienced killer could do what he said. "Not my eyes! Please! Mercy!" Reflexively, his eyes pulled in toward their sockets.

Tippet threw his gun aside and leaped on top of Bibix to pin him to the overgrown lawn. "If you're not the winner, you don't get mercy or justice! I know. I've watched my own people beg for their lives. And you know what? They died."

Fear gripped Bibix in a way he'd never previously experienced. His heart raced and his limbs froze. Being so very close to this enraged killing machine unleashed both his desire for survival and his prejudices. The human's unpleasant smell, wild hair, foul breath, and bad attitude combined to reinforce every negative thing he'd ever been taught about the species of Man.

Carl got to his feet. "I'm going to kill you, stone-cold dead, if you don't fight back!"

Bibix sprang fully upright. "I was wrong to do this. We should've gotten rid of your kind when we had the chance!"

Tippet picked up his weapon and charged it. "I'm sure you freaks gave it your best shot."

The Lapropod charged his antagonist. Something more than anger propelled him. There was a need that he simply had to fulfill, no matter the cost. Rational factors no longer applied. Instinct changed into something he couldn't name. The fat, slow, untrained Bibix surged forward to battle for his own safety and future security.

Carl backed away and raised his weapon. Using the simple sights, he fired a grazing shot that burned the small hairs off the top of Bibix's head. The superheated plasma bolt passed between the Lapropod's two eyestalks. Bibix fell. With a single kick to the head, Carl rendered his rescuer unconscious.

42 | Bibix

Turning off the power supply, he dropped the weapon and flopped onto the cool grass. His heart fluttered as he suffered conflicting emotions and the effects of the cancer cure. "I should just get out of here. There have to be enough supplies in the house to keep me going for a week."

The notion of killing just one more Lapropod appealed to him. The chance to eat real food and carry working weapons fired his imagination. The sinking sun reminded him of where he was. Looking over his shoulder at the ruined house made his skin crawl. "Sixty years and I'm still behind enemy lines. What in the hell am I supposed to do now?"

Bibix moaned and kept his eyes pulled inside his head. "You could stop hurting me."

Tippet looked at the bruised and bloody being. "You got what you deserved."

The hapless Lapropod rolled over and let his eyes rise from their protective cavities. "I suppose I should've seen that coming. The literature I found states that individuals released from cryogenic suspension don't feel like any time has passed. You're still fighting us."

"What is that supposed to mean?" Carl exploded.

Bibix wiped torn grass from his nose. "Humans and Lapropods haven't been at war with each other for a long time."

Tippet kicked at the ground. "That's what happens when you drive a species to the edge of extinction. They don't fight back quite so much."

Bibix lowered his eyes, then his head. "Was it really that bad?"

44 | Bibix

Carl didn't know how to answer. "Hell on Earth, Bibs. It was always cold. We were always hungry. We had just enough tech stuff to remind us how things used to be. I hated those camcorders. The old videos you're talking about were our way of coping. No, not really coping. More like documenting atrocities." He paused. "I think your drugs are getting to me. I hurt and I can't think."

The human's behavior puzzled Bibix. He wiped blood from his mouth and stood up. "My people developed a similar technology. We've got millions of hours of video that remind us of our home world. There must be two or three centuries worth of the stuff still floating around."

Tippet ripped grass from the lawn and ate it. "I was ten years old when you guys invaded. In the span of just five months, I went from clean underwear and shopping malls to battlefields and scrounging for food.

The people who used to call themselves journalists kept working, using solar powered cameras. Some of them did it just to stay busy. Others did it as a way of gathering information. A few had some lousy excuse about preserving the historical record."

The troubled Lapropod shook his bruised head. "So, it really was that bad. The material I've seen looks to be quite traumatic. Did your journalists have to spend so much of their time recording combat? What was the point? Really, it was hard for me to watch all the killing."

Carl looked right at Bibix. "You have to want your freedom. Sometimes you've got to want it bad enough to kill for it. You're not going to save anyone if you can't get muddy and bloody. I can kill you, and I'd like it. As much as I hate to say it, we might need each other, so…you get to live. For now."

46 | Bibix

Bibix began to take stock of his wounds as the yard darkened. "I think I'm glad that you see things my way. I also think I might understand where you're coming from. Before you knocked me out, I was…I felt…Please, don't laugh. This is hard for me."

Tippet replied, "It was hard for me, too. It was hard for all of us. When your ships came out of the sky, a lot of us thought you'd actually come in peace. We got the message pretty quick. Especially when you guys ate everything and everyone that wasn't nailed down."

Bibix trembled. "I…I've heard stories. My grandfather confided to me once, years ago. I always thought he was telling a tale. Fibbing. Everyone knows about the destruction of your farms and livestock, but… come on. We didn't really eat humans."

"Right down to the bone," the man confirmed with a grim stare.

The Lapropod started to cry.

Carl chewed some more grass. "So, the turdy little 'Pod people have a dirty little secret."

"You saw this with your own eyes?" Bibix demanded through his tears.

The callous scavenger nodded. "I was sixteen years old when I first ran into it. We were raiding. Our squad got the drop on a bunch of 'Poddies who camped out in the open. It was the stupidest thing you ever saw – no sentries and a really big campfire. It's one thing to hear about stuff like that, but it's a totally different thing to watch it happen. We were too angry to bother with the video camera. We did stuff. You know?"

48 | Bibix

The distraught Lapropod fought back a sob. "Please, tell me. I need to hear it."

Tippet remained unmoved by Bibix's pain as he dredged up the dark memory. "The 'Pods were cooking body parts and eating them. The wind was blowing away from us, so we didn't get much of the smell. We attacked – shot a few, knifed the rest. They had no guns. I can't remember how many there were. Fifteen? No more than twenty. We put their bodies into the campfire. I'm not sure if we were trying to take revenge for what they did or if we were just cleaning up the mess we'd made."

Fully engulfed in the visions conjured by the terrible revelation, Bibix retched. When the dry heaves had passed, he shuffled over to pick up his gauss gun. "I don't want to talk about this any more."

Carl couldn't resist one last, cruel jab. "Don't sweat it, Bibs. Humans ate humans long before you guys came along. We called it cannibalism. That grandfather of yours may even have had a nibble. Someday, you should ask him if he liked it. It could be something that the Lapropods have in common with the NorCons."

Bibix choked on his rage. The human was too dangerous to argue with, and he was still drowning in his shame. How could his people keep such an evil secret? "I've had more than enough reflection for one day. Will this weapon defeat NorCon armor?"

Tippet stumbled to his feet, grabbing his own weapon. "There's only one way to find out. We'll have to find one and shoot him. The other stuff you brought takes cartridge bullets. You know, those little copper-jacketed things? Most of those won't go through antiballistic weave. A little guy like you shouldn't waste your time with them."

"The principle is the same? Check the safety, point, and shoot?" Bibix asked as they walked back inside.

"Pretty much," Carl admitted, closing the door. He walked into the tiny living room.

Bibix, still unsettled by the nature of the conversation and the fact that the human still had a weapon, decided to assert himself. "Captain. Stop," he said with all the authority he could muster.

The scruffy man halted in his tracks when he heard the gauss repeater's initiator click.

"Put your weapon down," Bibix commanded. "I won't let you flout my authority." He took aim at the back of the human's head.

"Well, now, Bibs, I didn't think you had it in you." Turning slowly, the veteran unslung his rifle and activated it. Raising it one-handed, he checked his peripheral vision.

The Lapropod trembled at the sight of the weapon in the human's bony hand. "I didn't think I had a lot of things in me until a few moments ago. You can give up if you want to, but I won't. In a way, I don't blame you. If our roles were reversed, I'm sure I'd feel just as put out, burned out, and used up as you do. The NorCons are despicable. They use your kind for food. They use mine for slaves. I'm sorry that's not enough for you. Now, drop that gun."

"You're getting what you deserve," Carl repeated.

Bibix cringed but kept on talking. "You've already won that point, Captain. The conflict with my people is still fresh in your mind, as if it happened just yesterday. That was then. This is now. If you and I don't work together, here and now, there will be no humans or Lapropods outside of museums. The NorCons will see to that, and they'll enjoy doing it."

Tippet's drug-induced hostility flared. "That's pretty incisive for a guy who eats his own body weight in food three times a day."

Bibix raised his weapon, as he'd been taught. "You should take me seriously."

"I need time to think," the aggressive man admitted, conflicted.

Bibix decided to remain decisive. "Drop the weapon. Then start thinking."

Carl shook his head and adjusted his aim. The drugs in his system were making him much more irritable than usual. "It's not that simple. It's been sixty years. I know that, but I don't feel it."

Bibix tossed his own gun to the floor. "Fine. Does that make you feel better? In spite of your experience to the contrary, my species does not get violent when it really matters, like now. That's why we fell to the NorCons so easily. You're aching to kill me for things that earlier generations of my people did. I've heard your words. I've seen the scars on your body. I can guess how you got them."

Tippet's heightened anger caused him take a step forward.

Bibix spread his four arms wide in a show of total surrender. "Your service file says you and the troops under your command killed a hundred and sixty Lapropods, mostly with knives or your bare hands. I can only assume that you were low on ammunition.

54 | Bibix

The video we have in our vault suggests that you, personally, lived under terrible conditions. Everything you've said today makes me believe it. I've seen clips of you in action. 'Home movies,' I think they're called. I don't know by experience what starvation is, but it looks terrible on the big screen."

"You have no idea," Carl snorted, tightening his grip on the plasma rifle.

Bibix found it hard to stay calm. Everything he'd worked for was slipping away. "Intellectually, I know what it means to lose my home. I keep hearing stories about a world that doesn't exist anymore. It's all my parents talk about in their old age. A whole culture that was dead when our last ship left orbit; a place my elders still speak of fondly. It's a place I'll never see, except in a picture album or a NorCon museum. My 'loss' doesn't compare to being forced out of your cities, or being pushed out of your refugee camps, or picking through landfills while shivering in the rain so that your smallest children can have something to eat. I haven't experienced any of that, but I get the point. It hurts, a lot, but I do get the point."

Tippet lowered his gun and sat on the moldy couch. The little shrimp was right. Never mind the drugs in his body. The ruins of the surrounding city stank of defeat, and it was preying on his war-weary mind. The odor reminded him of the fetid, sweaty reek of infected wounds. That, and the transition from cryo, served to weigh him down. Even before the cancer had made him eligible for cold storage, he and the rest of his platoon knew they were fighting for a lost cause. Honor was dead, killed in the line of duty while defending compassion.

As Carl broke down under the weight of his many miseries, Bibix retrieved his gauss weapon from where he'd let it fall. The sight of a crying human was almost too much to bear, but he forced himself to stay in the room. Climbing into a rotten chair, he picked off some of the moss and quietly nibbled as the man released his grief.

Bibix gave Tippet a blanket after he'd calmed down. The emotionally drained human slept soundly, despite the nerve-rattling drugs coursing through his damaged body. Aware that he was treading a fine line, Bibix resolved to stay awake to prevent his reluctant teacher from escaping. Roaming through the dark house, he stayed busy investigating all the nooks and crannies he could find with his natural night vision. Randomly checking on the snoring soldier, he also had time to think and worry.

As the cold night wore on, his mind filled with unpleasant thoughts. The Lapropods had institutionalized their guilt about their unintended destruction of Earth's many civilizations. The translator band on Tippet's wrist hadn't been invented until well after the collapse of human resistance. When communication became possible, most of the surviving humans had surrendered in exchange for food, shelter, and other comforts. The rest had been hunted down or driven into the remotest of regions for the sake of public safety. It had been a task that the Lapropods had undertaken with great reluctance and regret as they covered up the atrocity of their use of humans as a food source.

Upon their arrival just three decades later, the NorCons had very little to do. The small gray quadrupods tried to put what they'd learned from the humans to good use, but they were quickly overwhelmed by the ferocity of their enemies. Human resistance, what little there was, impressed the NorCons. Popular gossip suggested that the armored conquerors would've enjoyed the chance to fight with the violent humans. Because the NorCons enjoyed the taste of human meat, they tended to romanticize and exaggerate what <u>Homo sapiens</u> might have been capable of in war.

As he wandered, Bibix wondered if he'd done the right thing by reviving such a dangerous creature. This one man could rampage and kill dozens of Lapropods before the NorCons caught him…if they caught him. The irony left a sour taste in his mouth.

The very thought of sharp, cold steel made his skin crawl. His decision to become militant hadn't beent made lightly. No self-respecting Lapropod would take a life unless forced. The humans had been driven to violence by accident. The historical record suggested that they might have actually welcomed the early landings with open arms, but that was just a speculation. Most records from that period had been lost due to NorCon malice.

Emotional conflict was hard for Bibix to rationalize. His highly ordered mind was, by the standards of his society, an impregnable intellectual fortress. As he prowled around the neglected dwelling, fear began to challenge his inner defenses.

Sitting alone in the kitchen, he ate, and ate, and ate. Even with a full stomach, his confidence suffered. "I could just go home. It'll be like none of this ever happened. I could kill Tippet, or just let him live in the woods like he wants."

He thought about what he'd just said. "Ew. No. Absolutely not. No more guilt or indecision. I need him, and he needs me. Huh. Will you listen to me? I'm a philosopher."

Bibix went back to the living room. Carl slept fully clothed under the blanket, the plasma rifle curled to his chest in both hairy arms. Bibix scanned the man's weather-beaten face in the dim light. Gaunt facial features intimated a lifetime of malnutrition. Uneven curls suggested infrequent, hasty haircuts. Stained teeth completed the picture of poor hygiene.

"You look like you smell," Bibix mumbled as he went back to the mossy chair on the far side of the room. Hopping onto the wooden frame, he scrunched until he got comfortable. Sitting still, he was slowly overcome by the cool night air. Sluggishly, both eyes retracted into his head. With a long, slow sigh, he slipped into a troubled slumber. The desire to fight or flee came and went several times as he mumbled incoherent protests through several traumatic dreams.

Chapter 3

Bibix fell out of the chair as the day's first light streamed in through a dirty window. Looking up from the leaf-encrusted floor, he extended his eyes to scan for Tippet. The couch was empty. The human was gone, and so was the blanket. Searching the house, he darted frantically from room to room until he remembered the apple tree in the back yard.

Going back for his gun, he found a fresh clip and changed it. He slowly probed into the back yard. Trees, grass, and weeds were all slick with dew. Increasing sunlight revealed that the apple tree had been picked clean. Sulking, Bibix knew he was alone.

62 | Bibix

A more determined search of the house and lev proved that most of his food and water had been taken. The plasma rifle and all four remaining power packs were gone, as were the firearms using bullets. The three boxes of ammunition were missing, too. Angry and embarrassed, he searched in vain for a farewell note. When he didn't find one, he sat in the living room and thought about his options.

Carl didn't understand the NorCon threat because he didn't want to. He was stuck in the past. Shaking his head, Bibix had to admit that he'd overestimated the human. The shaky videos that documented his exploits hadn't spoken of his inner pain or fragile state of mind.

When he'd first discovered them, those low-grade images had been inspiring. Alone in the museum's basement, behind a locked door, he'd watched them with the sound turned down low. The human warrior had scared him at first. With a translator plugged in, Bibix cringed each time Tippet yelled at the camera operator. The pep talks he had given to the men and women under his command were brief and full of swearing.

After several months of exposure to the recordings, he'd gotten used to the profanity and violence. The fear went away. He no longer vomited when he saw the humans eviscerate Lapropods. They were doing what they had to, just as he knew he must.

Pulling himself together, he set about the task of caching his weapon. He patiently sealed the precious device in slick plastiform to protect it against moisture. Going to his lev, he took a shovel from the back. He carefully buried his gun and remaining supplies. Taking his time, he packed up his personal effects and collected the trash. Something in Tippet's demeanor suggested that humans would do this. It implied a sneakiness that appealed to him at that moment.

Continuing his charade, he drove further south and booked into a coastal resort that catered to Lapropods. The formerly human facility had been adapted with the blessings of their NorCon masters. Prior to the arrival of the armored conquerors, the Lapropods had shunned most things human. Because the NorCons relished the spoils of war, it was easy for them to insist that their subjugated serfs do the same.

Alone in his rented room, Bibix nursed his abused body. A creative lie told to the front desk attendant suggested that he'd had a run-in with his supervisor before running aw…er, departing on vacation. Physical abuse passed as normal behavior for NorCons. With sympathies, he had been shown to his room and left to rest. Salve and bandages did nothing to hold back the nightmares when he slept.

Bibix woke early the next day and went for a swim. His pear-shaped body bobbed up and down on the waves. The cold salt water relieved some of his stress while the activity ensured that many witnesses saw him. Afterwards, he made a TransCall to the museum. In keeping with his overly meticulous nature, he pretended to be unable to enjoy himself unless he knew that all was well back in the archives.

"Somehow, I knew it would be you." The NorCon supervisor shook its helmeted head.

Gripping the edges of the panel, Bibix began his performance. "I knew I shouldn't have left. What's wrong?"

66 | Bibix

His master seemed utterly unaware of the deception. "One of the humans in cryo was stolen. Lubix has already investigated the matter. It's nothing you need to be concerned with."

"I've only been gone for two days!" Bibix pleaded with some sincerity.

Grilleck enjoyed the groveling of his underling. "I like your dedication, Bibix. For as long as I can remember, you've been the only 'Pod that really cares about our trophies. How would you like to be the deputy curator for this facility?"

The question shocked Bibix. He had no trouble extending his eyes in a gesture of genuine surprise.

On the screen, the bulbous helmet jiggled with laughter as mighty jaws cracked open ever so slightly. "The job is yours when you return."

Bibix was overcome with pride. "If I drive all night, I can—"

"No! I'm looking forward to having Lubix slow-roasted. It takes forever to make you people taste good. That reminds me, I need to have him arrested and cavity-scrubbed prior to spicing. Loyalty, Bibix. You're being promoted because you're loyal. Never forget that, or I may have to invite you to dinner."

Bibix starred at the blank screen for a long moment before going back to his room. Three days ago, he would have merely accepted the consuming of Lubix. The old suck-up was a disgrace to his kind, always willing to send museum staff out to steal anything the administrator demanded. In his newly liberated condition, Bibix found the idea of collaboration to be barbaric and unclean. Nobody truly deserved to be eaten. As much as it saddened him, Lubix would have to go in order for his plan to succeed.

That morbid thought refused to leave him as he struggled to enjoy himself. Eating, swimming, and hiking in the surrounding foothills that overlooked the resort barely held his depression in check. None of the activities improved his mood. After three days of unsatisfying recreation and troubled sleep, he stopped being mad at Carl.

Strolling through the resort's gift shop, he bought a book in the hopes that it might hold his attention long enough to allow him to sleep without nightmares or self-loathing. He settled on a popular reprint of a pre-Collapse classic, <u>The Poetry and Memoirs of Anne K. Nagel</u>. Like other Lapropods, he enjoyed human literature. Something about this author's struggle to find her place in an unfriendly world appealed to him.

* * *

Bibix was back on the job two days later. Dense rain poured from the sky as slate gray clouds stalked across the horizon, powered by harsh winds. Thunder boomed. Lighting flashed.

The chore of moving into his new office wasn't enough to prevent Bibix from watching the NorCons closely as each went about its assigned daily routines. They strutted around in their bulbous helmets and slab armor. The armor's appearance was deceptive. What appeared to be poor upkeep was, in fact, a deliberate show of past combat experience. Battle damage of any sort was highly prized. Some NorCons had colorful patterns emblazoned on arms or legs, though chest and helmet surfaces remained mysteriously bare. The pressure pump that each wore was clamped to the armor in a different place for each being. Placement of the pump seemed to depend on personal preference.

Grilleck and Veknar were having a heated argument in their native tongue when Bibix returned to his office with yet another armload of disks, chips, and crayleon bundles.

"Bibix!" Grilleck challenged, standing in the way.

The new deputy curator cringed just a little. "Yes, Greatness?"

The administrator failed to notice the lower than normal level of fear in his underling. "There seems to be some doubt. Tell us about the human that was stolen."

Bibix ignored the snort that the translator imparted. Going to his desk, he picked up a single printed page. He held it up for Grilleck to read through its helmet enhancements.

"Tippet, Carl. Captain, Alaska National Guard. Serial number—"

"Guard?" Veknar looked at his superior.

"National Guard. Reserve troops," Grilleck explained.

Disappointed, Veknar handed over its wager, which Grilleck took in one large, four-digited, mechanical claw. Bibix pretended not to notice the transaction.

Veknar's translator tried, and failed, to communicate its envy. "A captain? Whoever stole him must have had a tasty meal."

72 | Bibix

"I would believe it," Grilleck chortled as the two walked away, leaving Bibix to his work.

Unwilling to think about the human soldier he'd let loose, Bibix threw himself into his tasks. Lubix had been a poor leader and a worse record keeper. Before Bibix could rebel any further, there was much to be done so that nobody would suspect him. The Bibix they'd always known had to be seen doing his job. Calm Bibix. Queasy Bibix. Busy Bibix.

Trebix, the senior curator, had taken an immediate dislike to the younger Lapropod. Where Lubix had been easy to deal with, Bibix was not. His constant whining about accurate cataloging began to wear down the older being's patience. After two weeks, he couldn't stand it anymore. Trebix took his case to Grilleck.

"It's all here, under one roof. How much more cataloguing does it take?"

Grilleck put down its stylus. "Close the door, and let's talk about it."

Office gossip later claimed that Grilleck had eaten Trebix on the spot, unhinging the big jaws on its helmet. Employees at all levels spun details and described images that suggested how he had been torn into bite-sized chunks. The rumor didn't surprise Bibix, who had witnessed Grilleck's cruelty many times before. Most NorCons couldn't stand the taste of Lapropodian flesh without some exotic additive, spice, or sauce. Grilleck, it seemed, took its duties very seriously. Eating the unappetizing staff was just part of its thankless job.

When Veknar informed Bibix of his promotion to senior curator, the Lapropod was not surprised, although he pretended to be terribly embarrassed. The position held tremendous power. He, Grilleck, and Veknar, would be the only ones who actually knew what was in the museum. If Bibix chose to omit things from the inventory, they'd never know. The very thought made him shiver in fear and anticipation. That sudden rush made him think of Carl Tippet. "Please don't let me turn out like him!"

Making careful use of his new authority, Bibix went from home to work and back again as predictably as he could. Nobody questioned his purchase of the books on Tippet's list as he made improvements to the exhibits. The multitude of small, simple purchases baffled Grilleck until it began to see how its master's holdings were being improved.

"Amazing, Bibix! The appraisers have increased the value of this hall by nine percent. I didn't know that was possible. My master is very pleased."

Alone with the boss, Bibix feigned humble deference. "I live to serve, Greatness. I'm beginning to understand your concepts of value."

Grilleck held up a baseball, turning it over in one alloy claw. "Explain this."

Adjusting his breath mask, Bibix tried not to fret over how long he'd been in Grilleck's office. "Baseball. A team sport. That ball is thrown at a man holding a large wooden club. The club wielder, called a 'batter,' hits the ball toward a tall fence. A successful hit allows the batter to run for designated safe zones, called 'bases.' The winner of the game is determined by runs batted in – the total number of players who make it around all bases."

The administrator was unimpressed. "Why do we have seven hundred of these?"

Bibix rubbed his chin to hide some of his fear. "The game was very popular, Greatness. A common practice involved signing, or 'autographing,' the ball after a successful game. Only the successful players had this right. All seven hundred of our baseballs are autographed, which enhances their value."

Grilleck regarded its Senior Curator with what might have been kindness. "I would have liked to do battle with the humans."

Something in Grilleck's attitude and body language put Bibix on guard. "How so?"

The marauder waxed philosophical. "I miss the days of challenge. I'd like to think that, if we'd gotten here first, the humans would have given us a good fight."

"We tried, Greatness." Bibix sighed soberly, thinking that now would be a good time to show impertinence.

Grilleck put the ball down. "Don't patronize me."

Bibix lowered his eyes to show obedience. "No, Greatness. I would never think of it."

"No, I don't suppose you would," the NorCon fumed.

Grilleck's contempt inspired Bibix to start reading the books that Tippet was so certain would be of use. Time passed quickly. The weeks flew by and the season changed. Alone in the sanctioned privacy of his messy one-room apartment, Bibix hoarded supplies and read the books, bringing them to the trophy hall after finishing with them. Diminished daylight and increasing snow ushered in the long winter as the authorship of long-dead thinkers filled his head with new ideas.

The concepts of strategy and tactics weren't that hard to grasp. The deceptions and applications of force merely ran counter to Lapropodian instinct and logic. The term "pacifist" hurt, once he understood it. Words like "appeasement" proved to be most enlightening after translation.

Knowing that he was always under some form of surveillance at work, Bibix went out of his way to adopt antisocial behaviors that he knew would be disliked by his peers. They gossiped easily about "Bibix the work slave," when he wasn't around. Grilleck and the other NorCons who managed the trophy hall picked up on this convenient bit of intelligence. It reinforced their individual opinions that Bibix was uncharacteristically reliable.

Pleased with the success of his complex manipulation, Bibix used the leeway his new image afforded him to keep up a vigorous schedule of nighttime book reading and daytime sleuthing.

Lapropods were naturally incurious and apolitical when it came to things that they feared or matters that didn't concern them. Sedition and rebellion were unknown concepts to them. Armed with newfound political prowess, Bibix began to reevaluate his society and his place in it.

Successfully keeping secrets inflated his ego. This resulted in a smug demeanor that he often found hard to suppress. NorCons and Lapropods alike misinterpreted his newfound confidence. Bibix's mother gossiped proudly about her important son, whom she now suspected was dating an equally important female, and how the two would no doubt provide her with lots of podlings. Bibix's father was glad to see that his unusual boy had finally lost some of his shyness and was thought of positively. The NorCons who decided his fate on a daily basis began to rely on Bibix for his sound judgment.

Chapter 4

Late one night, six months into his tenure as Senior Curator, Bibix found a small, water-damaged fiberboard box with no label. Alone in the basement of the large, prefabricated structure that served as the trophy hall, he smiled and shivered with glee. It contained a stack of much abused optical disks. The logos on the disks indicated that they had once been the property of a local television station.

According to the receipt, the box had been acquired just ten years before. He recognized the name of the senior curator from that period. Excited, he made sure that he was the only Lapropod in the museum. The NorCons on patrol ignored him. Satisfied, he went to the AV lab and used recovery cleaner and fresh towels to carefully wipe each disk. They weren't numbered. Only one had a hand-written notation: 'Arrival, Day 50.'

Bibix held the scarred disk up to a work light. "Arrival?"

The prospect was intriguing. A conspiracy theory popular among Lapropods in college suggested that, prior to the coming of the NorCons, the Lapropod leaders had worked hard to expunge the public record of sources that mentioned the more unpleasant details of their landings on Earth. As his people embraced human technology and certain aspects of now-dead regional cultures, books and movies were made about their arrival on this watery blue planet. Actors and computer-generated images were used to simulate theorized human reactions, which were generally agreed to be unkind.

82 | Bibix

Sliding the object into a composite reader, he keyed the conversion system and waited. A one-meter display near his workbench lit up. Bibix pulled up a chair, and waited with great anticipation as the network introduction played out. The visual field jiggled frantically as the operator tried to keep up with a disheveled woman scrambling through a muddy trench. Her long brown hair hung in thick, dirty ropes that draped over her back and shoulders. Her light body armor and trendy clothes were caked in the muck she crawled through. Bibix recognized the wireless headset mike she wore. The trophy hall had three intact units in inventory.

"We are live on the perimeter of Kulis Air Base, where the creatures are attacking in force. Before we lost the national news feed, I was talking to Doctor Milo Hopkins from the University of Alaska. He was telling me about the latest failed attempt to communicate with the invaders. Come on, Bucky, keep up."

Bibix nodded to himself. "Reporter and cameraman. This is rare stuff."

He flinched when the camera's eye peered over the lip of the trench. A hundred meters away, thousands of Lapropods were rushing a line of human infantry. Hunkered down, the trained soldiers aimed and fired automatic weapons of all sorts. Gas-operated gunpowder systems banged away in rapid succession. Gauss repeaters thumped like rapid heartbeats as plasma-boosted flamethrowers belched out long, red streams of unquenchable fire. The muzzle flashes and explosive coronas reflected off the low cloud cover.

Despite this terrible slaughter, the wave of Lapropods advanced steadily over the partially frozen ground.

84 | Bibix

Bibix imagined that the cold weather was forcing his people to fight their way to shelter. On the big screen, the human troops fell under the weight of sheer numbers.

Looking at her cameraman, the reporter spoke her final words as a massive starship thundered by overhead. "I can see four more of their ships coming down now – one, maybe two, miles away. They're everywhere. I don't know what made us think we could welcome them. They won't talk to us, and they just keep coming. If anyone's watching this, fight back. For the sake of us all, fight back!"

The camera angle changed radically as a dozen Lapropodian hands reached for the reporter. The screen went blank as she started kicking and screaming.

Bibix shivered out of fear and revulsion. Seeing his people under those conditions gave him a greater appreciation for Carl's mindset. Their conversation, and his own words, played back in his mind.

"I'll never understand why my own people never had the good sense to form our own army. If we had—"

"You might be where I am now."

The revelation was chilling. Shaken, Bibix eyed the remaining disks with open worry. Tippet's show of apathy had been a lie. His breakdown might have been due to post-combat stress, but his hate for the creatures that had oppressed him was very real. Were Lapropods really that easy to manipulate? One look at the NorCon fixtures around the room gave him his answer.

"Does it work both ways? They manipulate us. Can we do it to them?"

Bibix took the box of disks home with him. He was only now getting comfortable with the need for violence. He didn't want anything else to cloud his judgment. In time, when he was ready, he could explore what was on the other disks. For now, he had a rebellion to start.

According to the author Clausewitz, violence was just another form of politics. Alone in his apartment's little bathroom, Bibix pondered this. The NorCon political view was much like that attributed to Genghis Khan. The strong preyed upon the weak. Possession was ownership. If somebody had a thing that you wanted, you took it. These disturbing notions gave him nightmares, preventing him from getting a full night's sleep.

Three days later, Bibix took the final item he needed for his first covert mission from a storage room near the back of the trophy hall. Pilfering didn't come easily to him. With a canvas bag slung over one shoulder, he felt bad about being so larcenous. He waited for the guard shift to change, and then snuck out to his lev unnoticed, driving away with his loot.

Gliding along the semi-smooth surface of a partially restored pre-invasion highway, Bibix guided the lev with increasing worry. He drove through the ruins of Anchorage, eventually turning east to approach the NorCon facility near Eagle River. Parking inside a ruined structure situated half a kilometer from the trophy hall, he turned off the vehicle and got out to open the rear hatch and unpack his gear.

Lapropod physiology did not lend itself to war gear. At least, that's what Lapropodian politicians had been saying since the first encounters with humans.

Fighting his way into a black battle smock made for the largest of humans, Bibix couldn't resist flexing his muscles as he slid two arms through each sleeve. The dense, dark fabric hid his smooth gray skin from the starlit night, making him feel powerful and threatening.

As he filled his shirt pockets with a variety of small items that might be useful in any number of disaster scenarios, Bibix found himself thinking of Carl. He pondered what it must have been like for other humans to wear all this equipment as they did battle with their enemies. It was effort to not think about the humans killing Lapropods.

Shrugging into a load-bearing vest, he clipped on a flashlight and combat knife. The sharp, steel blade hung upside down in a nylon scabbard. Worn in this manner, it could be pulled free with the point up and ready for use with just one quick move. Bibix could feel his stomach flutter. It felt strange to have a lethal instrument so close to his skin and his hearts.

As Bibix understood it, he was about to engage in the activity known as 'reconnaissance.' The NorCons fortunate enough to have trophy halls jealously guarded the buildings' contents. It was rumored that some NorCons attempted espionage in an effort to find out what was being hoarded by their competitors.

Bibix mumbled to himself as he put on black face paint. "If greed works like Machiavelli says it does, all I need to do is recon this trophy hall for the good stuff. Then I tell Grilleck. He tells his master and…I might not get hurt. If they end up killing each other for this stuff, I win." In spite of everything he'd learned, he doubted the success of his plan.

Lapropods cherished community living and the sharing of objects. It bothered him intensely to live alone. Hoarding guns, books, and other military support tools weighed heavily on his conscience. The only thing that kept him going was the knowledge that the NorCons must be stopped.

Satisfied that he was prepared to meet any circumstance that might occur inside the trophy hall, Bibix looked at the last item in his duffel bag. A scarred, rusted automatic pistol rested snugly inside a shoulder holster that was wrapped around it in a tight bundle. The loaded weapon bothered him because he'd never used a handgun before. It had been an impulse theft, one that he now regretted.

With confidence in his own abilities, he shut the bag and put it into the back of his lev. Locking the doors, he inhaled deeply before starting the slow walk toward his target.

NorCons had no fear of Lapropods. The contempt they felt for their slaves encouraged their belief that exceptional security measures weren't necessary to protect the trophy halls. As he snuck closer to the building, Bibix found himself fuming at their hypocrisy. "They think so very little of us, yet they send us to steal from their competitors. Admittedly, we do that stealing during normal business hours, but we do steal for them – if we don't we get eaten."

Due to his education, Bibix had risen rapidly through the ranks of the staff that managed the Anchorage trophy hall. He'd never been one of those chosen to enter a rival cache to steal loot for his NorCon masters. The novelty of what he was about to do caught up with him. "Calm down. I've had plenty of time to think about this. It's not like they're expecting me. I can do this."

Bibix

Moving as quietly as he could, the nervous Lapropod snuck silently on just two pods and slipped a glove on each of his four hands. He avoided the roaming night guard, used a small pry-bar to break the lock on a side door and entered the building. "I've got to be fast. It's only a matter of time until the guard notices that this door isn't secure. Unless…"

Bibix smiled as he went through the pockets on his vest. "Watergate break-in, 1972. Human burglars used fiber tape to force a locked door to stay open. A night guard spotted the tape and the burglars got caught."

Pulling a strip of clear plastic tape from a handheld dispenser, he made hasty repairs to the face of the broken lock. "Who says you can't be smarter than a human?"

Slipping into the large, metal-skinned structure, he closed the door behind him and made his way past many familiar exhibits to the Deputy Curator's office. Knowing that there might be more than one guard inside the building, he forced his breathing to remain shallow as he slowly padded along. If this trophy hall's D.C. was anything like the one who worked for him, Bibix reasoned that his intrusion, if it were even detected, would go unreported for fear of being eaten by the NorCon supervisor.

Bibix held the tiny flashlight in his front teeth and quietly rifled the files he found in an unlocked cabinet. For reasons that he didn't question too closely, the NorCons were surprisingly low-tech when it came to records storage. They disliked using computers. Reading as fast as he could, Bibix found himself pondering this strange behavior as he scanned the master inventory lists. When he found what he wanted, he paused just long enough to memorize a few item descriptions and shelf numbers before covering his tracks.

On his way out, he was tempted to have a look at the installation's cryo storage. It occurred to him that he might find another human soldier with Carl's experience and skills. Giving in to his curiosity, he evaded the single guard that he heard shuffling around the supposedly empty museum. Locating this facility's cryogenic suspension storage room wasn't hard, thanks to the strategically placed site maps.

Bibix had planned the theft of Carl for weeks. He felt his hearts pound in his chest as he considered a spur-of-the-moment heist. "Carl taught me a lot, but I need a human to stay and help me fight. I hope the NorCon who owns this place hasn't eaten all of his pre-Collapse humans just yet."

Their swift and sudden victory over the Lapropods had shocked the NorCons. Because they thrived on war and its many perilous moments, the effortless takedown of the pacifists had left many NorCons feeling cheated. The discovery of millions of cryogenically preserved humans, many of whom had been senior military personnel with notable combat service records, had sparked an unprecedented debate in the NorCon ranks.

It was quickly understood that the Lapropods had come into possession of these medically stabilized people when they'd overrun human triage centers, hospitals, critical care facilities, and mortuaries. Careful inspection had revealed that most of the stored humans suffered from debilitating diseases like cancer or any of a number of neural degenerative disorders. A precious few of them had been frozen because they were deemed to be politically important within their societies.

Tradition dictated that the NorCons should eat their defeated foes as a sign of respect. The invasion commanders were disinclined to eat the Lapropods, whom they regarded as weak and pathetic, not to mention foul tasting. They decided that, as a formal gesture of their disapproval, very few of the small, gray creatures would be eaten. The 'frozen meat' was divided among the invasion commanders and their subordinate ground force leaders.

It was quickly discovered that humans tasted very good. This encouraged the NorCons to scour remote and underdeveloped areas in search of the few remaining pockets of human resistance. Many of the resulting small-scale combats were quick and bloody, much to the liking of the NorCons. Using the last of their technologically advanced weapons, some of the human leaders led their men, women, and children to what the NorCons considered glorious deaths.

The myth of the warrior humans – and their great flavor – was quick to grow. NorCon troopers, seasoned veterans all, agreed that human beings were by far the best food source they'd ever had the privilege of subjugating. This social perception was enhanced when stories began to emerge about the conduct of revived humans. Nonmilitary personnel tended to beg for their lives. Politicians, in particular, attempted to bargain for their own safety in ways that most NorCons found obscene.

Men and women who had seen combat were a different matter. If allowed to regain consciousness without proper restraint and supervision, human warriors performed magnificently until put down. The amount of combat experience each of the many soldiers, sailors, and airmen had varied with nationality. This intrigued the NorCons. The majority quickly agreed that humans with military experience tasted better than anything else they'd ever encountered.

As a podling in primary school, Bibix had learned these grim history lessons with an open mind. Like any other Lapropod of his generation, he accepted the NorCon tales of revived human soldiers as just more poof that humans were dangerous. With these thoughts in his head, he peeked into the room labeled 'Human Storage.'

The long, high-ceilinged, two-thousand-square-meter room was stacked to the rafters with silver coffins. Green lights on each unit indicated that the cellular suspension technology was still active, thanks to nuclear batteries. Air conditioners blew cold air to keep the room cooled to less than fifty degrees

Fahrenheit. Bibix darted into the room and headed for the only desk he could see.

Finding the logbook, he read quietly. "Seven hundred and fifty-three units. Two hundred and sixty female homemakers. Forty male homemakers. Two hundred blue collar professionals. Eighty white collar professionals. Ninety federal level civil servants. Twenty state level civil servants. Ten from the U.S. Navy. Thirty from the U.S. Coast Guard. Five doctors. Fifteen nurses. One land surveyor, and two lawyers. Hmm. That's not much of a selection."

Disappointed, Bibix left the trophy hall as fast as he could. He deliberately tripped the antitheft alarm as he fled. His reading of Machiavelli had been correct. The NorCons thought so little of the enslaved Lapropods that they did almost nothing to guard against them.

100 | Bibix

He stopped to hide his gear, as learned from his readings on Ché Guevara, and then raced home, only to spend yet another restless night in contemplation.

The next day, Grilleck called him on it. "Bibix, you look like poop. What's the matter?"

"I've been checking up on the other museums in this region," Bibix replied, starting into his lie just as he'd practiced.

Grilleck had its own concerns. "Can you believe humans used to pay to get into trophy halls? Now we keep everyone out except our masters. I'm starting to think we might be missing out on something."

"I also think we are missing something," Bibix continued, despite his roiling stomach.

The administrator seemed incredulous. "How so? Has somebody found another cache of hidden human loot?"

Working with the tangent, Bibix took a risk. "The museum over in what used to be called Eagle River has a collection of papers that once belonged to the human general called H. Norman Schwartzkopf. I was thinking that, since we had some of this man's uniforms and medals, we should also have his collected wisdom."

The chance to fight over something caught Grilleck's attention. "That's very interesting. Are you sure about this?"

"My source does not lie, Greatness," Bibix replied humbly.

102 | Bibix

The NorCon considered its options. "I'll bring it up to my master. If they choose to trade, what can we offer?"

Bibix tried not to swallow his tongues. "Why should we give them anything? We know the papers are there. Why not just...take them?"

"What? That's very...very...That would involve a raid. A fight. A..." Grilleck looked down at Bibix, seeing him in a whole new light.

"Challenge?" Bibix offered meekly.

Grilleck's pressure pump worked overtime for several seconds as he considered what he would tell his master. "Why not? I know the administrator for that dump in Eagle River. We could kill the entire staff. Ha! While we're at it, we'll take everything they have. If my master approves."

Thinking of the staff, Bibix dared to speak up. "Greatness, if I may? It will be a lot of work to integrate their holdings into our own. We might need a larger building. It would be helpful if we could use the staff."

Grilleck trained all his attention on Bibix. Was it possible that one of these vile, tasteless creatures was finally starting to learn something useful? There was only one way to find out.

"Suppose that my master allows a few of them to live. Suppose that, for the sake of argument, I let you have them as part of your work force. How does this benefit me?"

The question made Bibix sweat. "Actually, Greatness, it does not benefit you. Most of them will not be able to measure up to your high standards. When we finish adding their trophies to our inventory,

104 | Bibix

you may have to eat many of them to make the point that they…we…are unworthy."

The veteran of more than a hundred battles appeared to stare in silence.

Bibix forced himself to keep talking. "You tolerate so very little, Greatness. I have come to respect and admire this drive for excellence. We are doing more than just cataloging the spoils of war. We are pleasing your master. I can think of no higher calling."

Grilleck's translator approximated laughter. "Stop! Enough! Bibix, you amaze me. Fine. If my master approves the attack, I'll bring you the 'Pod survivors. I make no guarantees, mind you. If any of the little nuggets survive, you can put them to work."

Once he was dismissed, Bibix tried not to flee. He stayed in his office well past quitting time, waiting for

Grilleck to come and eat him for being so foolish. In his desk drawer, he had a small bomb. The inventory listed it as a 'hand grenade.' He didn't know if it still worked, but he was willing to give it a try, if things went that far. When the night guard came by his office for the third time, Bibix gave up his deathwatch and went home.

That night, he read more about human politics. Most of it seemed easily relatable to the NorCons. Eating as he read, he tried to relate those concepts to himself and his own kind. More to the point, he wondered why his people had never developed many of the traits he was learning about. "How do you take advantage of something if you can't relate to it?"

Some of the books he read had detailed bibliographies, listing other titles on similar subjects. Clearly, more research was needed before he could rebel any further.

"I'll probably end up writing my own book, just to make sense of it all."

Chapter 5

Ten days later, when it was obvious to him that spring had arrived, Bibix went back to the ruined house where he'd spoken with Carl. Clouds rushed in and cool rain fell as he dug up the gauss repeater and took it inside. He disassembled the weapon and cleaned it with supplies he had brought from home. Amazingly, the roof of this abandoned building had few leaks. In the low light, he imagined the comings and goings of the family of humans who had once lived here.

"Freeze," Tippet said softly, touching the cold metal of a gun barrel to the center of Bibix's back.

108 | Bibix

The Lapropod put down his rag and raised all four hands. With some effort, he turned his eyes on their stalks to bring Carl into view. "I didn't think I'd see you again."

The mud-spattered human shrugged. "I said I needed time to think, remember?"

"And? How did that go for you?" Bibix asked without so much as a shiver.

Tippet holstered his sidearm and moved around to sit facing the little alien. "I owe you an apology. This whole screwed up situation was a lot to take in all at once. I've been places, seen things. I've been able to verify just about everything you told me. I get it now."

"That's why you're back?" The doubt in Bibix's tone surprised even him.

Carl scratched his shaggy beard. "Yeah."

Somehow, the industrious man had scavenged a change of clothes. Bibix marveled at the combination of synthetic flannel and faux denim. Both were rare commodities. "I don't remember who said it, but, 'Welcome to the revolution.'"

Tippet smirked. "Thanks, Bibs. That means a lot, coming from you."

Bibix gestured at Carl's dirty shirt. "Where did you get the clothes?"

The man reached down to brush dirt from his old, battered combat boots. "When you said the NorCons didn't make your slave gangs work underground, I started looking for basements. Alaska is a cold place. I got lucky. Anchorage has a lot of basements. I spent most of the winter in a basement. I found some pretty disturbing stuff, too."

Bibix could see that Carl didn't like whatever he'd discovered. "I can only imagine."

Carl folded his hands. "Look, Bibs. I've got something to tell you. You're not going to like it. A few months back, I was dodging a NorCon patrol when I found what's left of a local T.V. station. They had stuff on disk. I found a civil defense power generator, and got the equipment working."

"I know what you found." Bibix motioned for the human to follow him into the living room.

"How?" Tippet sat on the couch and fiddled with his wrist translator, as if checking the fit.

With some hesitation, Bibix told him about the disks he had found in the museum. "They must have been copies of copies. As much as I feel shame about what I saw, I can't turn my back on what's happening now. Not any more. Please, help me save the humans and the Lapropods. Defeating the NorCons is the only way we can make things right between our two species."

Carl raised both hands in submission. "You'll get no argument from me, Bibs. There's a human processing plant out in the Mat-Su Valley. It took me three days just to walk out there. Now that I've seen it, I'm a believer. The NorCons have got to go."

The passion in the man's words drove Bibix to straighten in his seat. "Great. Where do we start?"

112 | Bibix

Tippet grinned wickedly. "I've already been contributing to the war effort. What have you been up to?"

Bibix explained his opening moves, careful to relate them to the books he'd read. Carl stopped him after five minutes of animated monologue. "I haven't seen you in nearly seven months, and all you've done is plant half an idea in your boss's brain bucket?"

Bibix was hurt. "I suppose you've done better?"

"Oh, yeah." Carl huffed and walked out of the house. Bibix followed.

The irritated man pointed to a larger house down the block. "Come on. I have something you're going to want to see."

Ignoring the light rain that fell from high clouds, they entered the other house and went to the dining room.

Bibix stared in disbelief when he saw a NorCon helmet dominating the center of a long table. Along one wall, an assortment of rusty weapons leaned against mildewed sheetrock: shotguns, light machine guns, and even a NorCon particle projector. "Y-you killed one?" he stuttered.

Carl swung into a chair, and then turned to face Bibix. "I killed two. They must have been on patrol. Some kind of punishment detail, maybe. I waited until one's attention was focused on a bear. While he was busy, I dropped his buddy with a plasma shot through the chest. Man, they really don't like our air. Breach that suit, and they're toast. That reminds me, forget that gauss gun you've been practicing with. It'll just make 'em mad."

114 | Bibix

Bibix thought about his disassembled weapon. "I see. Their armor is really that strong?"

Tippet grunted. "I had to use plasma on both of them. I cracked 'em open, just to have a look under the hood. That's what I wanted to show you. Let's go out back."

Bibix followed him into the overgrown back yard. Inside a tool shed, Carl opened a sealed plastic bucket. Inside was a stinking mass of more than a hundred small, mossy green fishlike bodies. Bibix instinctively began to back away.

"This is about half of what's in one of those suits," Carl explained.

Ignoring the cold water dribbling down his back, Bibix pulled himself together. "That's incredible. Each NorCon is a community organism."

"What?" Carl asked, examining the mess in the bucket once again.

Bibix was intrigued. "We had something like these on our home world. Not this sophisticated, but something like them."

Carl put the lid down, and then sat on the bucket. "For those of us who haven't been there, please spell it out in simple human."

The Lapropod stepped into the shed. "You and I are made up of many parts. Each of our parts is made up of many cells. Community organisms are creatures of the same species that function together for a common purpose. Individually, one can't do much. In large numbers, they can perform complicated tasks."

Tippet shrugged. "Is this a common thing where you come from?"

Bibix nodded. "Many thousands of years ago, we Lapropods were community organisms. That's why I know about them, even though I'm not a biologist. We got this stuff in what you'd call grade school."

Tippet smirked. "Aren't you lucky? My schoolroom education stopped at fifth grade."

The curator snickered. "I don't hold it against you. I've seen examples of high-end academic material from Lapropodian universities that dates back to before we came here – essays and math that 'prove' the utter impossibility of bipedal life. Like humans, we assumed we were alone in the universe."

Tippet shuffled his feet and thumped the bucket with the heel of his boot. "So, here we are, sitting on a bucket full of community killers, being lectured by a reformed community pacifist."

Bibix raised all four index fingers to ward off the insult. "With one big difference."

"Come on." Carl stood and headed for the house.

Bibix followed, turning several times to look back at the shed. He could feel his worldview change, as if it were a thing crawling inside his brain. The NorCons were not so scary. Not any more. Now that he knew they were a lower lifeform augmented by technology, he could summon the courage to more proactively plot against them. Trotting into the house, he didn't stop to consider that Lapropodian science was responsible for his prejudice.

In the living room, Carl was stoking the fireplace. "The NorCons are white with little gray spots when they first come out of the armor. There's a lot of clear, sticky liquid, too."

118 | Bibix

Bibix shuffled closer on all four pods. "I'd guess that each of the individual organisms weighs no more than half a kilo. The green, slushy material could be any number of things. It could be their guts, or just a chemical reaction to the air." He paused. It feels so strange to know the truth."

Tippet moved away from the fireplace as the flames began to rise. "You guys scared the hell out of us when you arrived. Once we figured out just how breakable you were…"

Bibix thought he understood. "Now that I know what my enemy really is, I'm not so afraid. Tell me, once you understood something of our biology and anatomy, did it help you kill us more effectively?"

Carl tried to enjoy the warmth from the fire. "Yes. Yes, it did." He paused. "Look, I tested all the ranged weapons I could scrounge on the NorCon armor. It's some kind of crystalline slab matrix. Slugs can chip it, but they generally won't penetrate unless a lot of bullets rapidly hit the same spot. Lasers get reflected somehow. Plasma seems to be your best bet. My shots burned through every time. The rifle you salvaged is missing a lot of its accessories. With scopes and boosters, weapons like this can kill them from two thousand meters."

Bibix came closer. "We've got six more plasma rifles in the trophy hall – five on display and one in storage. There must be fifty power packs, which are also on display. You've got what we had in storage. It'll be hard to steal anything from the displays."

The soldier sat on a wooden stool. "The pump is their weakness. For some reason, it's not protected. I don't know tech stuff, but it looks to me like these pumps aren't part of the original equipment. They run on batteries, too. Any of the weapons we've got can take those out."

Bibix sat near the fire and grumbled out loud, "What do you expect from food in a can."

Carl jammed more twigs and branches into the growing fire. "Remember what I said about getting cocky? Don't underestimate them. You overestimated them before, so don't waste your time thinking about how damned superior you are. It didn't work for us, and it won't work for you."

Shamed, Bibix got up and went to the dining room. He picked up the NorCon helmet. Turning the scarred headgear over in his hands, he marveled at the interior mechanisms. Hundreds of tiny switches, connectors, and radial displays competed for space inside the cavity where a larger head should go. The visor system that would have protected a lifeform's eyes had clearly been adapted for eating. The very idea of several dozen NorCons swimming about in the confines of this device made his stomach turn with revulsion.

"It does kind of smell bad," he observed, taking the helmet back into the living room.

"You don't know the half of it." Carl offered Bibix a long strip of moss as he sat down.

Bibix took the food. "How did you know?"

The man laughed. "I can go nuts and still pay attention."

Carl's meal came from a silver packet, to which he added water. Bibix ate his moss and watched with interest as the human ate gray mush with an extruded synthetic spoon. "That must taste terrible."

"Don't care," Carl said with his mouth full.

"What is it?"

"Don't care." The human tossed the empty wrapper into the fire and reached for another.

As darkness fell, Bibix found himself enjoying the fire. Something about the light and heat appealed to him in a way that he couldn't define.

Walking back to his lev to get more food, he thought about his reaction to the NorCons. "How about that? I have a prejudice." Collecting his food, he hurried back to Carl.

Tippet's clarifications were painful at times. "We've all got 'em, Bibs. I guess it doesn't matter which planet you come from. Shucks, every time we had a war back in the old days, we'd dehumanize the other guy.

It's easy to knock somebody off when you think he's inferior, or food. The hardest thing we ever did before you guys showed up was to get along with each other."

Bibix couldn't help his keen interest. "But you did do it?"

The man scowled. "No, not really. We tried. We had lots of little wars instead of one really big one. I suppose the only reason we tried to be nice to you guys at first was because you weren't like us. It didn't do us any good, obviously."

Once again, Bibix found himself shamed into silence. Humans and Lapropods had each made so many mistakes. Knowing the secret of the NorCons didn't seem to provide much hope for either species. "Unless..."

Carl stopped poking the fire. "What?"

"Common cause. I forget which author said it, but I remember something about friends and enemies."

"'The enemy of my enemy is my friend,'" Carl replied, quoting Sun Tzu.

Bibix nodded. "That's the one. Humans will be food and Lapropods will be slaves until we stop the NorCons. After that, we can make peace with each other."

Carl snorted. "We can try."

Pleased with himself, Bibix got up and brushed the dirt from his body. "I'd better get home. I can tell anyone who asks that I was out with a lady friend. I'll come back in three days. It might be too dangerous to come back sooner. Will you be okay?"

The man smiled. "If I'm the only human outside of captivity, I kind of have to be."

Bibix enjoyed the dark humor. "I'm glad we could get this worked out between us."

Carl looked at Bibix for a long moment. "Three days. If you're not back here in three days, I'll move on. In the meantime, I'll think about what has to be done next. Scratch up whatever you can get away with and bring it with you – guns, bombs, bullets. It's all going to be useful."

"Human food is going to be a problem."

Tippet disagreed. "I've seen several moose and a couple of bears in this area. As soon as I can get a clear shot at one without alerting the NorCon patrols, I'll be eating like a king."

126 | Bibix

Bibix stood up. "It's good to see you again."

Carl stopped what he was doing, muttering, "I wish you hadn't revived me."

Chapter 6

Halfway through the following workday, Bibix was summoned to Grilleck's office. Donning a breath mask, he knocked and entered.

The administrator sat behind its large desk. It sounded like it was in a good mood. "Bibix, come in. Close the door."

The Lapropod choked, "Is there a problem, Greatness?"

Grilleck enjoyed his underling's fear. "Close the door."

"I'd rather not," Bibix admitted.

128 | Bibix

The NorCon enjoyed its laugh for several seconds. "This isn't that kind of meeting. Close the door. I have questions, and an assignment, for you."

Bibix reluctantly shut the door and took a seat.

"My master has approved my attack plan. If all goes well at the Eagle River site, we will attack other trophy halls in this region. My initiative will be rewarded if we prevail. Fresh troops are being brought in from home. It should be a good fight."

The news wiped away Bibix's fatigue and some of his fear. Carl would be pleased to hear that the NorCons would soon be killing each other over meaningless artifacts that they had no basis for understanding.

Sitting across from Grilleck, Bibix was revolted at the thought of hundreds of...things...swimming around inside the mechanized suit. He forced himself to take a filtered breath. "I am pleased that you are pleased, Greatness."

Grilleck accepted the groveling. "As much as I look forward to this fight, there are other matters. I've just come from a meeting with the sector security chief. Human war gear was found near the Eagle River trophy hall. It was hidden in a manner consistent with human military procedures. I have a list of the items that were found. I need to know if any of these things are missing from our inventory."

Bibix froze.

Grilleck misunderstood the long silence. "I could lose my chance to lead the Eagle River attack if it turns out that those items were stolen from this trophy hall. My master wants to see the complete inventory list today. Now."

130 | Bibix

Bibix blinked. Taking a slow breath, he spoke with a calm that he did not feel. "At the risk of being eaten, I swear that everything under this roof has been accounted for."

Grilleck might have actually been nervous. "Lapropods lie. You do it all the time. I know that you cover up your mistakes."

Bibix trembled. "Nobody wants to be eaten, Greatness."

The NorCon adopted a neutral pose. "The corps commander has ordered every trophy hall in this region to be audited. That action will take place in two days. Your lists must match precisely what is actually here on display or in storage. Do I make myself clear?"

Bibix nodded with intense sobriety. "If you fail, I fail. We all fail."

Grilleck said nothing for a long moment. Then it changed the subject. "I have seen a recon photo of the Eagle River site. Once we have its contents, we won't be able to fit them all under this roof. We will need a bigger building."

Bibix bowed his head. "I had thought of that, Greatness. Both buildings are prefabricated structures. We could take their building apart and use the pieces to make this one bigger."

Grilleck smacked a fist on its desk. "Your people make bad laborers. It could take weeks to finish such a project. My master would not stand for the embarrassment."

Recalling what he'd read about human labor unions, Bibix tried once more to sound humble. "Greatness. As I study your leadership tactics, I see…that is, I can't help but notice that your underlings tend to work harder than those of others because you care about what happens to them."

"I do?" Grilleck wasn't sure if it had been complimented or insulted.

Bibix watched the NorCon adjust its translator device. "Yes, Greatness. You care about what happens to the people under your command, and it shows."

Grilleck fumed. "My translator must be broken. What are you talking about?"

Licking his lips nervously inside the breath mask, Bibix struggled to find words that would not translate as 'compassion' or 'kindness.' "You and I are talking.

I've seen you do it with others of my kind. When we have good ideas, you use them. When we have bad ideas, you eat us. Trust me when I say that your good example has not gone unnoticed."

"Talking is caring? Is that what you are telling me?" the NorCon demanded.

"Yes, Greatness." Bibix remembered so show just a little bit of fear.

Grilleck thought it understood. "Talking to the labor battalions will somehow make them work faster? That sounds very foolish. My master would have me disciplined for being so stupid."

Bibix made his move. "You could let me talk to the workers when the time comes."

The NorCon sat still for a long moment as the community inside its armor struggled to make sense of what it had been told. The group craved military promotion and social advancement more than it feared treachery from a creature that it regarded as less than food.

Grilleck spoke as the will of the majority asserted itself. "You are, without a doubt, the smartest 'Pod I've ever met. You do a lot of good work around here. My master seems to think well of you. These are great accomplishments for something like you. If I could find a female 'Pod with your potential, I would force the two of you to breed. Your solution is acceptable. I shall put it forward as my own. Do you have any problems with that?"

"How much time to do I have to pack?" Bibix asked, his voice evincing real fear.

"What?" the administrator asked angrily.

The Lapropod risked his life to con Grilleck into giving up just a little more information. "I've given most of my adult life to this facility. I won't stand by while the exhibits are—"

Grilleck kicked at its desk in rage. "Be ready to move the contents of this building in ten days. That's all I can say."

The adrenaline racing through his veins caused Bibix to feel brave. He probed for more information. "You're looking forward to battle?"

Grilleck thumped its chest, which made Bibix shudder at the thought of what must be going on inside that armor. "I am. When the shooting starts, NorCons will be brought in from many parts of this region. If the trophy hall isn't destroyed, we will all have a good time."

Bibix realized that his translator might not be giving him an accurate account of what Grilleck just said. Regardless, NorCons would be fighting NorCons, and that was all that mattered.

He bowed his head. "I wish you well, Greatness."

"You should. If I get killed, Veknar will be in charge."

Bibix didn't know what to say to that. He bided his time, waiting to be dismissed. Trundling back to his office, he tried to avoid looking happy. If all the NorCons in this region were eager for a fight, they might not be paying attention to other things – like the human processing center Tippet had seen.

Chapter 7

The next workday passed slowly for Bibix. Using pen and paper that he brought from home, he drew maps of the food processing plant and its approximate location. He got the layouts and geographic details from a series of official photos posted on the wall near Grilleck's office. Late in the afternoon, he pretended to clean a dog sled exhibit so that he could eavesdrop on Veknar and Grilleck.

The administrator pretended to admire a collection of synthetic mountaineering gear as it gossiped with its deputy. "Are you serious? The fools at the Eagle River compound actually think their trophy hall was infiltrated by a human scouting party?"

The deputy wasn't so skeptical. "That is what I have heard. Ten items were found. My source tells me that only two of those items might have been taken from their trophy hall. If they weren't taken from our facility, that only leaves one possibility. There could be armed humans in the area."

Grilleck reached out with one of its mechanical claws to examine a long chain of carabiner clips. "How do they know that Lapropods didn't break the lock on the side door? I've ordered more than a few 'Poddies to steal things from that site, whereas we have not seen armed humans in thirty years. Is your source Administrator Velleck?"

Veknar knew better than to lie. "Yes. He was in my assault group during the invasion. We were assigned to the same assimilation team. The discovery of free-range humans has excited him."

The NorCon's casual use of gender terminology bothered Bibix. The very idea of a NorCon that could somehow be female made him queasy.

The senior NorCon couldn't bring itself to be so fanciful. "We all want to move on. We all want other conquests. Earth has been a disappointment. Stop looking for a fight and do your job."

Veknar walked away. The insubordinate move surprised the Lapropod. Grilleck went back to its own office.

Taking his cleaning supplies back to a janitorial closet, Bibix thought about what he'd just seen. "Dumb, Bibix. Really dumb. You shouldn't have buried those things."

The exchange between Grilleck and Veknar reminded him of two old friends having a causal chat after a long workday. His anger receded as he thought of Carl. "He's going to ask me why I buried my stuff so close to the trophy hall, and I'm not going to have a good answer."

He shook his head and wiggled his eyestalks to clear his mind. "Easy now. I'm not afraid of them any more because I know what they are. Remember what Carl said. Prejudice. Hate. I need to make my peace with this." He thought for a moment, and then shook his head ruefully. "I really should stop talking to humans."

Realizing that he was conflicted in ways that he could never describe, Bibix decided to seek philosophical guidance. When his shift ended, he packed his things and prepared to leave the trophy hall. His phone rang as he watched the last of his underlings go.

Bibix answered wearily. "Senior Curator Bibix, Trophy Hall Two-Five. How may I help you?"

His mother sounded like she'd been crying. "Bibsi, darling. Please come home."

He leaned back in his chair, smiling and rolling his eyes. "I'm not going to let you set me up on another date. I promise, I'll find a mate when I'm ready. I've just…I've got a lot going on right now."

The family matriarch sniffled through the connection. "Bibsi, it's your father. Sweetness, I'm so sorry. He's been eaten."

Bibix felt like he'd been clubbed by three NorCons at the same time. Even though he had decided to hide his militancy by adopting antisocial behaviors, he loved his parents.

They had mated before leaving their home world. The podling that would eventually become Bibix didn't generate until they'd been on Earth for twenty years.

142 | Bibix

His mother had feared she was barren. His father had feared he was impotent. The ten long years of hard work immediately after their arrival had kept them from having a stable home life.

"I'll be there as soon as I can."

He put the phone down and let his eyes retract into his head for a long moment. Tears filled his ocular cavities and the excess fell through the lower sinus cavities to stream out of his nose.

Thirty years of NorCon occupation hadn't numbed the Lapropods to the random, senseless losses inflicted by the callous conquerors. No family was left untouched. It was this chronic fear of being eaten for no apparent reason that had driven Bibix to his present state of rebellion. As he mourned the loss of his father, he wished he'd acted sooner to oppose the NorCons.

Keeping his eyes closed, he felt through the drawers in his desk for a handkerchief. He wiped his nose, feeling his skin temperature rise as his hate for the NorCons grew. He thought about Carl and the way the human had tried to provoke him. The ruthless man's words rang in his ears. <u>It's not enough to be morally outraged. You've gotta be really mad when you pull that trigger.</u>

With a long, hearty blow of his nose, Bibix pulled himself together. He wiped at his eyes as the stalks extended. Tossing the mushy handkerchief into a trashcan, he checked the contents of his briefcase. The hand-drawn map of the human food processing facility peeked out from behind a group of folders. After a slow and careful thought, he took the hand grenade from his desk and slipped it into the satchel.

Bibix left the trophy hall. The roaming guard ignored him as it tromped through the exhibit area. Flopping into his lev, Bibix dropped his things into the passenger's seat and drove to his family's home in the residential zone. Lapropodian society embraced community living. Most families, no matter how large, lived together under one roof. In recent years, younger Lapropods had taken to living in pairs or by themselves. Some said this was an emulation of human behavior. Others said it was merely youthful rebellion.

Because the Lapropods had fled their home world in great haste, they hadn't brought much with them. Using what the humans had left behind seemed like the natural thing to do.

Collective guilt over the destruction of an entire species had motivated males and females alike to do more than merely keep and use the items they found. Mastering the many tools, languages, laws, and social customs of the regions in which their ancestors had landed, each succeeding generation of Lapropods had become more "humanized" than the last.

Bibix thought about the way his people chose to remember the humans they had displaced. "We live in their dwellings. We use their tools and most of their manufacturing and agriculture techniques. We fear them and we're glad they're gone. If all that's true, why do we try so hard to be like them? Is this what human philosophers meant when they described hypocrisy?"

Gliding over clean pavement and through the brightly lit intersections, Bibix guided his lev past hundreds of homes that had once provided shelter for thousands of humans. He brought his vehicle to a halt when a traffic signal indicated a mandatory stop. Drumming his fingers on the steering column, he watched a NorCon cross the street and walk down the block. The armored suit moved with purpose. The visored helmet swiveled back and forth as it scanned the neighborhood for unauthorized activity.

Bibix found himself drawn to the sight of the single NorCon as the traffic light flashed green. "You're not afraid of anyone, are you?" he thought.

He turned and pulled over to the side of the road. As the lev idled, he watched the NorCon. A new thought occurred. "Stupid can of food. You're not expecting trouble, are you? You wouldn't strut around like that in a neighborhood full of humans."

Bibix sobered at the thought. Some of the books Carl had recommended dealt with the subject of guerilla warfare.

"Ambush," he murmured as the NorCon went around a distant corner.

Reaching into the back seat, he fumbled with his briefcase. Using just two hands, he pulled out the small device he'd been saving. It was one of the many undocumented items he had looted in the trophy hall. "Ha, that's funny. I don't actually remember how much stuff I took. Now then, what do we have here?"

Bibix examined the olive drab sphere. Tiny yellow letters on its rounded surface labeled the device as a small explosive. "Frag. Three-point-seven-five ounces. Effective range, sixty feet. Warning, may start fires."

The old mechanism felt cold and heavy in his hand. The silver pull ring slipped around one finger as if it had a will of its own. He identified his feeling as a longing to kill the patrolling NorCon. The certainty of that desire energized his imagination.

148 | Bibix

He shook his head as his enemy walked out of sight. Taking great care to put the grenade back in the briefcase, he quoted an old Lapropodian nursery rhyme: "Harming for spite is not right."

Bibix drove to his family's house in a mood that got worse by the second. He talked to himself on the way. "It's not like I'm trying to be a human serial killer. There's no pleasure in this for me. I've got a good reason to fight back against the NorCons. Why does this have to be so hard?"

His parents lived in a subdivision that had survived both the Lapropod and NorCon arrivals completely intact. The Lapropodian desire for conformity without adherence to divisive socioeconomic guidelines had resulted in a similarity between all the homes he drove past. The standardization would have gone unnoticed in most human societies. Looking for his parents' home address, Bibix found himself being irritated by the uniformity of colors, styles, and architecture.

He parked his lev next to the clean sidewalk and stared at the only dwelling he'd ever inhabited as part of a family. The customary baskets of cut flowers hung from porch rails and stanchions, indicating that the family was in mourning.

"That was fast," he muttered.

NorCon prejudice was widely feared. Because Lapropods showed their grief in such subtle ways, it was common for them to be harassed by their oppressors. Bibix was amazed to see that flowers had been put up so fast. Was that a family effort, or had the neighbors helped?

150 | Bibix

The streetlights came to life, their orange sodium glare contrasting with the darkness as the sunset faded. With a sigh, he turned off his lev and got out.

His grandfather came out of the house as he gathered his thoughts. The old fellow shuffled down the steps and across the lawn with a posture that suggested great purpose. Bibix took note of the elder's eyestalks. They were partially tucked in. His eyeballs were close to his skull, a sure sign of poor temper.

"Hello, Grandfather. I came as soon as I got the news."

The old Lapropod was surprisingly blunt as he came to a stop on all four pods. "Glad to hear it, Bibix. I'm pleased that you haven't given up all of our traditions. Unfortunately, the family doesn't think it's a good idea for you to be around just now."

The rebuke hurt like a slap. Bibix raised both eyestalks to signal his shock. "I don't know what to say. Can you at least tell me what happened to my father?"

The elder looked back at the house before softening his tone. "You know better than to ask me a question like that. I have no idea why he was eaten. I just know that it happened. We got the news from one of his coworkers. Look, blood of mine. You're too chummy with the NorCons. I don't blame you for it, but the others don't see things like I do. That and your antisocial behavior are just too much to tolerate right now."

Bibix took the criticism without comment. He had his prejudices and they had theirs. "Was it work related? Did they eat him because he made a mistake?"

The older being's white hairs bristled. "Do you see what I mean? Your mother doesn't need to hear that from you. Not now. Not ever again. Your father – my son – was a good 'Pod. Go back to wherever it is you call home, Bibix. We don't have a body, so there won't be a funeral. Don't give me any of that human logic, either. We'll grieve in our own way. When your mother is ready, she'll call you."

He bristled. "Mom asked me to come. That's why I'm here."

Grandfather shook his knobby head. "This is no time for your sass. 'Mom' is a human word, and I won't let you speak like that in our house. I know you're just trying to be an individual, but this is not the time for that kind of bad behavior.

"We've talked it over, and the majority agrees. You brought this on yourself when you moved out of our home. If you care for us at all, you'll respect our wishes and come back when we think the time is right."

Frustration boiled inside Bibix like an active geyser. With great effort, he held his tongues for a long moment.

His grandfather noted his restraint and sighed. "I don't like this any more than you do. Your father was proud of you. Do you know that?"

Bibix leaned on the front of his lev, looking to his left and then to his right. "He was so angry when I didn't follow him into civil service."

Grandfather laughed. "He wasn't angry. He pretended to be upset just to make the rest of us happy. Truthfully? When you weren't around, he defended you and your choices. He and your mother never let any of us forget that you are an important 'Pod.

The curator made an expansive gesture with all four hands. "There are a hundred families in this area, but you'd never know it. For as long as I can remember, this neighborhood has been as quiet as a tomb. Even if I hadn't made certain decisions, I'm not sure I could have stayed here."

"You broke with tradition, Bibix. We love you, but we can't ignore that." The old 'Pod pointed at the night sky. "You want to know something? I'm not as dense as you think I am. Every time I get full of myself, I just look up. This isn't our home world, and things will never again be like they once were. Most of us, with you being the exception in our family, try so very hard to hang on to the old ways because, when they're gone, they'll be gone forever."

Bibix blinked. "I never meant to turn my back on the family."

Grandfather nodded. "In your own way, you're still attached to us. You come for regular visits, and you come when your mother asks you to. It's the new way of doing things. It's normal for you, but it's still scary and strange to the rest of us. Pity us if you need to, but let us have some leeway. Give us a chance to mourn this loss before we welcome you back."

The younger 'Pod lowered his eyes in defeat. "Tell Mother to call me when you're ready."

Grandfather went back into the house.

Bibix got into his lev and went back to his apartment. He studied his hand-drawn maps, trying, and failing, to ignore the shame he felt. He fell asleep while reading.

He arrived at work three hours early the next day to make final preparations for the internal audit that would precede the inspection that was so important to Administrator Grilleck's future.

As planned, his 'adjusted' inventory perfectly matched the actual contents of the trophy hall. The small army of auditors pronounced the exhibits to be in complete order after just ten hours of scrounging and scrutiny. The administrator shared this news with its subordinate while Bibix was nearby.

Veknar had news of its own. "I've been told that the war gear found near the Eagle River site included a small-caliber handgun. Most of the objects were missing from the official inventory of that trophy hall."

The administrator raised one of its mechanical hands. "You're not going to convince me that humans have come down from the hills. They are food, nothing more."

Veknar continued to ignore Bibix's presence. "Two of the long-range patrols were lost this winter. Another patrol is overdue. Lapropods didn't do that. Humans could."

Grilleck pointed to an exhibit on the far side of the trophy hall. "This region is populated by grizzly bears. The troops who have gone missing were new to this world. Like you, they probably did not pay attention to their sector briefings. If you had been more observant, you would know that we are vulnerable to certain large mammals which are common to this world."

"What about the war gear?" Veknar demanded.

158 | Bibix

Grilleck turned to lay one large, cold claw on Bibix. "I do not know, and I do not care. Our inventory was flawless. Once I bring this news to our master, we will be free to plan the attack on that poorly defended position. Their loot will be ours, and there will be no more stealing in this region. There will also be no more talk of humans."

Bibix remained quiet and motionless until both of his tormentors were out of sight. Then he went back to his office to calm down.

The rest of the staff had been sent home. As Bibix rested in his chair, Grilleck stomped into the small room. The Lapropod cringed as he tried to straighten his posture. "Yes, Greatness?"

"This facility will be closed until the morning of the inspection. Anyone who reports for work before then will be eaten. You will inform the others before you leave this building."

Bibix made the required phone calls. All of the Lapropods under his supervision were just as surprised as he was. With that chore completed, he turned off the lights in his office and left the building.

Chapter 8

Returning to his apartment, Bibix ate leftovers and sorted through his stockpile of weapons and equipment. Many things still troubled him. He didn't sleep well.

Early the next day, he packed his things in a suitcase and left. Driving with his usual caution, he tried to make sure that he wasn't being followed.

Carl had moved his lair to another house. He showed Bibix where to park and hide his lev, and then directed him into a building that was hidden from view by a swath of overgrown shrubs. He went through the new supplies as the nervous curator talked.

Bibix told him about the attack Grilleck was planning. "It felt like the right thing to do."

Tippet looked up. "Good for you, Bibs. It's not going to hurt me to see them kill each other. Who knows? It might be just the distraction we need. While they fight, we can break into that food processing plant. I don't know what we're going to find, but it's one sure way of getting more troops on our side."

Bibix munched on a snack while he talked. "I thought you might see things that way. If one human is dangerous, lots of them should be overwhelming."

Carl paused in his rummaging, and then held up an olive-drab military issue bra. He eyed Bibix strangely.

The Lapropod talked with his mouth full. "I don't know what that is. Can you use it?"

"Let's hope not." Carl tossed the garment aside.

Bibix sat down. "Carl? Did you get along with your parents?"

The human examined the odds and ends of military equipment on the floor in front of him, and then started putting something together. "Yeah, Bibs, I did. Why do you ask?"

The troubled Lapropod lowered his eyes. "My father was eaten yesterday."

Tippet stopped his tinkering. "I'm sorry to hear that. I lost my dad, too."

Bibix shuddered at the implications. "Did my people kill your father?"

"Yes." Carl glanced at him before finishing his assembly of what turned out to be a grenade launcher.

Bibix tried not to sigh. "I'm sorry."

The soldier pointed his new weapon at the far wall. "Do you have any rounds for this?"

"What is it?" the curator asked.

The hairy man opened the breach to look down the long black tube. "A forty-millimeter grenade launcher, effective to seven hundred feet. Just the sort of thing you need to shake, boil, and then fry a NorCon."

Bibix pulled the suitcase closer and pawed through the contents. "I found parts for two plasma rifles. Forty-millimeter rocket-propelled grenades are hard to come by. We have six of them in one of our exhibits. Here. I think this is what you want."

Carl took the offered shell and held it up to eye level. "Sweet. See this tip? It's armor piercing. Just what we need."

The guilty Lapropod gave up his search. "We've only got one?"

"We only need one," the soldier said as he scratched his dirty beard.

Bibix tried to ignore the fleas that jumped off the mud-covered man. "I don't understand."

Tippet grinned. "I've been out to see that food plant for myself. It's one big building, out near Wasilla. Security seems to rely on locked doors more than anything else."

The Lapropod nodded. "The NorCons don't fear us. You, on the other hand, will be a different matter."

The veteran laughed. "I'm counting on their arrogance. If they actually do start fighting with each other, we could catch a break. If they pull troops away from that death camp, we should be able to take them by surprise."

"I don't know when Grilleck plans to attack."

Carl shook his head. "It'll happen soon. Do you have more equipment?"

The alien patted the nylon lid of the suitcase with two hands. "Enough to fill this bag one more time. I had more, but I lost it."

Bibix was relieved when Carl didn't seem to care. The human held up an assembled plasma gun. "This is a carbine. It should still have enough punch to take out NorCon armor. Use it just like that old slug thrower. That reminds me, have you been practicing?"

"No," Bibix admitted.

The man looked at him with unfiltered contempt. "You are a credit to your species."

Bibix threw up all four hands. "Before we came to Earth, my species never fought a war. Not once, ever. Humans killed each other all the time and, I might add, in very large numbers. I'm sorry that this isn't normal for me. No, wait. I'm glad it's not normal for me. I don't want to be a killer like you."

Carl put a power pack into the carbine and handed it to Bibix. "Bibs, I'm twenty-four years old. I should be in college, growing a beard, chasing girls, and getting bad grades. I'm not. Everyone I ever knew is gone. All the places I've ever been were wiped off the map. Instead of being tormented by one alien race from outer space, I'm forced to deal with both Lapropods and NorCons. Suck it up. We can't always have what we want."

Bibix took the weapon, cradling it in two quivering arms. "You sound like my father."

Tippet sat back and brushed dirt from his torn shirt. "I thought you guys were all hugs and kisses. No violence and all that. Was your dad in your version of an army?"

The nervous Lapropod fidgeted with the settings on his gun. His eye stalks pivoted in different directions as he attempted to avoid looking right at Carl. "My father was a civil servant. He worked for what you might call our government. He used to tell me that it was okay to be afraid of the NorCons. When I was small, he'd say that we didn't have to like what they were doing to us. I didn't really understand what he meant until much later."

Carl yawned. "I have no idea what you're talking about now. Please, explain."

Bibix licked his lips. Checking to make sure his weapon was in safe mode, he laid it on the floor. "There's an old saying. 'If you don't know why you're angry, it's a bad thing.' We are taught from childhood to understand what makes us angry."

Tippet blinked. "What do you do about it?"

Bibix locked both eyes on the human. "Excuse me?"

Carl shook his head with frustration. "What are you supposed to do when you figure out what makes you mad?"

After a long pause, the Lapropod replied, "I don't understand your question."

Tippet sighed. "Do I need to hurt you?"

Bibix recalled the first time Carl had beaten him. "That's right. I wanted to harm you, too. I was angry. I wanted to make you stop hurting me, and—"

Carl eased up. "That's right. Sometimes, the only way you get the other guy to stop what he's doing is to give him a taste of the pain he's dishing out."

"I understand that here," Bibix replied, pointing to his head, "but I don't understand that here." He pointed to his hearts. "I want to be militant. I want to be violent. I know it's the only thing the NorCons will understand. I'm just not getting off to a very good start."

Tippet leaned back and tried to relax as the daylight faded. "I remember the last time I saw a television broadcast. Some guy in a suit was telling us that the military wasn't going to bother with the formal recruitment process anymore. They were going to start handing out guns and gear to anyone who asked for it. National Guard armories were ordered to give their stuff away on a first come, first served basis. We were all being encouraged to form guerilla bands. The T.V. signal faded out while the guy in the suit was still talking."

The idea made Bibix shiver with sympathy. "We forced you to that."

Carl nodded. "The NorCons are forcing you to act now. There's no shame in that. We used to say that freedom isn't free. You can't just write these guys a stern letter or talk trash about them when they aren't around. You've got to act."

Bibix reached into the suitcase for his maps. "Let's plan our first action. I can come back here to get you when Veknar and his troops start their attack on the Eagle River site."

Tippet moved in closer to look at the maps. "I've been in one place for too long. It's only a matter of time until one of their random foot patrols finds me. There's another house a few blocks north of here. The aboveground portion has collapsed, but the basement is still in great shape. I'll move my things after dark. When the time comes, just drive slowly through this area. I'll flag you down."

172 | Bibix

The Lapropod picked up the plasma carbine, holding it casually with just two hands. "You're trusting me with a lot of information. Why?"

The scruffy human ran his dirty fingers over the diagram of the food processing plant. "I've been thinking about what I'm going to find in here. It gives me nightmares. You know? I keep dreaming about Nazi death camps that I saw in the old black-and-white documentaries. I've got to trust somebody just now or I'll go insane."

Bibix nodded. His eyes wobbled on the ends of their stalks. "I spend so much time away from my family that I feel alone, too. I know its wrong, but I have to do this. I hope that, someday, they'll understand."

Carl folded the maps and laid them inside the suitcase. "Sounds like you're on the outs with them. What happened?"

"My father," Bibix reminded him.

Tippet frowned. "Now it's my turn to be in the dark."

The worried Lapropod fidgeted with his gun. "My family doesn't want me around for the funeral. They don't hate me. It's not like that. It's just that I spend too much time away from home. I think they're afraid of me."

The human yawned. "You're asking me to be sympathetic about things I don't understand. Even with the handy-dandy translator, I don't comprehend some of what you say. Look, Bibix, you still have a family. My parents got mad at me sometimes, too. You know what? They never stopped loving me. Let your people have their grief. It's what they need."

"I wish I knew what I needed," Bibix replied rhetorically.

174 | Bibix

Carl stood up. "You need a girlfriend. Go home and get some sleep. Leave all this gear with me. Do whatever it is you little freaks do to relax and wait for the spit to hit the fan. Leave the rest of the battle plan to me. You'll feel much better after you've had your first taste of combat."

Bibix felt his stomach lurch. "I doubt that very much."

Chapter 9

Bibix went back to his apartment. Driving through the light rain in the dark, he tried to reevaluate Carl Tippet. The human was rude, brutal, and profane. Alone in the front seat of his lev, Bibix tried to make sense of the man's many, apparently unrelated, contradictions. How could a rational being speak so calmly about doing violence and still be capable of discussing family matters?

Sleep wouldn't come to the restless Lapropod. He showed up for work the next morning with a mild headache and bloodshot eyes. Arriving early, he briefed the staff on the protocol for the official inspection.

176 | Bibix

Grilleck summoned him to its office as the inspectors began their counting. Bibix put on his breath mask and shuffled in with more confidence than he felt.

Behind its desk, Grilleck looked down on its minion. "If the assessors find anything to be missing, I'll eat you in three bites. I have brought spices and sauce to get past the bad taste."

Bibix couldn't help trembling. He knew that Grilleck meant every word it said. "I would not blame you, Greatness. We have had enough time to prepare. I see that you have polished your military decorations."

Every scratch, scrape, and chip that scarred the NorCon's armor had been left unrepaired to show off its war fighting experience. Grilleck's combat awards, service medallions, and honor stripes were all buffed and clean. The contrast stood out in Bibix's mind as a philosophical hypocrisy, though he kept his thoughts to himself.

"I need to show my master that I am more than a simple administrator, that I am front-line combat material."

"You must be looking forward to the attack," the Lapropod observed.

Grilleck thumped its chest with one sharp claw. "The fool who runs the Eagle River site deserves to have it taken away from him. I don't expect you to understand, but this fight will keep us strong. This is an impoverished world. Its lack of skilled combatants is not good for us. Those of us who can do so will gain promotions so that we can leave this miserable place."

Though he stopped speaking, the administrator didn't dismiss Bibix. The Lapropod became terrified when he realized that Grilleck intended to keep him nearby until the inspection was complete. The NorCon remained silent and brooding for two full hours.

Bibix jerked out of a sullen trance when the master inspector entered the pressurized office. It stomped into the center of the room and gave its brief report. "The inventory of this facility is one hundred percent accurate. All conquest trophies are accounted for. There is nothing extra. There are no items missing from the register. You are to be commended. This is the report I will make to your master. Do you have anything to add?"

Grilleck stood and replied, "I live to serve."

Bibix tried to breathe quietly as he paid close attention to the examiner. The servo-assisted, armored suit that housed the composite being lacked some of the unidentifiable attachments that were commonly found on NorCons with more battlefield experience. Bibix also noted that the master inspector was unarmed and its armor showed few battle scars. Remembering what he'd read about human samurai warriors, he suspected that unarmed NorCons were somehow less important than those who went armed.

"Your remarks are noted," the being acknowledged blandly as it left.

Grilleck sat and turned to address Bibix. "My master will order the attack soon. You must begin packing the inventory. When we are victorious, parts of both trophy halls will be combined to create a larger structure. We will, of course, add to this facility. You will not have much time. Ten days at the most. I suggest that you get started at once."

180 | Bibix

Bibix heard the dismissal in the administrator's tone. He stood and backed out of the room without saying a word. In the corridor, he pulled off his breath mask and wiped sweat from his brow. A pair of eyes peeked at him from around a nearby corner.

Raising all four hands, Bibix flashed an 'okay' signal to the cowering Lapropod. Word was quickly passed to the rest of the staff that he had saved the day. With his popularity at a temporary high, Bibix decided to enjoy the moment while it lasted. He would wait to break the news to them about the packing orders.

Recalling what he'd read about making friends and influencing people, he used the occasion of a midday supervisor's meeting to be both diplomatic and authoritative. "We have been given a great honor. We are to immediately start packing everything for temporary storage. No half-measures. I don't want anyone to be eaten. If we can do a good job, most of us can stay off the labor gangs that will be used to improve this facility and make it bigger."

The two dozen Lapropods who made up the trophy hall's fearful staff talked about him after he left the room. His apparent regard for their safety made them all feel better about the coming move. A few of them actually thought he was brave. One or two whispered that Bibix might even be a leader who could deal effectively with the NorCons.

* * *

Unaware of his fame, Bibix endured many threats and insults heaped on him by Administrator Grilleck, Deputy Administrator Veknar, and other NorCons as he quietly urged his reluctant subordinates to work long hours during the next several days. The difficulties associated with finding suitable packing materials frustrated him to the point of insomnia.

Seven days slid by in a blur of panicked packing, loathsome item logging, and working with boxes that were either too big or too small. Spurred on by his good example, the Lapropods who labored under his bleary-eyed gaze began to think that Bibix was a harsh taskmaster. He might also be insane.

"Don't make me take this to Veknar!" he shouted at the end of the eighth day of hot, sweaty, backbreaking labor.

His loss of temper took them all by surprise. They called him names when they were sure he wasn't around. There was no longer any doubt. Bibix had gone mad. In the end, though, they feared the deputy administrator more than they feared him. The pace of work sped up slightly. The quarrels over boxes and tape became a little less frequent.

That evening, Grilleck called an exhausted Bibix into its office. "The trophy hall will be closed tomorrow. We will have extra guards on duty, and you will not need to be here. Tell everyone to stay home."

Bibix pulled on a breath mask and settled on to all four pods. "We're not done packing!"

The administrator was in no mood to be trifled with. "Don't start with me. My master has set the date for the attack. You are not entitled to know more. Troops are lined up on both sides from all across this hemisphere. I have been given a front-line command."

"It sounds glorious." Bibix tried not to squirm as adrenaline shot through his tired body.

184 | Bibix

Grilleck laughed until it overloaded its translator. "Glorious? Ha! It'll be fantastic! Bibix, I called you in here because I want to use a human weapon in this battle. Pick something suitably lethal, and bring it to me. Now."

Bibix hurried to comply. Recalling what Carl had told him about ballistic weapons and their inability to penetrate NorCon armor, a wild idea popped into his head. Running through the halls, he ripped off his breath mask and yelled for assistance. With the aid of six junior archivists, he brought Grilleck a very large machine gun.

"What is that?" the NorCon soldier demanded when it saw the long weapon being wheeled into its office on a hand-trolley.

Bibix shooed the other staff members away as he squirmed back into his breath mask. He hurriedly explained, "It's a heavy machine gun, Greatness, built by a human named Browning. It fires twelve-point-seven-millimeter projectiles at a rate of more than six hundred per minute."

Grilleck clearly liked the size of the weapon, though it remained dubious. "What about their energy weapons? This is an old human weapon. I wanted something with more punch."

Bibix was ready with his answer. "We have more than ten thousand pages of literature that feature this weapon. It's a classic. Nothing else says 'human warrior' quite like this belt-fed killing machine."

Grilleck paused. It placed one claw on the gun's firing mechanism. "I have seen this weapon depicted in human video dramas. The little human with big muscles and no shirt, what is that character's name?"

186 | Bibix

Bibix bowed his head and lowered his eyes. "Rambo, films One through Four."

The NorCon actually nodded. "Rambo is the name, and I believe he used an M-60."

The senior curator bobbed his head, ready with an explanation. "We have many such dramas on disk, greatness. But the weapon you see here is larger than what you refer to," he offered, as if it were a secret.

Grilleck rose to its feet and took the weapon in both mechanized hands. Bibix watched it raise the weapon and sweep it around the room. A small aperture on its helmet adjusted as if Grilleck were squinting down the length of the barrel.

"Where did this come from?" the administrator asked.

Bibix pointed to a nearby map that hung on the wall. "The Fort Wainwright infantry armory."

Grilleck raised the machine gun to eye level. "Is it loud? Does it make a lot of noise?"

The stunned Lapropod choked ever so slightly on his answer. "I expect so. A weapon of such power would have to be quite loud."

Grilleck dropped the weapon back on to the trolley. "Bah. Its ballistics will not penetrate NorCon armor. Will they?"

Bibix struggled to bend the truth. "I wouldn't know, Greatness. We have seven hundred rounds of ammunition for this weapon. All of it is labeled as 'armor piercing'. I merely presumed that's what you were looking for in a human weapon."

188 | Bibix

The NorCon veteran snorted and went back to its desk. "I will take it. Have the ammunition brought to me at once. Once I clear it with my master, I will practice with it. After the battle, if I like it, I may ask to keep it."

Bibix said nothing as he fled the scene. With any luck, Grilleck and all its unseen organisms would die in battle. If it could be fooled into carrying an inferior weapon, it would get what it deserved.

With this ember glowing in the back of his mind, Bibix informed the staff of their unscheduled time off. "Don't come back to work until I personally call for you. If you come back before I give you the all clear, they'll probably throw you in chains and put you to work on the labor gangs. The battle for the Eagle River site should be over in a few days, I think."

Some of the staff gathered in the parking lot after they'd been dismissed. They talked among themselves about Bibix. All of them were grateful to be spared the pain and injury of the chain gangs. Most were grateful to Bibix and his apparent political power, though a few still thought he was out of his mind. A pessimistic few thought he would be eaten any day now, just like his father. His family must surely be cursed.

As he packed his things to leave, Bibix overheard Veknar bragging. "The battle will last for at least a week. When it is over, there will be room for many promotions. I checked the battle roster and we have more experienced troops than they do."

The inside information gave Bibix more hope. A seven-day battle would mean even fewer NorCon survivors. It also meant he and Carl could deal with the food processing plant slowly, rather than having to make a mad rush of it.

Fear made his skin crawl as he went home. In the safety of his apartment, he ate slowly and waited for midnight. Looking around, he considered the very real possibility that he might never come back to this domicile. Memories competed with gnawing fear as he tried to sort it all out. He packed a few precious keepsakes. The many books he'd collected over the years stared back at him accusingly from their shelves. More than a thousand books would be left behind if he never returned. "I'll just have to find a way to get back here."

Chapter 10

With the inside of his lev packed uncomfortably tight, Bibix forced himself to drive sedately out of NorCon-controlled territory. Making limited use of the vehicle's navigational lighting, he drove aimlessly for an hour, sweating all the way, before going to meet Carl.

The unkempt man came out of hiding after Bibix had driven past his location three times. Dressed in mended camouflage, the bushy-haired man looked scary to Bibix. He followed the human to a secluded location.

"You've got a lot of stuff in here," Carl said, opening the back hatch.

192 | Bibix

Bibix shivered in the cold night air as he turned off the vehicle and got out. "I wanted to be prepared for any eventuality. If things don't work out right, I may never be able to go home again. Living in the woods may be normal for you, but I've never done this kind of thing before."

Tippet reached for a duffle bag. "Help me get this stuff inside."

Bibix ignored the cold and helped with the unloading. Carl stopped him after two trips into the ruined house with gear. He offered the Lapropod a military jacket. "This ought to fit you. It's made out of synthetic fibers. As long as you don't bleed into it or set it on fire, it should last for a couple of years."

The Lapropod noted the coat's unusual construction. "Did you sew an extra set of arms into this?"

"Yeah." Tippet continued moving gear into the ruined house, struggling under a heavy load.

Bibix hurried after him with the last of the equipment he'd brought. Inside the surprisingly warm basement, he found a place to drop his cargo. "When did you learn how to sew?"

The soldier pulled a canvas flap over the crude entry to the underground hiding place. Lighting a long white taper, he sat on the dirty floor. "Three years after the invasion. Nobody had clean clothes anymore. The only way you got new clothes was to make what you could from the rags that other people left behind. We became the ultimate recyclers."

Bibix turned the camouflaged coat over in his many hands. "I don't know what to say. This is very practical. I just can't see you taking the time to sit and sew."

194 | Bibix

Carl tore open the wrapper of a desiccated military-issue protein bar. With some effort, he bit off a piece. "I spend most of my daylight hours hiding from the NorCons. I've got more free time than you might think. My dad taught me how to make needles and salvage thread. My mother taught me how to use them. Just another one of the many job skills for the human survivalist on the go."

"I like it," Bibix admitted as he slipped into the baggy garment.

Tippet spoke after a moment of fierce chewing and one hard swallow. "I've noticed that you guys aren't big on clothes. How do you survive the winters?"

The Lapropod busied himself with the many flaps and zippers on his coat. "My people have never worn clothes. Anyone who saw me in this thing would laugh. No, really. We stay inside when the temperature drops. It's like my mother says, only humans go outside when…never mind."

"It's okay," Carl said after a drink from his canteen.

Bibix pulled the long zipper up to the middle of his chest. Both of his eyestalks remained stationary. "No, it's not okay. I've got prejudices I didn't know I had. I wasn't taken out of the pouch yesterday. I know that you put up with me because I'm useful. You're useful to me, too. I pretend that you don't scare me, even though you do. This whole thing is going to end badly if we can't find a way to get along.

"Honestly, Carl, I'm afraid of what happens if we succeed. You love battle, but those NorCons guarding the food processor could kill me. If I survive that, your people might kill me just for spite."

Tippet eyed the fidgeting Lapropod. "Are you done?"

196 | Bibix

Bibix pulled on the sleeves of his coat. "Did any of that make sense?"

The human tapped the electronic device on his wrist. "I think I got it."

"So?" the tormented being demanded.

Carl blinked. Screwing the lid onto his canteen, he put it aside and scratched his beard. "I don't know what to tell you, Bibs. Those are big concerns. Sometimes you've just got to learn by doing. My people did a lousy job of getting along with each other, but we kept on trying. Politicians and diplomats devoted their entire professional lives to the process. Sometimes they got it right. Sometimes they only made things worse."

The observation appeared to satisfy Bibix. "Are we making things better?"

Tippet shook his head. "Neither one of us is dead yet, so I'm going to say yes, in our own way, we're making things better. Do you know when the attack out in the valley will start?"

Bibix shook his head. "They sent us home with orders to stay away until we were called back. Grilleck seemed to be very eager to get started with the killing. My guess is they will start shooting at each other some time tomorrow."

Carl reached for a synthetic fiber sleeping bag and tossed it to Bibix. "If those slug buckets are as military as you say, they might've already started in on each other."

Bibix took the insulated bag and laughed. It was a deep belly laugh that boiled over into a euphoric arm-waving guffaw. "Slug buckets! I like that!"

198 | Bibix

Tippet rolled out his own sleeping bag and laid on it. "That concludes tonight's show. I'll be here 'til morning. Please tip your waitresses, and have a good night."

Though the bemused Lapropod didn't understand the reference, he got the idea. Taking a deep breath, he blew out the flame wavering back and forth atop the candle. Wrapped in the warmth of the jacket, he slept. He dreamed about his father. Together, they laughed about slug buckets when they weren't busy running from nightmarish hordes of rampaging humans.

* * *

Bibix awoke when his bladder was full. He stretched all four arms and wiggled his pods, yawning deeply as his eyes came out of his head, the stalks becoming erect. Both eyes scanned in separate directions. His breath fogged in the early morning cold. The white wax candle was lit again, and Carl appeared to be working quietly.

The human looked up from what he was doing. "Hey, Bibs."

The somnolent curator sat up. "I don't suppose you've got a bathroom down here, do you?"

Tippet pointed to a large bucket in the far corner. "If that doesn't work for your anatomy, I suggest you go outside. Don't do your business in this yard. Walk 'til you can't see this place. Then, do whatever it is you do."

Bibix split his gaze to look at Carl and the bucket at the same time. Shaking his head, he got up and went outside. The warmth trapped inside his jacket negated the predawn chill. The cold air caressed his face with an unkind touch that helped to wake him up. Shuffling through the yards of two damaged homes, he rounded a corner. Finding a place behind a long shrub, he relieved himself.

On his way back to the hiding place, he paused to look at the skyline to the north. Tiny strobes of unnatural light flickered silently. He thought it might be the promised battle for Eagle River. The very notion changed his frame of mind. He considered what it might be like for NorCons to be killing each other. His imaginings gave him no joy. He went back into the ruined basement, closing the canvas flap behind him as he trundled down the old steps.

The human proudly held up a pair of plasma weapons. "Two carbines with all the bells and whistles: scopes, coolers, and laser rangefinders. I don't care who you are, that isn't bad. They'll go full-auto, so we'll have to watch it. We may burn through all the power packs, but I think we can adapt the power supplies from the NorCon guns."

Bibix sat on his sleeping bag. "I brought some paper diagrams of NorCon power systems. You can look at them later. I saw lights on the horizon. I think the battle has started."

Carl laid the guns down and gave Bibix a bottle of water. "Drink this."

Bibix was thirsty. He drank the tepid water without hesitation. "Pre-combat hydration. I read about that. Something about sweating."

Tippet examined the power packs for the plasma carbines. "You'll sweat like a pig when the spit hits the fan. Your calorie use goes up, too. Since this is your first time, you don't get to eat anything."

202 | Bibix

The nervous Lapropod chugged his water. "First time? Oh, you mean first time in combat. Is that a human ritual? I recall reading that some of your tribes had big meals before fighting."

Carl hid his chuckle with a mighty scratch of his dense beard. "I wish I could say it was a ritual, but it's not. The truth is that most people throw up some time during their first battle. That's a waste of good food."

"I'll have to remember that," Bibix mumbled.

Tippet reached into a pocket and took out a small device. "This is a handheld computer. I found it in the basement of a government office building last winter. It runs on batteries, but it'll recharge if you leave it out in the sun."

Bibix took the personal data device with two hands. He examined it casually. "Oh, yes. We found a lot of these after…after…you know. They're quite useful. The NorCons like them, too. I understand that humans were addicted to the use of this kind of electronic tool. Is that true?"

Carl grinned. "A lot of the older people I used to know kept theirs, even after we'd been pushed out of the cities. My dad used his to store pictures and some video. Mostly he used it to keep a journal."

"Yeah," Bibix mumbled as he fumbled with the tiny display and keyboard.

"What?" Tippet asked as he leaned forward.

The squirming Lapropod felt his eyestalks twitch. "The…um…Look, there's something I want to tell you that will likely make you angry. Please don't hit me."

Carl tucked his hands into his lap. "Shoot."

204 | Bibix

Bibix reached out to put the PDD on the floor next to the human. "A lot of your people used these things to record their experiences after our arrival. Many of your people used some rather extreme language. Murder, extermination, and genocide are not in our lexicon. We never needed those words before we came here. As we recovered millions of these devices, we…we deleted the data in them. It was a reflex. The words and pictures we found stored in them were like hate speech to us. I'm sorry."

Tippet picked up the black square object and turned it over in his calloused hands. "Bibs, what exactly are you talking about?"

The Lapropod checked his translator. "Some of us who work in the trophy halls feel badly that we've destroyed so many of your electronic records. I just thought that you might feel that way, too. When you said you found a PDD, I thought you might have found a survivor's account of…things. You know? Angry words. Pictures of things you'd rather not see."

Carl opened a shirt pocket and took out a dozen small information storage cards. In the dim candlelight, he shuffled through them slowly. "All of these once belonged to people I never met. Each card is completely full of data. Everybody tells the same sad story – invasion, and then the famines. Some battles. Searching for food, shelter, and clothes for the kids. Funny thing is, the words bothered me more than the photos. It took me a while to get used to the way those words would light up in my sleep."

The curator bowed his head in abject sorrow. "I really don't know what to say."

Tippet put the data cards back into his pocket and cleared his throat. "There's nothing to say, Bibs. They're dead, gone, just like everyone else I ever knew. Some blabbermouths wrote down everything that came into their heads. A lot of them didn't survive the first or second winter. I don't blame you guys for erasing what you thought was offensive. We would have done the same."

Bibix sat up. "Really? I thought humans loved their pasts. I've seen some very impressive libraries and science museums – art, history, literature. In our trophy hall, my subordinates have catalogued more than a million personal diaries written by men and women from different eras in your past. We always thought you kept them for social research or sentimental reasons."

"We did," Carl admitted.

The Lapropod rubbed his chin. "I'd be angry about something like this."

The human picked up the PDD and pointed it at Bibix. "I've got a clean data card in this thing. Let me take your picture. Just look right at me and say you name."

Bibix giggled. "That device doesn't have a speech filter in it. Any human who watches this won't understand a word I say unless he's got a translator band."

Tippet lined up the image of the fidgeting Lapropod on the small readout. "You're not much to look at, either. Stop flapping your eyes around and look at me. Say your name."

Bibix tugged at his camouflage coat to pull out the wrinkles. He looked right at Carl. "Hello. My name is Bibix. I am a Lapropod. I'm here in this lovely underground hideout with a human named Carl

Tippet. He is my friend. We are about to go and rescue a lot of humans."

Carl shut off the device and clipped it to his belt. "That's the thing about history, Bibs. You can always make more. We'll shoot some more video after we've rescued somebody."

The eager Lapropod held out one hand. "This should be a joint effort. Let me record you. If this does make it into somebody's historical archive, I'd like my kind to know that I did this with the best of intentions."

Tippet removed the computer and tossed it over. "On the first menu that comes up, you'll see a 'slow record' option. Turn that on and clip that gadget to your jacket. Pin it up high, and it'll see most of what you see for the next thirty-two hours."

Bibix activated the video recorder and attached the little PC to his jacket. Then he looked at Carl. "It's your turn. What words do you have for posterity?"

Candle light flickered as Carl tried to think of something serious to say. "Hi. I'm Carl Tippet, on loan from the Alaska National Guard. If you're watching this, I'm probably dead. The fat guy with the goofy eyeballs is called Bibix. He really is here to help you. Pay attention to what he says, and follow his advice. Don't hurt him unless you really need to."

The Lapropod turned off the PDD with an agitated swipe. "That wasn't very nice."

Carl smirked. "Sorry. It's an old habit. Lots of us used to record short messages before we took off on a raid. Most of the time, we used digital audio recorders."

Bibix looked down at the device clipped to his jacket. "I think the word I'm looking for is 'smart-ass.' I understand the need to be funny so that you can hide being nervous, but that comment was uncalled for."

Tippet handed one of the carbines to Bibix and deliberately changed the subject. "My memory is a little fuzzy, but I can still remember when my family would sit down for an evening meal. Back in those days, you could eat all you wanted. There was never a lack of food. My stomach doesn't like me to talk about it, and my brain doesn't like it when I remember. Those were good days."

Bibix didn't reply. He knew that Carl was dangerously close to recalling something else linked to what the human would call "the invasion." Rather than suffer through another grotesque tale of torment, he resolved to get to the task at hand.

The would-be warrior focused both eyes on his weapon. Several green lights shone back at him from the black plastic. He smiled. "I don't think I've ever seen one of these with green indicators. Can you show me how it works before we go?"

Carl picked up his own weapon and raised it to his shoulder. "This is a little hard to do in a sitting position, so pay attention. See where my thumb is? Push that little stud down until it clicks, and the gun is ready to fire. Look through the holographic sight. Don't squint."

"I can't squint," Bibix insisted as he raised and lowered his eyestalks.

Tippet lowered his carbine. Pointing with a greasy finger, he explained some of its features. "This thing practically shoots itself. Chances are very good that you'll hit anything that you see through the camera sight. That little round thing on the front of the stock is full of coolant. As long as that's on nice and tight, you can shoot as fast as you want. This gray box on the side is your power pack. It'll live longer than you will. This long black tube on the back is your ammo. When they're new, you can get sixty shots out of them. We've only got one for each gun, and I don't know how reliable they are."

The Lapropod picked up his weapon to follow the lesson. He turned it on. "This works like the gauss gun. Safety on, safety off. Point and shoot."

Carl nodded approvingly. "Don't touch the front of that thing after you've pulled the trigger. Let's go outside so you can squeeze off a few rounds, then we'll pack our gear and hit the road."

Bibix turned off his weapon and slung it over his shoulder. "I'm still not sure how we should do this.

Do you have a plan, or are we going to make this up as we go along?"

Tippet struggled to his feet. "Fast and loose, Bibs. Works every time. I'll give you the basics while we drive out."

They went outside to stand behind a tall hedge. Bibix aimed and fired his weapon three times, as instructed. Each plasma bolt made a hissing sound as it ripped through the moisture-laden air. Satisfied, Carl helped Bibix put their gear into the lev.

The human was quite specific about what he wanted to bring and what he wanted to leave in the basement shelter. As they worked, he recounted rules for preparation and conduct. "Don't take more gear than you really need. Never take more than you can carry by yourself. Always assume that you might lose whatever you take into any battle. If something breaks, drop it and forget about it. Don't start picking over the loot until you know for sure that all the bad guys are dead."

Bibix watched as Tippet closed up the basement. The human spread extra debris over the footpath to the entrance. Stepping back, he wiped loose dirt from his camouflage shirt and pants. "You might have to come back here by yourself. Memorize what you see. If it rains while we're gone, this location will be harder to find than you might think."

The Lapropod began to swing his eyestalks around. "Land navigation and terrain camouflage. We have a two-hour documentary on this subject in our digital media storage. I think it was a U.S. Army production." He paused, considering. "Yes, I think I can find this place again."

Carl rapped his knuckles on the side of the lev.

"Okay, then. Let's go."

Chapter 11

During the long drive to a position overlooking the food processing plant, Tippet hid under a blanket in the back seat and explained his plan to Bibix. As the sun rose, they were able to see a gray haze in the sky above the approximate location of the Eagle River trophy hall. Bibix kept one eye on the smoke cloud and the other on the road ahead. Going around the projected battle site took two long, frustrating hours.

"No checkpoints?" Tippet asked as they glided through the ruins of Wasilla.

Bibix turned both eyes forward. "The NorCons don't think they need road patrols out this far. I'm probably the only Lapropod in a fifty-mile radius."

"Lucky you," Carl muttered.

The curator smiled and licked his teeth with both tongues. "Nobody is allowed to live out here. That's too bad. My people are fond of large forests and mountains."

The human shifted his weight in an effort to get comfortable. "I'm surprised. This used to be good farm land."

Bibix guided his vehicle around a large hole in the crumbling road. "The NorCons allow us to grow fruits, vegetables, and grains in places that never see snow. Their reasoning has something to do with 'conservation of resources.' I think it's cheaper for them to keep military garrisons in warm places."

Tippet raised his head to look out a side window. "It was that way for us, too."

218 | Bibix

Driving slowly to get around a tree that had fallen into the road, Bibix halted his lev behind a pile of crushed automobiles. He turned to look at his passenger. "We are good farmers. We could do a lot with this land. Who knows? Maybe, after things get better, we might be able to come out here to dig in the dirt and raise families."

Carl sat up to relieve the stress on his back. "I know that you like moss."

Bibix rested all four hands on the steering column. "We can't eat many of your non-citrus fruits. Legumes, in general, are some of our favorite foods. We even had something like what you call a potato on our home world."

Tippet yawned. "Beans and 'taters. Let me out, I've got to take a leak."

Bibix pushed a button to open all the doors. Cool air swept through the lev's interior, wiping away the smells of sweat and unwashed clothing. After a ten-minute break, they got back in the vehicle. Carl went over his plan one more time.

Bibix had very few objections. In his nervous state, he tried to think about something else while his stomach fluttered. "Honestly, I don't know how you survived through the winter. Moving from place to place. Scavenging. All that cold and snow. I couldn't handle being lonely and without food. I wouldn't know how to do it."

"If this doesn't work, you're going to find out," Carl quipped from underneath his ratty blanket.

When they arrived at the agreed upon hilltop location, Bibix waited for the human soldier to scan the food processor's compound with a pair of chipped, dusty binoculars.

Leaning on the front of the lev, Carl liked what he saw. "Single structure. Sheet metal skin. Seven stories. About the size of four football fields. No fence. No guards. The loading docks are on the far side. I saw them last winter. There are two very large landing pads on the south end of the structure. Are those what I think they are?"

Bibix pulled his eyes in close together. "Docking stations for assault landers. The NorCons use their combat ships for heavy lifting. You can hear them long before you see them. The ground shakes and the air vibrates."

The soldier turned in the direction of Eagle River. "Let's hope these guys aren't scheduled to send or receive anything today."

Bibix studied their target. "We are half a mile away and the ground is flat. There are no places to hide. Is that why you called it the direct approach?"

Tippet let the binoculars hang around his neck. "Not quite. Being direct can sometimes mean that you don't sneak around. In this case, we're going right up to the front door. It's the last thing they'll expect."

"Are you ready?" the nervous Lapropod asked.

Carl went to the back of the lev and opened the hatch. "I was born ready."

Bibix helped him to move gear. "Please don't take this the wrong way, but I can't help worrying about the security cameras. What if a guard manages to activate an alarm?"

Carl thought about that. "Hmm. Security cameras. Electronic locks. Sure, I can see that. Back in my day, one person with his finger on an alarm button could guard a place that big. If the NorCons are so eager to fight over a junk pile, I'm willing to gamble that they won't leave many guards to watch their food supply."

"I wish I could be so confident."

Tippet took off the binoculars and climbed into the back of the lev. He turned to sit facing Bibix. "How many people do you figure they have in a place that size?"

Bibix shrugged. "Humans? Sixty, maybe seventy, thousand. Why?"

Carl reached for a plasma carbine and placed it within easy reach. "Before you guys showed up, my Uncle

Rosco earned his pay by being a night guard. I never once heard him say anything good about the job. Boring, boring, boring. Seventy thousand humans could only be boring if they were either tranqued out of their minds or under lock and key. There can't be that many in there."

Bibix thought about the night guard at his museum. Then he thought about what he'd seen while sneaking into the Eagle River trophy hall. "Bored people make sloppy mistakes."

Tippet knocked on the roof of the lev. "And how. See? We're close enough. They should be looking at us right now with their surveillance gear, but they aren't."

Bibix took off his jacket and put it in the lev. He then used several blankets to hide their guns and equipment. "I've read about the element of surprise. I wish I had more faith in it."

Carl pointed at the facility. "I do. The unlucky parasites guarding that place are missing out on a fight they know is going on just back that-a-way. They're bored and jealous. If we tempt them with the right kind of bait, they'll be surprised and dead before they know what happened."

The worried Lapropod wanted to throw up. "P-please, explain it to me one more time."

Tippet bristled. "You know who owns that museum they're fighting over?"

"Yes," Bibix admitted through rising bile.

Carl took a deep breath and let it out. "Great. Here's how it goes. This is his – her – its territory. He's going to send his loyal guards a little snack. My cousin Ivan used to deliver pizza, so I know how this will go down."

"What is pizza?" Bibix asked, curious in spite of his fear.

Tippet bit down on his irritation. "I'll show you later. Come on, Bibs. Pull yourself together! I'm going to lie down and play dead. Just drive up and knock on the door. When they come out to get their goodies, I'll pop 'em. All you have to do is stay out of my way."

It was the sort of scheme that only a human mind could conjure. Ten minutes later, Bibix drove his lev straight up to the official administrative entrance to the facility. The scent of industrial-grade cleaners gave the air an unpleasant tang. He stopped just long enough to towel off some of his fear-induced sweat.

226 | Bibix

"I can do this. Fear is just a state of mind. I will not be killed. Nobody is going to eat me."

He got out of the lev and opened the rear hatch. The guard promptly challenged him, the intercom carrying its translated voice through a speaker near the large door. "Who are you? What are you doing here? This facility is closed!"

Bibix stepped away from the hatch so the guard could see the limp human in his vehicle's cargo space. "I have orders, Greatness, from Administrator Velleck. His master has ordered him to reward your vigilance. I was told that the battle goes well."

The guard took note of the Lapropod's fear. It was hard-pressed to believe its good fortune. Velleck was not known for its acknowledgment of subordinates. The battle for Eagle River must truly be going well. Velleck's master must be planning something.

It remained unwilling to open the door. "Leave the food and go."

Bibix took one step away from the lev, assuming a bashful pose. With eyes lowered, he lied with all of the pitiful demeanor he could summon. "Greatness, please. If I don't do exactly as Velleck commands, my wife and podlings will be without me this evening. My youngest child has just come out of the pouch. I don't want to be eaten."

The sentry was about to chastise the squirming sycophant when it noticed the worn and tattered camouflage fabric that clothed the incapacitated human. It placed one claw on the door as it adjusted its visual sensors. "Is that a human warrior?"

The Lapropod kept its eyes pointed at the ground in a show of utmost terror that wasn't hard to feign. With all four hands folded, it spoke slowly. "Yes,

Greatness. I supervised its removal from cryogenic suspension. It is fresh. Will you come out and take it, or shall I bring it inside?"

The guard opened the secured door and stepped outside with its particle gun pointed at Bibix. "Velleck's master is generous. What can you tell me about this human's military record?"

Bibix stood aside so that the guard could approach the lev. "I don't know soldier stuff."

His answer had the desired effect. The NorCon's helmet swiveled. It moved in closer to evaluate its prize. "The lack of hygiene and grooming could mean that this human was in combat."

"He may have been quite dangerous," the Lapropod suggested. He noted the pump resting on the right shoulder of the being's mechanized armor.

The NorCon's translator approximated a sneer and a laugh. "Perhaps I should revive it."

Bibix glanced at the open security door. "Can I go now?"

Carl watched through squinted eyes as the NorCon turned to face Bibix. The Lapropod shuffled away from his tormentor. With a sudden jerk, the human sat up and pulled his plasma carbine from hiding. Thumbing off the safety, he fired with one hand. Three bright, hot bolts ate through the protective shell to boil the community organisms within the armor. The guard died, its suit spewing liquid and pulp. Its translator seemed incapable of processing the being's scream.

Bibix ran to the open facility door as the NorCon clattered to the ground. He held it open with two hands and used a third to wipe away some of the slick sweat running down his face. "What took you so long?"

Tippet wiggled out of the lev and bounded to his feet, the hot gun still in his hand. "This is your first ambush, Bibs. Don't complain. I can tolerate you, but I won't feel bad for very long if you get capped. Now grab your gear and let's go."

"No alarms," Bibix observed as he slipped into his jacket and reached for his gun.

Carl pulled on his vest and walked to the open door. "He could be the only guard. Then again, his buddies are probably just as bored as he is, so they're not watching the security cams. You go first. Run, and don't stop. Look for signs on the walls. We've got to find their security command post. If we find trouble, stay out of my way."

The Lapropod tossed a breath mask to the human, and they rushed into the large building. Each being put on his breathing filters as they plunged into the pressurized, nitrogen-rich interior. Bibix loped along in a "one-two" pod rush while Carl walked quickly. As he jogged, an accidental nudge activated the video recording function of the personal data device clipped to his collar.

"Move it!" Carl demanded.

The senior curator tried not to choke on his tongues. "I'm going as fast as I can. I'm not an athlete. See that sign? 'Security and Detention, Level Two.' We need to find stairs or an elevator."

Tippet kept his weapon ready as he scanned the drab concrete walls. Harsh fluorescent lighting made him blink. He moved out ahead of Bibix. "Who built this? Humans or Lapropods?"

"I don't know," Bibix wheezed as he struggled to keep up with the speeding human.

Carl came to a quick stop as they reached the first intersection of corridors. "There aren't very many doors. Where do they hide the elevators in this joint? Hey, wait a minute. Do you smell that?"

Bibix lifted his mask for just a moment to spit. "It's the atmosphere. It'll play tricks on your nose."

Tippet shook his head. With one scarred hand on a cold, concrete wall, he paused. "No stink. Haven't you ever been to—No, I suppose you haven't. Lots of people means lots of body waste. No stink means no people."

The Lapropod trembled at the thought of failure and what it could mean for the future of his own people. "I'm sure you must smell worse than the average human. It's possible that the NorCons could have bathing facilities here. We should keep moving."

Bibix took the lead. Following the signs, he led Carl to a ramp that sloped up to the second level. "The sign at the top of the ramp says 'Detention Area and Malcontent Storage.' There's a strict warning that goes with it, too: 'Armed Access Only.' The sign right next to me here says that animal storage is located at either end of the building. No wonder we couldn't smell humans. They must be too far away."

Carl scanned the ceiling. "I haven't seen anything that looks like a video camera. Then again, I don't know what I'm looking for. Are you sure that sign says 'Malcontent Storage?'"

The curator rested his weapon in two arms. "I know how to read NorCon. The word is literally the English equivalent to malcontent, as in, 'not happy' or 'disgusted.'"

Tippet smiled fiendishly. "I don't think they care about how happy their food is. Clean or dirty, I think that's a holding area for criminals and troublemakers."

Bibix glanced at the sign, and then at the human. "No! Hold on. I'm not having anything to do with criminals! I—"

Carl moved in close. He grabbed the Lapropod's left eyestalk. "Less talk, more sneak. If you mess with me again, I'll rip this thing out and beat you with it. I don't care if we find criminals or saints, we're going to release those people and sort it all out later."

Paralyzed with fear, Bibix watched the human soldier release his grip and advance up the ramp without him. With his weapon raised, the man turned right and stepped out of view.

Twin waves of anger and self-loathing crashed over Bibix as he regained his nerve. Tears fell from his eyes as he shuddered in agony and rage. Tippet's hostility had been dormant for so long that he had actually dared to hope that it had gone away. At the worst possible moment, the man had violated his trust and his dignity in one show of naked aggression.

With revenge on his mind, Bibix stormed up the ramp with his gun at the ready. He was met with a hail of fire from a charged particle weapon. Emboldened by his own bad attitude, Bibix sighted down the length of his carbine and fired three quick shots into the charging NorCon. One of the plasma bolts burned through the center of the community organism's torso armor while it was still forty feet away.

236 | Bibix

The angry Lapropod fired once more at the dying entity. Splitting his vision, he quickly took in his surroundings. Two NorCon husks lay motionless on the bare concrete floor near an open door. A long corridor to his right contained the downed wrecks of two more guards. Bibix brought both eyes to bear on the NorCon he had killed. In his hearts, he truly hoped all of the creatures in that vessel were dying slowly and with great pain.

He advanced on the foaming carcass and fired at the pump mounted on one arm. The device exploded in a shower of metal, plastic, and ceramic. "I'm never going to be afraid of you again!" he yelled.

"Are you talking to him or me?" Carl asked from behind the partially open door.

Bibix pointed his rifle at the door. "I'm definitely talking to you. Come out here, you filthy human! I've had all the crap from you that I'm going to take. It's bad enough that I have to fight with motorized food. Now I've got to deal with kill-crazy humans, too? No. You'll do what I say, when I say, or I'll kill you where you stand!"

Carl stayed behind cover. "We don't have time for this, Bibs. There could be another guard. We need to keep moving. You can kill me later."

Bibix stomped towards the door. "The guards are dead. Come out."

Tippet muttered something obscene. "Knock it off, Bibs."

"I'm not a child! Stop calling me that!" the angry Lapropod screeched.

238 | Bibix

Carl stepped out into the open. He closed the metal door with a kick. His carbine was slung over one shoulder. Both hands were open and away from his body. He moved slowly. "Man, you picked a bad time to blow your top. If you're going to shoot me, do it now. Please. We're behind enemy lines and there could still be more of that 'motorized food' out there, so you need to make up your mind. Who bothers you more, me or them?"

Bibix looked at the weapon in his hands. He walked over to the NorCon he'd fired on. With one eye on Carl and the other on the shattered armor, he reached inside with a free hand to extract one of the many creatures that made up the larger social group. The lump squirmed in his grasp as it turned green. With both eyes on Carl, Bibix jammed the creature into his mouth and ate it. Chewing ferociously, he swallowed with great purpose.

Tippet looked towards the ramp, then down the length of corridor. "I guess you showed them."

The agitated Lapropod held up his sticky hand. "I won't be afraid of NorCons any more."

"How was it?" Carl asked after a second look down the corridor.

Bibix flicked some of the gunk off his fingertips. "Exotic. Reminds me of fish. Something like the red salmon that are common to this region, but without the bones."

Tippet became serious. "I'm really glad for you Bibs, but we've got to go. If what I saw behind that door is correct, the only humans in this place are being held on the ground floor in the southeast corner. The rest of the holding pens are empty."

Wiping his hand on his jacket, Bibix regarded the shiny metal door. "That's very specific. What did you see in there?"

"You don't want to know," Carl said gravely as he went to the ramp.

Chapter 12

Bibix quickly went to the door and opened it with deliberate haste. Raising his weapon, he stepped inside the operations room, ready for a fight. What he saw made him scream as only a shocked Lapropod could under such circumstances.

The terrified being lurched out of the room, allowing the door to swing shut as he fled. With both eyes pulled firmly into his skull, Bibix fell to the floor and retched. Bile and small pieces of NorCon fell from his lips as he fought to avoid letting loose a full-throated rush of vomit.

Tippet peered down the ramp and then went to Bibix. "Take a breath and calm down."

"They were eating somebody in there!" The Lapropod rolled into a standing position.

Carl searched his pockets for a rag. "Get a grip, will you? All I saw were arms and legs. I tried to protect you—"

Bibix allowed his tear-filled eyes to rise from their sockets. He took the improvised handkerchief that was offered. "I really don't know what to say."

The human stepped back. "I ought to kick you! That was stupid."

The Lapropod emptied his runny nose with a long, sloppy blow. "I'm sorry. I really am. It's one thing to hear about this kind of thing, but it's something else to actually see it. Is that what you saw? Is that what you lived with?"

Tippet recalled the story he'd told Bibix about the night his group had encountered Lapropods eating humans. He nodded unsympathetically. "Bad situations can drive us to do bad things. That's how some of us justify staying alive. Nobody deserves to be eaten. Take their lives before they take yours, but don't eat them. Cannibalism is a mindfreak that nobody comes back from."

Bibix pulled a clot of masticated NorCon out of his mouth. "You let me do that."

Carl nudged the weapon that now lay on the floor. "You pointed the gun at me. I didn't have anything to say in the matter. You made your own choices."

Bibix flicked away the evidence of his crime. The undigested material struck the far wall and stuck. "I lost my head when I saw the bone pile. What else did you see in there? How do you know where the humans are being kept?"

Tippet strained to hear any sound that might warn of approaching guards. "That room is a camera station, with lots of monitors. Most of them are turned off. There was also an electronic map on one wall. The only active monitor shows a holding area with lots of people in it. I matched the symbols on the readout with the symbols on the map, and they correspond to the southeast corner of the ground floor."

Bibix picked up his gun. "You killed all these NorCons and read the map that fast?"

Carl went back to the ramp. "I'm used to working on a tight schedule. Let's go."

The Lapropod gestured with the barrel of his carbine. "Check the holding area."

Tippet rubbed his beard. "You do it. Hurry. Run, and don't mess around."

Bibix ran from cell to cell, peering through transparent security doors. With the taste of NorCon still in his mouth, he was afraid that he might find captive humans in the cells. He was also afraid that he might not. Would they be glad to see him?

A two-minute search turned up nothing but locked and empty rooms. With a roiling stomach, Bibix went back to Carl, his feelings a nerve-wracking combination of relief and sadness. "The cells are empty and the lights are off. I'm sorry."

The man kept his eyes on the ramp. "Don't sweat the small stuff, Bibs. Empty is good. Keep your eyes open when we go down this ramp. There could be roaming guards. I'd be willing to bet you a hot meal that they've got people watching the folks in the holding area I found. I'll go first, you follow."

The Lapropod took one last look around the detention area. He charged his weapon and steadied it with three hands. "We've only been in this building for fifteen minutes. I came in here feeling righteous and civilized. I'm going to leave feeling confused and dirty."

Carl touched him on the shoulder and then started down the ramp. "Cheer up. You've still got plenty of chances to get killed."

"How can you be so flippant at a time like this?" Bibix demanded as he followed.

Tippet risked a look up and down the corridor before making a fast right turn. "I've been in the trenches for almost ten years. I've had cancer and everybody that

I ever knew is dead. I'm inside a modern death camp with a pacifistic idiot who's playing soldier, and I'm on my way to rescue people who are under the thumbs of two alien races. I've earned the right to enjoy some gallows humor."

Carl ran the length of the building, rushing past signs he could not read and doors of all seizes that were shut. His imagination came to life with grainy black-and-white images he'd seen in old video clips about extermination camps in Nazi Germany and certain Balkan countries during the late Twentieth Century. Memories of full-color news clips recounting the atrocities in the Middle East punctuated his troubled thoughts as he fretted over what he would find in the holding area. Would those people speak English? Or would they be mute and uneducated?

Tippet came to a stop under bright fluorescent lights as he neared a T-shaped intersection at the south end of the massive structure. The reek of cleaning chemicals assaulted his nose as Bibix labored to catch up.

He urged the wheezing Lapropod to be quiet as he approached. "Ease up. I think what we're looking for is just around this corner."

The curator leaned against the cold, gray wall. "I hear air conditioners. It could be the building's ventilation system. Please, just let me catch my breath."

Carl risked a peek around the corner. Turning back, he crouched and moved closer to Bibix. "Looks like thirty meters of corridor and a large sliding door. There's one guard, just standing there like a block of wood. Do you know if these guys talk to each other by radio?"

"If they talked to each other by wireless comm, they would act differently. To us, it would seem like they were telepathic because we'd only be getting bits and pieces of certain conversations. If they are food – community organisms – it's possible that they can't stand to be around certain electromagnetic fields. The creatures we harvested for food on our home world stayed away from our cities because the residual EM hurt them."

Tippet checked his weapon. "Do they carry handheld radios?"

The Lapropod nodded as his heart rates slowed. "I've seen them use both hand units and console systems. They scavenged all of the human wireless telecommunications networks shortly after they landed. Why does this matter?"

Carl smiled when he noticed that the PDD clipped to the Lapropod's coat was recording him. "Military protocols. If there's a guard on this side of the loading dock door, there'll be at least one on the other side. These guys would talk to each other before anyone opened that door. Even if we're fast, we won't be able to take the other NorCon by surprise."

The problem didn't bother Bibix very much. "I knew there would be situations like this. That's why I brought you along. What is your plan?"

Tippet stood up to relieve the pressure on his calves. "Turn that recorder off and give me a moment to think."

Bibix deactivated the device and put it in his pocket. Leaning his weapon against the wall, he unzipped the coat and wiggled out of it. Dropping the garment to the floor, he waited. "I've seen you make that face before. Let me guess. I have to go first. You're going to use me as some kind of bait."

Carl laughed into his sleeve to muffle the noise. "The word is 'distraction.' Look, all you have to do is do a little more of that play-acting that got us past the front door, and I'll take care of the rest. Just get that slug bucket to open the door."

Bibix's reply echoed an old Lapropodian grade school joke. "If this gets me killed, I'll never speak to you again."

Tippet flipped up the sighting reticule on his carbine and grinned. "I can't miss at this range. All you've got to do is get that guard to open up. If he won't cooperate, I'll tap him just as soon as he's not looking in my direction."

"Don't shoot me in the back."

Carl gestured in the direction that Bibix was to go. "Don't sweat it, Bibs. You're short. Every shot will go right over your head."

The Lapropod snapped, "Do you always have to be so rude?"

Tippet reached for Bibix's weapon. "If I live through this, I promise to think about being nicer. Now, get moving, you little freak."

Chapter 13

Bibix allowed his anger to carry him around the corner and into full view of the guard before his brain could process his fear and act on it. Walking with all the deliberate purpose he could muster, he put one pod in front of the other without looking back.

"Halt!" the NorCon commanded.

The Lapropod stopped fifteen feet from the guard as it raised its weapon. "Good afternoon, Greatness. I was instructed to inform you that there are more…human parts…in the detention area."

The guard adjusted its aim. Its helmet turned slowly from left to right. "I have not been able to communicate with anyone for several minutes. Is there a problem with the intercom system?"

Bibix glanced at a nearby control panel that would allow a user to access the building-wide intercom. He pointed. "Greatness, that system is down for maintenance. The problem came up suddenly. I've got my people working on it. Why haven't you used your own radio?"

The NorCon's speech device emulated a grunt. "Onboard communications are for battlefield use only. The ferrous metals in this structure would interfere with reception. How long will it take you to make repairs to the intercom?"

The harsh fluorescent lights made Bibix look even paler than he was. "I don't know, Greatness. I'm just making this up as I go along. Would you please open that door and let me pass? I still have work to do and I'd rather not be eaten."

The guard was in a non-combat zone and very bored. It assumed that the Lapropod's obvious fear was just a normal display of groveling. "This is a restricted area. We are holding dangerous humans for immediate disposal. You will have to be quick. I will supervise."

"Yes, Greatness." Bibix bowed his head with all of the false humility he could manage.

The NorCon failed to notice that Bibix wasn't carrying any tools. It turned to punch numbers into a recessed keypad with one of its claw-like fingers. The large folding door slid out of sight with a loud hydraulic hiss.

Carl ran from cover. Holding one plasma carbine in each hand as if they were large pistols, he fired, his voice splitting the air in a battle cry. The NorCon dropped after it was hit with ten shots that destroyed its helmet, armor, and pressure pump. The creatures inside died slowly as oxygen penetrated the holes that appeared in the armor's arms, legs, and torso.

Bibix was pleased. It appeared that Tippet's aggression was rubbing off on him, as he had hoped it would. He liked it. He might never get over his fear of humans, but he'd have the satisfaction of knowing that nobody was going to push him around, anymore.

Carl's charge took him past Bibix and into the loading dock, where he surprised a single guard. The NorCon fired one shot from its particle projector that nearly hit Bibix. The armored being collapsed under a hail of plasma bolts.

Tippet circled the vast open area in search of his objective. He found the captives on the far side of the platform, staring at him with wild eyes from behind thick security glass. None of what he'd seen since being revived prepared him for the shock.

Bibix came running when he heard Tippet scream. He slowed, and then stopped when he saw what Carl was looking at. He resisted the urge to hide as the trembling man approached the large window that separated him from more than thirty frantic humans. Twenty-one women and fourteen men slapped at the glass and shouted. None of the noise they made got through.

Tippet moved closer. Long hair cloaked the naked bodies of some. It hung in long, limp ropes on others. None of the captives seemed to mind their own nudity.

The numbed Lapropod kept his eyes on Carl. The human set his guns down and put both hands on the cold, clear barrier. Some of the captives fought with each other to place their own dirty hands near his. The pleading gestures made his throat go dry.

"How do I get them out?"

Bibix came closer. "That's not a window, it's a gate. See that, to your left?"

Tippet went to the locking mechanism. "Hmm. Electronic keypad. That glass has to be two inches thick. I've got some explosives, but we can't risk it."

The curator noticed that the captives were quietly watching him. He nudged Carl. "I've seen that look before. They're not happy to see me."

Carl glanced at Bibix, then at the prisoners. "Yeah, but look again. I know what it is to hate you little freaks. That's not hate. It's something else."

Bibix picked up one of the plasma carbines. The humans followed his every move with great interest. "They're talking to each other. I've never seen humans argue like that."

The soldier examined the sturdy metal frame of the windowed gate. "Bibs, we've got to move. A place this big might have more guards. Go back and get your jacket. Keep your gun warm and watch that hallway until I come get you. I need a minute to look at this gate. If I can figure out how it works, I should be able to burn through the mechanism with what's left in my carbine."

Once the Lapropod left their field of view, the captives became animated. Carl rapped his knuckles on the glass to get their attention. "Okay, so you know what Lapropods are. We can deal with that later. Right now, I need somebody to tell me which way this gate swings open. Look at my hands. Gate. Open, closed. Which way?"

The men and women watched him carefully. When his charade failed, he mimed opening and closing an imaginary door. After some debate, the majority answered with hand gestures that told Carl that the gate opened out and to his right.

He smiled at the silliness of his situation. "Back it up. Back. Move away," he said, gesturing as he spoke.

The anxious crowd stayed pressed against the glass. Pointing at his gun, and then at the corner of the gate frame, Tippet fired a single shot. Super-heated metal flew in sparks that forced him to take a step back. He swore when the prisoners stayed in place to cheer. Taking a long step back, he began to destroy the gate with one shot after another.

The captives didn't retreat until their cell began to fill with smoke. When he had spent his power pack, Carl used the butt of the carbine like a hammer, pounding until the locking mechanism was broken and the gate swung loose on its hinges. The dozens of exuberant people who grasped at his beard and clothing quickly overwhelmed him, knocking him to the floor. With cheers and shouts of joy, they pounded him to show their affection.

Shouting to be heard, Carl fended off his jubilant attackers with limited success. Probing hands ripped open the Velcro pockets on his combat vest and made off with the contents. Several strong grips combined to wrench the plasma rifle from his hand. Fingers gently stroked his beard. The cacophony of so many loud voices at close range drowned out his words, and deafened him. His thrill of victory was quickly turning into a tangled, claustrophobic tantrum.

Sucking in a deep breath, he fought back against the press of hands and faces. A series of kicks and punches impacted his nose, chin, and forehead. His skull was bounced off the floor several times before he lost consciousness.

Chapter 14

Carl awoke several minutes later to find Bibix staring at him. He sat up. "Where did they go?"

The Lapropod pointed at the loading dock and the distant tree line. "<u>Thra, ill tont.</u>"

Carl rubbed his head. "What?"

"<u>Othra. New ill othra</u>," Bibix insisted with a smirk.

Tippet wrapped one hairy hand around his left wrist. "I don't believe this! They took my translator. Did I just get mugged?"

"<u>Ohsay</u>," Bibix nodded from where he sat, and then gave an even deeper belly laugh.

The man assessed himself. Parts of his scalp were bleeding. The back of his head throbbed. He probably had a slight concussion. All of his vest pockets were empty. His carbine, pistol, and knife were gone. One of his sleeves had been torn completely off.

"That's just great," he fumed.

Bibix cleared his throat. In his best English, he said slowly, "Car-all, I do not think they were glad to see you. We should go now."

Tippet tried to stand and failed. "I'm not doing so good."

The curator put his weapon on the floor and reached into a coat pocket for some medicine. He offered it to the battered man. "Pain killer. Take one. I will get car and we go."

Carl watched the Lapropod zip his jacket, pick up his gun, and leave. From long experience, he knew that he was in shock. Trying to make sense of anything just now would only result in a more painful headache. Looking at the nearest NorCon carcass, he focused both eyes on the shattered armor until his vision cleared.

The attack shouldn't have surprised him. As a combat veteran, he knew better than to approach large groups of desperate people. He'd seen crowds turn on relief workers sent to help them more than once. In his early teens, he'd even been one of the rioters. Why had he ignored that wisdom? Did he really think that the people in this nightmarish future would be glad to see him?

Bibix arrived in his lev just in time to put an end to Tippet's caustic self-assessment. Crawling on his hands and knees, the human slithered into the vehicle. Unprompted, Bibix put his translator band onto the human's wrist. He then retrieved both of the NorCon particle weapons that had been dropped by the guards Carl had killed. Seconds later, they sped away from the food processor.

"Do you have any broken bones?" Bibix asked his passenger.

Tippet fidgeted with the translator. "No, I don't think so."

The Lapropod kept his eyes on the road as he increased speed. "I think my English is getting pretty good. Unless you've got a second tongue that I don't know about, you're probably not going to learn how to speak like a Lapropod any time soon."

Carl didn't reply for a long moment. "You must have a lot of regrets about what happened back there. I know that I do."

Bibix shrugged. "When we first met, you said you were going to beat me like a drum, and you did. I don't have to like your kind of violence, but I can accept it for what it is. When I saw those people, I was prepared for the consequences. While I was afraid they'd turn on me, I thought they'd be happy to see you. I'm sorry they beat you, but I'm glad you sent me away before it happened. Look on the bright side. There are at least thirty violent humans out there now. I can't wait to see what they do to the NorCons."

Tippet tried to get comfortable in the passenger seat. "This isn't working out like I wanted it to. I should be with them. If they don't have some direction, the NorCon patrols will swat them like flies."

The Lapropod steered his lev to the side of the road and parked. "In case you hadn't noticed, we just got very lucky. If they're so willing and able to hurt you, I don't want to think about what they'd do to me. If you want to chase after them, I won't argue, but I won't go along, either. What's it going to be?"

Carl opened the passenger door and slid out. "Open the back and let me get some gear."

Bibix turned off the lev and got out to help the human unload. "The NorCons are persistent. If they pick up your trail, they'll hunt you all summer."

Tippet took the remaining plasma weapon and the half-pack that was offered to him. "I'll find some way of getting their attention. Then I'll lead them deeper into the woods. It'll take me a few weeks, but I'll work my way back to that basement hideaway. I don't know what we'll scavenge along the way, but I know there's enough clothing to be found in and around Anchorage to get us through the winter. Can you bring food?"

Closing the rear hatch, Bibix leaned on his vehicle. With one eye, he scanned the high clouds moving quickly across the bright blue sky. "I can't possibly steal and hide enough food to feed thirty people."

The soldier rummaged through the pack. He seemed to like what he found. "I've got another pistol and fifty rounds in here. It's no good against NorCons, but very effective against unprotected humans. I underestimated those people. It won't happen again."

Bibix stood and went to the driver's side door. He took off his coat and threw it to Carl. "Don't you mean to say that you overestimated them?"

"Everybody is mean where I come from. Those guys did the same thing I would've done."

Tippet returned the camouflaged jacket. "Keep that. You're going to need it. Besides, I don't want to try to explain the extra sleeves."

The Lapropod folded the coat and laid it in the back of his lev. "I'll meet you in the ruins four weeks from today. If I…um…don't show up, you should assume the worst. Lapropods don't get trial by jury. We get eaten, and it tends to happen rather quickly."

Carl slung the pack over one shoulder and steadied himself. "Hey, what do you know? I didn't fall down. Okay, Bibs. We meet in twenty-eight days. I'll wait for three extra days. If you don't make it, I'll take what I can carry and hit the road. You've got to do the same thing. If I'm a no-show, take what you can use and walk away. Never go back to that spot."

Bibix got into his lev and drove away. The parting left him feeling sad and alone. Carl's easy familiarity with death was still hard to take. Every act of violence he participated in had left the Lapropod feeling strangely disconnected. It was as if his eyes no longer cared about what they saw and his hearts no longer worried over the profundity of his actions. Was he at last becoming the killer that he needed to be? Or was he going mad from the stress of exceeding his own capabilities?

The drive back to his apartment was long and miserable. Taking care to go around the Eagle River battlefield, he felt nothing when one of his wandering eyes caught sight of the smoke that rose high into the azure sky. Red flashes of light punctuated the haze as energy weapons burned through airborne particles and ignited oxygen.

With all four hands on the controls, he felt a little better when he thought about how easy it had been to make the NorCons fight each other. No self-respecting Lapropod would ever consider fighting over a building full of junk left behind by a dead species.

That line of reasoning made him shake his head. "I wish my father was here to share this with me. I killed NorCons today, and I liked it. I'm the only Lapropod who knows that the humans are on the loose again, and I want to throw up."

The curator returned to his messy apartment as the sun set. Orange streamers of light filtered through the plastic blinds to show the cluttered living room. He tossed his equipment onto an old couch and slumped into his favorite chair. An automated piston swung the neglected door shut.

Once again, he was truly alone. The semi-darkness appealed to his tired eyes. Pulled under by a mixture of fatigue and depression, he slept without dreaming.

* * *

A knock at the door shattered his uneasy calm. Without opening his eyes, he shuffled to the portal and opened the door. The smell of cooked food found his nose at the same time he registered the scent of a female. Instinct forced both of his eyestalks to rise and his eyes to open. Sudden awareness caused him to shake his head and blink. Soft sounds from nearby apartments buzzed in his ears momentarily as his eyes adjusted to the corridor lighting. Within seconds, all he could smell was the being standing nearby.

She looked at him through prescription lenses, each held in place by a wire frame that conformed to the individual eyestalks. Her eyes were a shade of gray that most Lapropods regarded as a sign of keen intellect and sharp wit. Her hair was braided in a style that was popular among academics and some of the more freethinking students. The curves of her body suggested that she might be just as out of shape as he was.

"Can I help you?" he asked, keeping two hands on the doorknob.

She smiled with the kind of perfect teeth that would appeal to any sane male Lapropod. "Hello. I'm sorry to disturb you at this hour, but you have some books checked out from the university library that I need."

He turned to look at the pile of books and papers that dominated his eating table. "I do? I mean, yes. I do.

I must. Those must be the books you're talking about. Please, come in. I don't entertain much. Watch your step, please."

Her eyes swung from side to side as she followed him into the dark apartment. "I understand better than you think. Do you know if the walls have ears?"

Bibix closed the door after she entered. "I don't get out much, but I still look for eavesdroppers. I'm sure they'll sneak one in if I do anything they don't like.

The female nodded as she walked slowly through the clutter. "I don't get out much, either. My apartment was bugged last year. I'm a professor at the university. My specialty is Human Studies. I know that must sound silly, but I am fascinated by them."

Bibix turned on the nearest light. "I've got a degree in Human Studies. Just a bachelor's. Nothing special."

She blushed. "I know who you are. The librarian told me. When I heard that you were the senior curator for the trophy hall, I didn't think you'd mind letting me have a look at those books. You know, professional courtesy. Egghead to egghead?"

He laughed. She mixed human words with Lapropodian speech so easily that she was more than entertaining. She was a pleasure to hear. "Well, Doctor, have a seat, if you can find one, and let's see if we can find what you're looking for."

She pulled out a chair and moved a canvas bag to the floor. "My name is Bevf."

"I'm Bibix."

Her eyes centered on the table and its many treasures. "There are only six 'Pods in my department. How is that I hadn't heard of you before now?"

He pulled out a chair and sat. "I'm not very ambitious."

Bevf snickered as she picked up one book after another to examine its title. "You're the senior curator for a NorCon trophy hall. That makes you the most ambitious 'Pod I know."

"I'm not a politician," he countered.

"I don't know any politicians," she replied, giving him a tight smile.

He pointed at the book in her left hand. "That's a good one, if you like fiction."

She put the dusty volume aside. "I got permission to do a study of American political systems, as they existed prior to our arrival. I'm looking for anything you may have borrowed from the library that was written by local, state, or federal lawmakers after 1970."

Bibix pointed to a stack of books near the center of the table. "There."

Bevf was pleased. She handled the books with all four hands. "Yes, I recognize some of the titles. If you don't mind my asking, why does a curator need so much background on republican government? I thought most of what your kind did was object identification."

"My kind?" he queried, one eye raised slightly above the other.

She stopped looking at the old books. "I didn't mean anything by that. It's just…you know. I could never work so closely with the NorCons. How do you do it?"

"It's my job, so that's what I do," he said with a shrug.

Bevf gestured at the clutter that surrounded her. "I'm fascinated by humans, too. Is that why you work in a trophy hall? How did you ever get such a ghoulish job?"

Bibix thought about Carl and what he must be doing at that moment. "My grandmother died shortly after we came to Earth. My grandfather talks about our home world so much that I feel like I've been there. My father was the only member of our family who talked about the NorCons like they don't belong here. When I was small, my mother used to try and scare me with human tales. Once I figured out that humans were real, I just had to study them."

"How come you're not at the university?"

He looked away. "That's not important."

"Tell me," she implored.

He straightened. "I was young and angry. I had lots of unrealistic ideas flying around in my head. Once I understood what the trophy halls really were, I decided to— Look, this really isn't important. Which of these books do you need? Everything on this table is checked out from the library. Take what you want."

She folded all four hands into her lap. "Tell me. What's so special about the NorCon junk piles? I'd really like to know."

He bristled defensively. "You're the doctor. You tell me."

Bevf bent over and picked up the canvas bag that she'd taken out of the chair before sitting and held it in two hands. "The NorCons let us look at books, movies, multimedia disks, and old computer files. We don't get the kind of hands-on experience you do. Humans were more than words and images. They were toolmakers, much as we are. Like the NorCons, we have just one culture. Humans had hundreds, maybe even thousands, of cultures. Can you imagine what that must have been like?"

"Chaos," Bibix declared with Carl foremost in his mind.

She opened the bag and put the contents on the table. "It was chaos to us, but not to them. They built whole countries that lived next door to each other for centuries without fighting. Look at what you've got in this bag. Variety. It's a kind of variety that we just don't have. You understand what I'm saying, don't you?"

Bibix worried when he saw a hand grenade mixed in with the items his guest had taken from the bag and set on the table. "I know that our variety is less likely to explode. Please, be careful with those things. A few of them are really quite dangerous."

"Like what?" she asked.

"Like that one right there." He pointed.

She picked up the fragmentation device. "This little thing? It's hardly big enough to be dangerous."

He reached out with two hands to take the weapon from her warm grasp and placed it on the table. "It's a high explosive fragmentation grenade – a hand-held bomb. This example is in very good condition. Pull the pin and throw it. The sphere comes apart into a thousand or more little pieces, each moving very fast. The end result can be very loud and very messy."

"Would this kind of thing work against the NorCons?" she asked.

"Excuse me?" He couldn't believe she'd asked that question.

Bevf looked right at him with both eyes. "Haven't you ever wondered if human weapons could be used to stop the NorCons?"

He stood up. "Don't be ridiculous. Why would I do that? Would you like something to drink?"

"Come on, Bibix. You don't read books like this without having certain thoughts. I can see it in your face. I'm not asking you to help me kill NorCons. I just want to talk. We can kick this around without getting into trouble. I won't tell if you won't. Okay?"

"You sound just like a human," he grumbled.

"Takes one to know one," she shot back.

"I'll get us something to drink." He went into the kitchen, turning on a small lamp as he went by. "Have you ever noticed that Lapropods are becoming more like humans?"

The professor gathered the items from the table and put them back into the canvas bag. "Why does that surprise you? We use just about everything they left behind that the NorCons didn't claim as war booty. Did you know that in some parts of the world, Lapropods wear human-style clothes? It's true. One out of every seventeen words you and I are using right now didn't exist in our language until after we beat the humans."

Bibix returned to the table with a pair of juice glasses. He turned on another light before sighing. "Did you just say that we beat the humans?"

She took the offered glass. "Well, yes. We broke their ability to resist and the NorCons did the rest. Arrival history isn't my specialty, but I know that much. Our thirteen billion against their eight billion, and we won. I know there's still some guilt about that, but it'll be gone in another few generations."

"Accidental genocide?" he suggested, not really wanting to hear her answer.

She drank and then put her glass down. "That's the worst part of the whole thing. So many cultures, gone, just like that. How many opportunities did we miss? Art, science, literature, and commerce. Humans had so many things going on, all at the same time. I'm not surprised that we've borrowed from them. I only wish they were still here to help us defeat the NorCons."

Bibix folded two of his hands to keep the other two from shaking. "That's quite the wild idea you've cooked up. How does a nice girl like you have a thought like that?"

She looked around the apartment. With better lighting, she saw more. "I see books, movies, maps, guns, knives, and swords. There's lots of other stuff that I can't identify. If your boss is anything like mine, you'd get eaten if he knew you had these artifacts. Haven't you ever thought about using any of these things? Don't you want to stop the NorCons from hurting our people?"

"I don't really know what to say," he croaked, his throat having gone dry.

Bevf gave him a hurt look. "Do you like working for the NorCons? Is that it?"

Both of his hearts raced. He forced himself to look at her with at least one eye. "I...that is to say...me...I might not be ready to go that far just yet."

She brightened. "You have thought about it?"

He lowered his eyes in the only gesture he could think of to hide his true feelings. "I've considered it, and I've rejected it."

"Why?" She clasped her hands.

He took a drink to moisten his throat. "Look, we're getting off on the wrong pod here. Why don't you take the books you want, and we can get together some time and talk about these other things. It's nice to talk to somebody who shares my interests, but you're asking me a lot of difficult questions, ones that don't have easy answers."

She picked up one of the books. "Why are you spending so much time with this material if you're not going to put it to good use?"

"You can't just run out and start killing NorCons. Most of the human weapons are useless against them. That armor they wear is proof against small caliber ballistics. On top of that, we just aren't cut out for that kind of violence."

Bevf looked sternly at him. "How do you know these things? Are you guessing, or have you actually tried to…to…kill?"

He snapped his fingers. "See what I mean? Right there. You can barely even say the words. Besides, any Lapropod who was dumb enough to start a fight with the NorCons would be hunted down and eaten like a three-course dinner."

She sighed and put the book aside. "I'm sorry, Bibix. You're right. It's just that…I wish…Well, you know what I wish, don't you?"

"I do," he admitted, nodding solemnly.

Bevf sat back in her chair. "You're a breath of fresh air, you know that? Thanks for putting up with me. You're not afraid of the NorCons. I should just shut up and be content with that. It's funny, but I really thought I was the only one who wasn't afraid of those bucketheads. I should just take these books and go. Can we talk again some time?"

He smiled. "The NorCons are busy killing each other. They're fighting over the ownership of that trophy hall out near what used to be called Eagle River. They could be at it for days. I suppose that means I'm on vacation until they tell me to come back to work. Sure, let's get together again. I'll check out more books, and you can come to borrow them."

The professor blinked. "Aren't you afraid of what people will say about us?"

He stood and began to move about. "Let them talk. I work for a very cranky NorCon trophy hall administrator who happens to like me. Nobody's going to say anything to my face about what I do in my spare time. Do the NorCons ever spend any time at the university?"

"No," she giggled.

"There you have it."

Bevf got up with a stack of books held close in each of three arms. "The humans did have energy weapons, you know. I'll bet you've got some on display in your trophy hall."

"Out!" He pointed with all four index fingers.

He held the door open as she left. When she was gone and the door was locked, he shuffled back to the table. Half of the flat, simulated wood grain surface was now visible. "Carl was right. The lies do get easier. Now how do I tell the truth without getting killed?"

Chapter 15

The question wasn't as disturbing as he thought it would be. Perhaps it was a sign of his new toughness. He locked the door, turned off the light, and went to bed. While sleeping, he dreamed about Bevf and the taste of NorCon flesh.

He woke the following day to find that he'd slept through the entire morning. Raising one eye, he spied the digital alarm clock on his nightstand. Noon. Slow movements of each limb and all four pods revealed that he was bruised and sore from the previous day's combat. A quick sniff from his dirty nose suggested that he stank like the NorCons he had dreamed about eating.

"Ow," he mumbled several times as he crawled out of bed.

Hot water from the shower brought some relief to his muscles. Two capsules of low-dose painkiller from the medicine cabinet put an end to his headache. Lunch cured the rumbling in his stomach, and his increased blood sugar levels improved his attitude. Shuffling around the disorderly apartment, he opened a few curtains and rolled back some of the blinds. From his window, he watched Lapropods come and go as the bright, yellow sun shone down upon them.

There was no one else to trust, so he confided in himself. "Look at them go, like they've got important things to do. Sheep that barely need watching. I'd give almost anything to tell my secret to just one person who wouldn't laugh at me, or turn me in."

294 | Bibix

A knock at the door made him jump. One heart skipped a beat while the other raced. Nobody ever came to visit him. His eyestalks swung wildly as he realized that the bright sunlight from the open curtains and blinds revealed the stash of human artifacts cluttering his apartment. When the unknown visitor knocked a second time, he covered his mouth to prevent a scream from escaping.

Shivering, he approached the door. "Who is it?" he asked slowly and clearly.

A feminine laugh echoed in the hallway. "It's Bevf. I was wondering if you'd like to go out somewhere and have lunch?"

Bibix leaned on the doorframe to recover his nerve and steady his breathing. Using one eye to scan the apartment for anything that should be hidden away, he looked himself up and down with the other.

Running over to the couch and coffee table, he gathered up the bullets and power packs. He used all four hands to toss the forbidden items behind the couch, where they landed in a series of thumps, thuds, and jingles.

The professor knocked a third time. "Have I come at a bad time?"

He lunged for the door. "Yes. No! Argh! Give me just a second, and I'll be—"

Bibix unlocked the door and threw it open before he could finish his sentence. "I'm really sorry about that. I'm really lost without my job. When the NorCons gave us time off from the trophy hall so they could fight their stupid battle, I just had to try and catalog some of the stuff in my…um…you know."

She laughed in her usual easygoing way. "I do. Now, how about that lunch?"

He stepped out into the corridor, pulling the door shut behind him. A quick touch to the coded thumb pad locked the portal. "You're looking very nice today."

She blushed as sunlight from a nearby window glinted off of her prescription optics. "For a Lapropod who's been playing with human artifacts all morning, you look surprisingly neat and clean. What's your secret?"

He pointed to the exit and they started walking. "I've been around human stuff so long that I guess I know how to handle it. Actually, I clean it. That's my real secret. I know you're supposed to leave it as you find it, to preserve the historical record, but the NorCons don't want the dirt and rust in their displays."

Bevf followed him out of the building on to the nearest walkway. "I never did think it was very smart to preserve every human artifact. Who cares about what condition it was found in? It's not like a human is ever going to show up and say, 'Hey, that one is mine.' Most of their stuff is nothing special. You know that, don't you? Turn here. We can go to that place at the end of the street."

Bibix nodded and slowed so that she could walk next to him. "It's popular. Do you really want to try and get in there now?"

She pointed. "It's under new management."

He focused his attention on the restaurant they were approaching. Her use of the old euphemism didn't faze him at all. He took in the new sign and the obvious lack of customers. "That's too bad. I hope they still serve the same food."

"They do," she assured him. The two entered and sat near a large plate glass window.

There was an awkward moment when they both reached for the same menu. Her gray skin was warm to the touch.

He pulled away slowly. "I've been thinking about what you said last night. Are we becoming humanized? I think the answer is yes. It's as you said. We use their tools, and we've adopted many of their social conventions. I don't think we want to be them. They just displayed traits that we admired, even if they scared us. That's really what the assimilation is all about. Using the objects left behind by the people who still give us nightmares just happens to be our version of what they called 'therapy.' We put an end to our fears by becoming just a little bit like them. I only wish we could apply that to the NorCons."

Bevf looked up from studying the menu. "That's what I was trying to say last night."

The Lapropod who took their orders appeared to be the same one who prepared the food. As Bibix chatted with Bevf, he paid attention to the new apparent owner. The older 'Pod slightly resembled Bibix's father, which made him think about his mother. When would she welcome him back into the family?

"What's on your mind?" Bevf asked when she realized he wasn't paying attention.

He tried not to fidget. "I was just thinking about what we might learn from the humans. You might be right. Could we learn how to fight the NorCons by studying them?"

She looked around the empty dining room before responding. "I have a theory."

300 | Bibix

Bibix placed two of his hands on the table in an effort to center his focus. "I'll bet you do."

"Why are you looking at me like that?" she demanded.

He lowered his eyestalks. "Suppose I was to admit that I've had a similar thought?"

The professor took note of his language. "You're making an awfully large assumption, aren't you? How can you really know what I'm thinking if you haven't spent the last few years reviewing the same material that I've been so involved with?"

Bibix waited silently while the proprietor served their food. When the being walked away, the curator reached for his fork and ate slowly. "I know what you've seen. I've read some of their books. I can guess at some of your conclusions."

Bevf picked at her food. "I'm not suggesting behavior emulation. We're Lapropods. We're not predispcsed towards that kind of violence. I am suggesting that certain techniques may be applicable. Process identification, if you will. Defining what we're actually capable of and doing it. Do you disagree?"

With a growing knot in his stomach and a lump his throat, he nodded.

She flinched as if she'd been slapped. "You disagree? Really? How?"

Bibix thought about his recent experiences. "Now that I've studied the various forms of violence, I find that there are more than cultural barriers to be overcome."

"Such as?" she asked indignantly.

302 | Bibix

With a knife and a fork in separate hands, he paused for a drink of water. "Knife, fork, and spoon. The only interchangeable item is the spoon. Humans invented it. So did we. We have seven different words for 'spoon' and, in some circles, it's socially acceptable for our people to eat with four different spoons at any one time."

Bevf remained on guard. "You're talking about weapons development. We can do that. We're not stupid. We just haven't been exposed to—"

He waved his eating utensils and raised a third hand. "Since we got to this planet, we've been exposed to more violence than our species had ever previously seen! During the worst of the human period, we made use of improvised weapons and existing tools. We did what we had to. Then we forgot most of what we learned. After that, the slug buckets showed up."

She laughed at the slang. "You're just full of surprises."

Bibix put down the extra utensils and finished his meal. "I'm telling you that it isn't as simple as you make it sound. We can't just wake up one day and decide to fight off the NorCons. If we did it at all, we need to…work our way up to it. Step by step. A subversive process like that could take years, during which time we'd risk betrayal by anyone who had a change of hearts or didn't want to work that hard. The more I look at this, the more I think that we're not cut out for war."

Bevf sat back from her empty plate. "The two of us might be good at subversion,"

He thought about that. "You may be right. We are, in our own way, political. We plot and scheme for office promotions. We lie to save ourselves from being eaten. My experience suggests that the NorCons might be vulnerable to subterfuge."

She perked at the observation. "Have you read Machiavelli?"

He nodded, casting a one-eyed glance around the room. "I've done more than that."

The prospect of such stimulating intrigue made her restless. "Can we go? I've got a class to teach and you've given me a lot to think about. I don't really know what else to say, except that I don't feel quite so alone anymore. Bibix, if we're right, we could really start something."

Bibix thought about what he'd already started. They each paid their share of the bill, and then he walked with her halfway to the university. "Based on what I've learned so far, I can tell you that guns and knives don't make physical combat any easier. If anything, it gets scarier. We don't get the same thrill from taking lives that humans do."

"We don't?" she asked pointedly.

He cringed at his mistake. "You've seen the movies and read the literature. They get off on that stuff. Their ability to kill is somehow life affirming. Surviving the combat is more than success. It's a form of rightness that they can't stop talking about."

"What do you know that I don't?" Bevf asked quietly.

Bibix turned away. "I'm an idiot."

Bevf looked at him closely with both eyes. "Is that a scar on your left shoulder?"

He brushed at the healed wound as if it were lint. "Administrator Grilleck tried to take a piece out of me.

306 | Bibix

You know how it is with NorCons; eat first, ask questions later. I was lucky to survive."

"I'll bet you were."

Bibix could tell that she didn't believe him. With his emotions in turmoil, he said his goodbyes and went home. She'd been so easy to talk to that he'd let his guard down. Now she'd figured him out. He felt both good and bad at the same time, and he didn't like it one bit.

Without the demands of his job to occupy his time, Bibix roamed through the shopping district. He was anxious and afraid. Bevf didn't actually know anything, but she clearly had her suspicions. He wracked his brain in a futile effort to recall what he'd said that might have tipped her off. Obsessed with his own safety, he panicked. He couldn't remember what he'd told her. He couldn't remember specifically what she had said, either.

He stopped pacing to look at himself in the reflection of a large storefront window. "I'm losing my mind! Okay, okay. Calm down. I can do this. Sheesh. I sound like a human. There is no danger." He smiled at his reflection one more time. "I am fine. There is no danger."

"I'm glad to hear that," somebody said as he passed by.

Bibix went into a store for some groceries. The simple truth was that he'd gotten used to rebelling against the NorCons by himself. Now that he was faced with the possibility of having an ally, he didn't know what to do. Leading the staff at the trophy hall wasn't the same as leading troops in battle. He understood that much.

308 | Bibix

Returning to his apartment with two sacks of food, he put his purchases away and then sat on the couch to think out loud. "I'm getting ahead of myself. Bevf is a smart 'Pod. She wants what I want. I'm afraid of betrayal. I'm afraid she'll turn me in. Grilleck would eat me one slice at a time if he knew what I was doing. No. I've got to trust somebody. It might as well be her."

With his mind made up, Bibix cleaned his apartment. The chore kept him busy well into the night. By the time he finished dinner and went to bed, his home was as orderly as his thoughts. The act of cleaning and organizing had taken his mind off both his family and his fear of being caught. By the time his eyes slipped into their sockets, he was looking forward to his next encounter with Bevf.

Bibix woke early. The reflex to prepare for another day on the job was strong. He cleaned up and had breakfast. Pulling open the curtains that covered his living room window, he watched the rising sun for a few minutes. Lapropods of all shapes and sizes were already on their way to work or running errands. He watched them shuffle up and down the sidewalks. Very few levs were on the street.

The sight of so much normal activity was gratifying. "This is how we should live. No troubles. No fuss. No bucketheads. I don't know how I'm going to make this work, but I promise I'm going to give it my best effort."

With his pledge made, Bibix went for a walk. He rode a monorail and got off near the trophy hall. He walked up to the guarded structure.

The sentry was not happy to see him. "You will be called when you are needed."

"Who's winning?" he asked.

As the NorCon's responded, its translator approximated something that sounded like pride. "I am told that victory will be achieved soon. Perhaps within the next day. Resistance is fierce. You are not expected to understand."

"Yes, Greatness," Bibix muttered.

He walked to the nearest transit point and boarded the monorail. During the long ride home, he thought about the guard and what it actually was. On their home world, Lapropods had excelled at aquatic farming. The community organisms that inhabited the NorCon motorized armor still reminded him of the creatures he'd learned about in grade school. Those water-breathing invertebrates were said to have been a staple food source.

Should he tell Bevf? Or would he have to show her what they really were by arranging a NorCon death? He shuddered. She was an academic, a university professor. He'd have to show her. It would be the only way he could win the argument.

He returned home to make his plans. The actual killing wouldn't be so hard. Not this time. Not ever again. The real challenge would involve selecting the target and the mechanics of the ambush. He'd have to be quick about it, too. No more stalling, waiting for the perfect moment to carry out each step of the plan.

Looking at the phone, he thought about calling his mother. "I don't need them to think I'm pushy. Grandfather was right. She'll call for me when she's ready."

* * *

312 | Bibix

Bibix received an automated phone call early the next day, telling him to report for work within two hours. He arrived at the trophy hall within the prescribed time limit. Amidst the chaos of returning workers, Veknar confronted him.

The NorCon had a new set of markings on its armor. "We were victorious. The inventory of the Eagle River trophy hall now belongs to my master. Grilleck is dead. He was killed in battle. The human weapon you selected for him was most impressive. I have recovered it, and I will keep it for future use. You will get more ammunition for it. I will authorize the necessary trades if the cartridges can't be purchased through normal channels."

"Yes, Greatness. It shall be done," Bibix replied, bowing slightly.

"I have ordered the construction of a larger and more heavily fortified trophy hall. You will organize its construction." The NorCon raised one mechanical claw in a gesture meant to convey threat. "I have ambitions that Grilleck did not. I expect more from you. If you fail me in any way, I will have you tortured. I will personally eat you, slowly, in a very public place, so that the others can see."

"Yes, Greatness," Bibix said with all of his false humility.

The new administrator was pleased. "With a few more victories, I will have enough promotions to merit leaving this miserable planet. Even if my transfer request is denied, I will still hold enough rank to be free of this hall and any other jobs like it."

Bibix nodded. He, too, was at the top of his career field, and he knew it. The only reward he could hope to bargain for would be his own continued existence.

Acting on sudden inspiration, he clasped all four hands together. "Greatness, I would like to get started. I'll need time to organize the manual labor assignments, and you will no doubt wish to consider a properly defensible construction site for the new facility."

Veknar liked what it heard. "How does a pathetic creature like you learn such things?"

Bibix made a show of looking for eavesdroppers. "You were always the one I paid close attention to, Greatness. Grilleck was an able administrator, but you are clearly the better soldier. I've told the staff many times, organizational skill is good, but attention to detail and flexible thinking is better. Have I misunderstood what you taught me?"

The NorCon looked at Bibix. It examined its audio and video inputs carefully. Inside the articulated armor, the dozens of lifeforms that comprised Veknar debated. None of the Lapropods it could remember had ever shown such clarity of thought. Was it lying or was it truly intelligent in a way that was rare for its species?

Bibix took note of Veknar's long pause. Could all of those <u>things</u> inside that suit be confused or somehow divided? He cleared his throat. "Greatness?"

The ambitious NorCon lowered its arms and turned to walk away. "I will study this matter and give you my decision later. I have already prepared the order that will allow you to draft as many Lapropods from the local population as needed to complete the new trophy hall. You will give me the first list by the end of tomorrow's work day."

Bibix choked for a moment when he realized that he alone would decide who would join the labor gangs and who wouldn't. He rubbed his upset stomach as he watched Veknar walk away. "I think the human word for this is 'collaborator.'"

Chapter 16

Bibix was surprised when Veknar visited him in his office just two hours later. The administrator closed the door. It towered over Bibix for a long moment.

"Yes, Greatness?" the worried Lapropod asked, genuine fear apparent in his voice.

Veknar pointed to a map on the wall that showed the local terrain. "During the battle, humans attacked the food processor. The guards were apparently taken by surprise. If we are fortunate enough to have more combat with humans, my master's holdings must be secured."

318 | Bibix

Bibix put down his writing box. "The humans are subjugated, Greatness. They are your food. How can they attack anything?"

The NorCon struck a pose. "Any species with a true warrior tradition can't be kept down indefinitely. If you had come from aggressive stock, you would know that. We have always known that one percent of all humans were not accounted for when we initiated our mass capture programs. That was thirty years ago. They have had more than enough time to breed and raise new combatants."

The Lapropod continued to play the part of the puzzled inferior. "Even if such resistance does exist, what difference can it make? The most they can hope to do is scavenge old weapons and live off the land. That would hardly be a threat to the mighty NorCons."

Veknar relaxed. "Yours is the only pacifist species we have ever encountered. Some have wasted valuable time trying to negotiate. In the end, everybody fights. One day, even the spineless Lapropods may resist."

Bibix rolled his eyes in what he hoped was an expected show of disbelief. "Greatness, if we were going to resist, we would have done so by now."

The NorCon couldn't fault the curator's logic. "Bibix, you are such a waste. There are moments when I think there must be a real brain inside your head. Then there are moments like this when I realize you are just another Lapropod."

"Yes, Greatness," Bibix replied as obsequiously as he could.

The administrator turned to leave. "You've had at least one good idea today. Perhaps I will evaluate the other trophy halls for future acquisition. It would be just the sort of thing to impress the High Command. They like that sort of innovative thinking."

"They do?" Bibix asked, suddenly inspired.

Veknar's translator emulated a laugh. "What would you know about innovation?"

The Lapropod saw his opening, and took it. "Trophy halls are fine and well, Greatness. However, if the humans truly are resurgent, it might be wise to do more than collect their leftovers. I have heard you say that it's important to know your enemy."

"What are you suggesting?" Veknar demanded.

Bibix took a deep breath. "So far as I know, there is no facility dedicated to the study of human warfare. I'm sure that I can find a few Lapropods capable of gathering that information for you. It wouldn't amount to much, and it would certainly cost very little, but the effort would demonstrate your ability to anticipate a future need."

The little being's suggestion sounded a lot like intelligence gathering, an activity always looked upon favorably by the chain of command. Veknar was tempted. "What can we learn that we don't already know? We have been examining human military literature for the last three decades."

The senior curator picked up an item from his desk. It was a broken night vision device. "The humans made war with machines. Now they don't have any. Greatness, I'm not a soldier, but even I know they would certainly find ways to fight without machines."

The observation was rational, too rational to have come from a Lapropod. The NorCon leader inspected

Bibix very carefully. "Guerilla war. Is that what you are saying?"

"I don't know what that is," Bibix lied.

Veknar stormed out of the office, leaving the door open as it departed. Several pairs of eyes peeked over or around office furniture as the bravest members of the staff tried to see whether or not Bibix was still alive. They gossiped with fear and amazement. Once again, the hard-to-please Bibix had survived a run-in with an irritated NorCon. What was his secret? How did he do it? New hands and senior specialists alike were baffled.

Bibix kept working. Unsure of his success, he braced himself for the moment when Veknar would return to eat him. The NorCon had always been quick to anger. Bibix had seen Grilleck use that to its advantage many times. When confused or embarrassed, Veknar would hide behind its anger to avoid any further indignities. It was a trait some Lapropods shared. In his youth, Bibix had relied on tantrums himself to avoid responsibilities.

"Know your enemies as you know yourself," he mumbled.

Bibix went home at the end of the normal shift. On his orders, most of the staff would work late into the night. The remaining exhibits would be packed and prepared for shipping within two weeks. Everyone was encouraged to turn in a list of family members so that they could be excluded from the upcoming labor assignments. This generous act sparked more gossip about Bibix and the many possible reasons for his growing political power.

Once inside the relative safety of his apartment, he called Bevf on the telephone.

"Would this be business or pleasure?" she asked.

He sighed. "I was hoping for a little of both. In three days, the NorCons will announce a new labor draft. I…know the 'Pod who is going to make the assignments. I have some thoughts I'd like to run by you before I go to him with my recommendations. This could be good for both of us, and that thing you'd like to do."

"Really?" She sounded intrigued.

He paced from the living room to the kitchen with the wireless phone in one hand. "I was being an absolute human the other day. I'd like the chance to apologize for that, too. I was taking you seriously, but other things were also distracting me. I think it's great that you want to do that thing we talked about. I want to help."

She quietly closed the door to her office. "Thank you. I really mean that. Thanks a lot. I was beginning to think— Well, you know what I was beginning to think. I didn't realize this would be so hard."

"Neither did I," he laughed.

She went back to her chair. "I have to finish prepping a class assignment. I should be done in an hour. Let me stop off and get something. I'll bring it over to your place and you can cook. How does that sound?"

He was flattered by the overt, suggestive gesture. "I'd like that."

Once she hung up, he rushed to prepare. Social custom among Lapropods relied on hospitality as the barometer for relationships. The sharing of food could mean many different things, each depending on location. The evening meal was most often reserved for family, close friends, or lovers.

Although many Lapropods around the world had embraced the various human traditions of wedding, most still chose to pair voluntarily based on emotional preference. The interpretation of the act of a single female bringing food to the domicile of a single male was still a matter of debate among older Lapropods. If she brought prepared food, it was assumed that the female was a close friend. Otherwise, they would eat in public. If she brought food for the male to prepare, she was expected to be his lover.

Bibix had turned his back to social convention many years ago. His decision to fight the NorCons had consumed him, robbing him of many chances to socialize, date, and mate. So much of his time had been spent avoiding detection and capture that he no longer recalled what the proper etiquette was for some situations. Was it good enough to have an open mind and a clean apartment? He didn't know, and that bothered him.

Bevf was talkative when she arrived. She held up a shopping bag. "I got to the market as it was closing. They gave me a good deal on salmon. I hope you don't mind. It's one of the few things you can get in this part of the world that I actually like."

He took the bag from her and headed for the kitchen. "You're not from around here?"

She followed. "No. My family lives in what they used to call Florida. Actually, I think they still call it Florida. I miss the humidity. But this is where the job is. You know how that goes."

"I had plans to do other things when I finished with college, myself."

She pulled up a chair and sat to watch him cook. "Let me guess. The NorCons picked you to work in their local trophy hall."

He laid the large fish on a cutting board and reached for a knife. "You got it right on the first try. Have a prize."

She waited patiently for him to pluck out one of the fish's eyes. He carefully fed it to her.

She smiled. "Were you serious about what you said over the phone?"

He kept one eye on his work and the other on her. "Fighting the NorCons? Yes. Absolutely. We can learn a lot from the humans when it comes to killing people and breaking things. It's not just an intellectual proposition. We've got to overcome our natural dispositions. Humans were not always the dominant species on this planet. Even after they industrialized, they still had to protect themselves from other lifeforms."

She relaxed. "I can't imagine what that would be like. I know the humans still have the power to scare us, even though they're gone. The NorCons scare me, but it's not that visceral, instinctive fear that would make me reach for a weapon."

He moved the knife to fillet the bright red meat of the salmon. "What would make you reach for a weapon? More importantly, what would make you use it?"

"I've spent the last two years trying to answer that question. We don't lack the instinct for self-preservation. We successfully proved that by leaving our home world because we faced extinction. We overcame the humans, and we've adapted to the

NorCon presence. In many respects, I think we are the ultimate survivors."

Bibix programmed his cooker and began to season the fillets. "Do you think there was ever any chance that the humans might have welcomed us to Earth?"

She shook her head. "Absolutely not. I, and others, have studied the historical record. There's no official account of any attempt by any human government to make positive contact during our arrival. It's a popular myth, unsupported by any shred of proof."

He thought about the videodisks he had viewed within the past year. "I've been told by certain contacts I have that our own leaders may have…sanitized the official record. The NorCons have certain media archives in their possession that strongly suggest that at least one of the human governments did truly attempt what they called 'first contact.'"

"You've seen this material for yourself?" she asked.

"I have," he admitted as he placed the fish in a ceramic dish.

Bevf watched him put the food into the cooker. He was testing her. She couldn't blame him for it. In their own way, they were plotting rebellion. If they were caught, the penalty would be death. Not even their fellow Lapropods would spare them. She had been bold enough to share a forbidden thought with him. Now he was doing the same. Her reply would either earn his trust or push him away.

She cleared her throat. "Assuming what you say is true, how does that impact our fight against the NorCons? If we can't learn from our mistakes, we don't deserve our freedom. The humans are gone – subjugated. Raised like cattle and processed accordingly. We didn't do that to them. We have nothing to feel guilty about."

He looked at the skin and entrails left on his cutting board. "We have plenty to feel guilty about, and we do. It gets passed from parent to child. We've enshrined our guilt in the textbooks that our children learn from. It was our good fortune to overcome the humans. It was our great shame to stand by and let the NorCons round up those who were left.

She was curious about his lack of anger. "Ah. You almost had me there. Do you really think we accept our status with the NorCons as punishment for what our ancestors may or may not have done?"

"I do."

Her eyestalks rose with mounting interest. "I see. No, I really mean that. You kept this to yourself for the same reason I did. You didn't think anyone would believe you."

He nodded.

She was speechless for several seconds. "So, have you really killed a NorCon?"

He nodded again.

She searched for the scar on his shoulder. "I don't know what to say. I'd really like to know how you did it. I can't imagine anyone charging off to find the nearest NorCon and kill it. I assume that you planned it all out in advance. I've had a theory that we may not be capable of killing without premeditation. At the very least, one would need a very high degree of rationalization."

334 | Bibix

Bibix felt as if he were in freefall. He'd lied to her about his career start only because he didn't think she would believe him. How could anyone harbor thoughts like these for so very long without going insane? She was clearly acting on her thoughts much sooner than he had. Did the 'safe' university environment give her an edge that he didn't have, or was she just smarter than he was? There was only one way to find out.

"What do you know about the NorCons?" he asked as he disposed of the fish entrails.

Her eyes came close together as she thought. "Earth doesn't seem to be their favorite place. It certainly doesn't have their preferred atmosphere or gravity. They appear to be genderless, which could mean they contain both sexes in the same body. I believe the term is 'hermaphrodite.' It's possible that they aren't mammals. I've heard some people speculate that they could even be an aquatic species."

"Really?" he asked, amazed.

"Oh, yes," she declared with academic supremacy.

He thought about the fish in his cooker. "What do you think they are?"

"I don't know," she replied slowly.

He liked her answer. "Would you like to find out?"

She sat up. "Of course I would. If you really have killed one, I'm sure you can tell me. Unless you didn't bother to look inside the armor."

He began to pace. "I looked. Believe me, I wish I hadn't."

She waited for him to go on.

He took a deep breath and stopped pacing. "Each NorCon is a community organism. It's possible they're aquatic. I don't really know. There are dozens of them in each suit. I haven't had a chance to sit down and examine the liquid in the armor, or even to get a good look inside. I think the interior is full of switches. It might be some sort of instrument system they can read."

Bevf's mind raced with the possibilities. "What do they look like?"

He gestured with all four hands. "Each one is about the size of an adult's hand, shaped like an oval, with an uneven surface. I don't remember seeing gills or fins. Their natural color is white or beige. They excrete green foam when exposed to the air. They die fast, and they taste like salmon."

Both of her eyes twitched. "Say that last part again."

He cringed at his own embarrassment. "Please, don't judge me. You had to be there. I was very mad. Angry. Very…angry."

She studied him. "Is that what it takes to kill? Some level of anger that's hard to reach?"

He fought the urge to mention his involvement with Carl. "Yeah. That's about it. When my safety was in doubt, I felt differently about being violent. I wanted to be aggressive. I was aggressive. I was very aggressive. I don't know how else to say it."

She misread his tension as further embarrassment. "How did you do it? I assume you used a weapon of some kind. Please, tell me. I won't judge you."

He wanted to laugh. He was well aware that she was already judging him. "I used a human plasma gun. Regular ballistic weapons are no good against NorCon armor. I put several holes in…it…and it died. Motorized food."

Bevf found herself nodding. "Yes, I can see how you might think that. There was a lifeform on our home world that we thought of as a community organism." She laughed.

"Krellum," he replied, pronouncing the Lapropodian word with unnatural care.

She sobered. "No, please. I'm not laughing at you. It's just that you called them 'motorized food,' and that struck me as being really funny. If our people knew they were being lorded over by something that looks a lot like food from home, they'd go nuts!"

"And then they would die because we have no concept of organized resistance," he predicted, pulling a sour face.

Bevf started to protest, but thought better of it. "You really have thought about this. If we're not careful, millions will die in a failed revolt. The NorCons aren't subtle. They might decide to use us for food, or they could…"

Bibix went to his cooler and took out some vegetables. He began to make a salad. "I don't care if I ever get credit for doing any of this. The last thing I want on my conscience is genocide, theirs or ours. The NorCons are still here because we've made it easy for them to stay here. They don't try very hard to keep us in our place. We do a very nice job of that on our own. We are our own jailers. You and I need to approach this carefully. We need to recruit secretly."

She blinked. "I'm fat, slow, and I can't see without my glasses. How am I going to inspire anyone to…to…you know? I suppose you can teach me how to shoot a gun."

He stopped what he was doing. "Brains before strength. We need thinkers who see things our way. We Lapropods may not be great fighters, but we are great thinkers. We can do anything we set our minds to. As I've learned from the human books I've read, there is more than one way to fight a war. We need to think of this as a multigenerational conflict. It could take decades. We also need to be thinking about the unsavory options."

She took a piece of vegetable from the counter and nibbled it. "What's more unsavory than fighting from the shadows? You are talking about deceit, deception, and misdirection."

Bibix put down his peeler. Both of his eyes met hers. "Be honest with me. What's the scariest thing you can think of?"

"Humans." She blushed. "The NorCons are mean – brutes, really. Humans, from what I know about them, were vicious killers who were capable of eating their own. In some recorded instances, they did."

He folded both sets of arms over his pudgy chest. "Right. What do you think would happen if the humans fought the NorCons?"

She shrugged. "I expect they'd be eaten. That's what happened before. What makes you think things would be any different a second time around?"

He raised a hand. "Think about it for a moment. What if we could organize them into a joint resistance force, melding our strengths with theirs?"

"You can't be serious! Even if you could find humans left outside of captivity, you'd never live long enough to speak with them. They'd have to be feral by now, which would only make things worse."

He finished making the salad. "I've done some interesting research that leads me to believe humans are always dangerous, with or without civilized behavior. It's their instinct we need. That, and their taste for violence. The real problem we face is diplomatic. How do we make friends with them? They don't have any reason to like the NorCons. They don't have any reason to like us, either. If we could reason with them, we might gain allies."

She shrugged. "Would you listen to what you just said? That's the stupidest idea I've ever heard, and I have to deal with grad students all the time. Where on this planet could you possibly find a human who would sit still long enough to hear your proposal? I know that the human strategist, Sun Tzu, said that the enemy of my enemy is my friend, but you're reading a little too much into that."

He placed the salad in a large bowl and put it in the cooler. "That fish will be done in another five minutes. Look, I'm not crazy. I've already found one human who is willing to work with me."

She scowled, and then folded two of her arms. "Prove that to me, and I'll join your war effort after I have your child."

Bibix forced himself to stop and think. There was no turning back, and Bevf was too smart to be deceived any further. "You're quite right. Today's humans are a managed resource. Cattle. Food. At best, they retain some of their pre-Collapse language and knowledge base. That stuff is probably handed down in story form, from one generation to the next, in the same way that our own people used to preserve knowledge."

She was unmoved. "You're not telling me anything I don't already know. How did you find this oh-so-rational human and when can I see it?"

He fidgeted. "As you say, today's humans are out of our reach. But yesterday's humans are not."

She urged him to continue with a series of hand gestures.

He continued. "It may not be common knowledge, but the NorCons still have some humans in cryogenic suspension. On rare occasions, they revive them and eat them. Certain things I've overheard suggest that the NorCons regard pre-Collapse humans as a sort of delicacy, or gourmet food. They particularly enjoy humans who have military experience."

Bevf was unsettled. "You're right, that's not common knowledge. I thought the whole 'canned human' thing was just a conspiracy theory. Something for the truly sick among us to talk about late at night."

Bibix continued slowly. "Most of the cryo systems in use at the time of our arrival were self-contained and portable. Those that could be moved were put into long-term storage. Those that couldn't be moved were destroyed. The NorCons took possession of every last one that remained when they defeated us. The humans were classified by social status and profession, and given out as rewards. Most found their way into the trophy halls, where they are kept for…um…special occasions."

The professor had no reason to doubt him. "I assume the subjects human doctors chose for the cryogenic process were generally rich, famous, or war heroes."

He wiped a bead of sweat from his forehead. "Yes. In some cases, the subjects appear to have been chosen for their specialized knowledge. More than half of the stored humans I've seen had an incurable illness of some kind. I'm just guessing, but it may be that those who paid for the suspended animation process were hoping to avoid the worst of the invasion."

"Invasion?" Bevf bristled.

He shook his head. "You know that's what it looked like from their point of view."

She relaxed slightly, accepting his comment with a slight nod. "I have to admit, we did show up unannounced. Please, continue."

He went to the cooker as it beeped. He turned it off and put on a pair of oven mitts. "We had a human soldier in our trophy hall, a young man with a long combat record. He was very fierce. He also had an illness for which we now have the cure. I intended to use that cure as leverage to keep him in line after I woke him up. Stealing him was easy. Reviving him was hard. Keeping him under my influence was…not possible."

She waited as he removed the hot dish from the cooker. "If I didn't have some sense of who you are, I'd think you were lying. Where is this man, and when can I meet him?"

Bibix put the baked fish on a serving platter and took it to the dinner table. "I don't know where he is at the moment. We parted company after our last mission."

Bevf helped him set the table. "You're asking me to believe a lot. This isn't Bigfoot we're talking about. I want to meet this man from the past. Just out of curiosity, how did you avoid being killed by what's-his-name?"

He finished the place settings with plates and napkins. "His name is Carl. He and I have…an understanding. He's not my friend. He tolerates me, and…I'm learning to tolerate him. He's a lot to take, even in small doses, if you know what I mean."

"Did he give you that scar?" she asked after taking her seat.

Bibix placed one hand over the old wound. "He did hurt me a few times."

She waited for him to get the salad and pour drinks. "Probably his way of negotiating."

He sat across from her and laughed. "You could be right about that. His language skills are excellent.

There's just one problem. He claims to have seen certain things which would be a little…inconvenient to explain."

Bevf offered him her plate. "You're the host. You serve. What exactly are we talking about? Are you saying that he witnessed atrocities?"

He put food on her plate. "You could say that. Lapropods eating humans. I think he'll stay quiet about it, but only for a while. He's very opinionated."

She accepted the full plate as it was given to her. "You said he has great language skills. How much education does he claim?"

Bibix served himself and began to eat. "Middle school. He might have called it 'junior high.' He can read and write. I've seen him do it."

"Do you speak English?" she asked.

He nodded because his mouth was full.

"Show me," she urged.

He used his best classroom English. "I am fluent, which is to say that I don't need a translator band to speak English. Did you know that Lapropods have six known regional dialects, but humans used more than a hundred variations of the English language?"

"One hundred and fifty," she corrected.

He put down his fork. "Wait one moment. I have something to show you."

She watched him leave the dining area. He moved with a casual confidence that was rare for most males of her species. His intimate knowledge of the NorCons had definitely changed his worldview. He wasn't afraid of them. He showed no signs of the timidity that she'd come to dislike so much in others. Would she have to experience combat before she could feel that secure?

Bibix returned with a personal data device in one hand. He gave it to her. "I've got video on this PDD. I've gone over it in my mind a hundred times, but I still can't find the right words to explain what you're about to see."

She picked up the small device and turned it over in her hands. "This thing is dirty, cracked, and chipped. I'm amazed it still works. What's that black stuff?"

He quickly sat down. "I think that might be dried blood."

Bevf dropped the PDD on to the table and wiped her hands thoroughly with a cloth napkin. "That's disgusting! Yuck! Did you really have to do that?"

He suffered quietly through his embarrassment. "There's going to be a lot more spilled blood, if you're serious about being a rebel. I thought I'd seen enough human movies and combat videos to be prepared for the blood, but I was wrong. I don't think anyone in his right mind can get used to it. The best you can do is to learn to live with it."

Bevf reexamined the PDD with one eye and him with the other. "I'm sorry. I didn't mean to offend you. You're telling me things that I don't want to hear…showing me things that I'd rather not see. I can do this. I can learn to live with it. Please, just slow down and give me a little more time to adapt."

He moved the PDD to the far side of the table. "We can deal with this some other time. Let's just relax and enjoy the meal before it gets cold."

She ate in silence for several minutes. "NorCons really taste like fish?"

He brandished his fork. "Salmon."

With academic precision, she ate the last of her cooked fish. One eye wandered as she analyzed the food in her mouth. "We might just be able to eat our way to victory."

He waggled his eyestalks in a show of outrageous humor.

She made happy noises. "I'm glad that we met. I'm really happy to be here. You're an amazing 'Pod, Bibix. You really are. Your family must be proud."

He pushed his empty plate off to one side. "I'm sure they are. At least, I think they are. My mother still hasn't called me. She must be taking my father's death harder than I thought."

Bevf held up her glass. "Half full or half empty?"

He looked at the liquid level. "Half full."

She smiled with approval. "You never did say. What did your father do?"

"Civil service," Bibix replied glumly.

She straightened. "You say that like it's a crime. We can't all be senior curators, you know. Tradition dictates that I don't ask you about your mother during her time of mourning, but your dad's a different matter. Tell me about him. Please?"

Bibix motioned for her to follow him into the living room. They sat on the couch. He collected his thoughts before responding.

"He was young when he came to Earth. He and my grandfather used to tell me stories about the home world and the exodus. My grandfather had plenty to say about the humans and what they put us through, but my dad never said a word on the subject, not even when I asked.

"I don't know what he did right after the landings, but I have the distinct impression that he suffered. There might've been hunger and starvation, maybe something worse. I just don't know."

She squirmed to get comfortable. "What did he do before the NorCons came?"

The curator shook his head. "I don't know that, either. My mother has hinted that he went through several jobs. None of them stuck until he went to work for our government. He managed to keep his job after we capitulated to the NorCons. He never liked them. He told me so, on more than one occasion. He was very disappointed in my career choice when I went to work in the trophy hall."

"Did he get over it?" she asked.

Bibix smiled. "Yes, I think he did. He put up a hostile front to keep my grandparents happy, but he never said a harsh word to me about my job. Not ever."

Bevf thought about her own relatives. "It must be a generational thing. None of my grandparents are happy with life on Earth. I like hearing stories about the home world, but it's gone and we won't be going back. This is our home now. We need to send the

NorCons on their way so that we can get down to the business of making peace with the humans and salvaging our society."

"What's to salvage?"

She made an all-encompassing gesture. "Come on. We had this conversation yesterday at lunch. Bibix, we are broken. Our social growth is…arrested. We came here in such a hurry that we failed to make a good transition. We're caught between the humans and the NorCons, and we don't know what to do next. That's why I think we need to defeat the NorCons. As a civilized species, we can't go on much longer like this."

He wanted to agree with her. He'd lived with his secrets for so long that it was extremely difficult to part with the truth. "Please, just give me a moment.

I've never been able to talk to anyone like this, and it's…hard."

Bevf went back to the table. She was moving too fast, and she knew it. In the sanctuary of their offices, Bevf and her fellow academics had similar conversations like this all the time. However, they were never so direct, and the discussions were always conducted behind closed, locked doors. Speaking so openly with Bibix made her hearts race. He was both intimidating and informative at the same time. His reluctance and circumspection contradicted his confidence.

The curator watched his guest eat her food. He could tell by the way she studied him that she well knew he was in over his head. She was attractive, opinionated, and informed. Her militancy was both sexy and scary. Her intellectual aggression clashed with her physical uncertainty. He was certain they could learn from each other. There could be more to the relationship if he could overcome his misgivings and shortcomings.

Bevf squirmed. "You're staring at me."

He averted his gaze. "I'm sorry. Like I said, I'm just not used to talking to anyone else about this kind of thing. How do you share something like this?"

She relaxed. "Behind closed doors, some of my colleagues talk 'at' subjects like this, but I've never met anyone like you, who speaks about it from experience. I can think of at least five 'Pods who would love to meet you."

He shook his head. "Please, no. I'm not ready for that."

360 | Bibix

She didn't know if he was being humble or simply afraid. "Did you sleep well last night? I didn't. I'm not sure how to live with this."

He thought about the labor lists that he was tasked with making. "That's one lesson I've learned the hard way. If we're really going to do this, we'll have to live with a lot of unpleasant truths. We may have to do many things we don't like."

Bevf smiled and reached out to take his hand. "I can't think of anything that would be worse than what we're talking about. You notice how we dance around it?"

Bibix held her hand and bowed his head. "Veknar is going to build a new trophy hall. It will contain all of the things the current one has, plus all the items we gained from capturing the Eagle River site. My job…is to decide who gets assigned to the labor pool.

I've been given…permission…to select anyone from this area."

The revelation left Bevf speechless. Her grip remained firm as she recovered. "I'm so sorry. A lot of 'Pods are going to hate you when they find out. You…may never be able to go home again. I'm sorry. I really don't know what else to say."

He looked at her with both eyes. "Does the name 'Edix' mean anything to you?"

"No," she lied.

Bibix rolled his eyes. "I looked it up. He's the last Lapropod on record who had anything to do with selecting work gangs after the NorCon's arrived. The official record says he was the last labor supervisor to oversee NorCon construction projects in this region.

362 | Bibix

Six weeks after the last work battalion was demobilized, he was…um…They killed him."

She looked away for a moment. "Does anyone else know about this?"

Both of his hearts sank. "The staff at the trophy hall. I had to tell them. I've even promised exemptions to them and their families. Bevf, I haven't seen the engineering specs on this new trophy hall, but it's going to be huge. They're going to want…need…demand a lot of strong backs. How do we stop the NorCons if we can't—"

The kind 'Pod put a warm hand to his mouth to silence him. Then she moved in close. "I'm sorry. I don't know what else to tell you. You've opened my eyes to so many things. I wish I could save you from this. I can't. That means we need to find a way to make it work for us. Humans aren't the only ones to adapt. We can do it, too. We need to find a way to…thrive…on this adversity."

The curator laid his head on her shoulder. "Are we too stupid to save ourselves? Why do we keep looking for human solutions to solve Lapropod problems?"

The questions sounded like something one of her colleagues might have asked, but only behind a very large and heavy locked door. "NorCons expect resistance. They prefer it. Humans have been predators and prey on their own world. In their own way, they prefer to live in a constant state of conflict that is totally alien to our way of life. Bibix, we're not killers, but we are thinkers. That counts for something."

He sighed. "That's why I went out of my way to find Carl. He thinks and kills in a way that would make your head spin. We don't need the kind of sneakiness that can get you a job promotion. We need the kind of sneakiness that can set us free."

His observation made her sit up. She held all four of his hands in hers. "I think I get it."

"Share it with me, please," he implored.

She released her grip and stood up. "If this human of yours is so dangerous, we need more of them. More humans." She held up a hand to stop his incipient interruption. "Now, hold on. Work with me for just a moment. For the better part of a thousand years, human writers said that wars were won at three different levels: violence, adversarial politics, and economics. Bibix, those are all quality of life issues. If this construction project makes a lot of Lapropods miserable, we can recruit them."

He glanced at the dining room table and thought about the PDD with the video recordings Carl had made. "Okay. I can see how we might, possibly, get more humans to take up arms against the NorCons. I've been thinking along those lines for a while now. How can we recruit our own people to join this fight? I'm in this thing up to my eyeballs, and I don't want to be involved. We don't have wealth or high position. How can we possibly make them listen to us? I've thought about this before, and I'm stumped."

"Are you done?" she scolded after he finished ranting.

He moved away from her.

She let him go. She had secrets of her own. "Don't you see it? They've given you the opportunity! Yes, you're being set up to take the heat for the labor assignments, but you're also going to be in a totally unique position. Bibix, you can recruit more Lapropods who think like we do!"

Bibix didn't like the idea of being hated by his own people. He struggled to find the right words to convey his unhappiness. "I've just been making this up as I go along. I've never been a good judge of character. Somebody would figure out what I'm doing and turn me in."

"Let me do it."

He blinked. "Excuse me?"

Bevf softened her tone. "Let me handle the recruiting. I can already guarantee that half of my department will participate. No, let me finish. Bibix, your hearts and mind are in the right place but, honestly, you're too insecure. You can't do this by yourself. I know it's hard for you to share this with me. Let me in. Let me help."

Bibix stood up and shuffled on all four pods. "You're right, again. Veknar trusts me. I can use that to our advantage. I'm sorry to be so difficult about this. It's been very hard for me to get this far." He paused. "I couldn't live with myself if anything happened to you."

Folding her arms, Bevf watched him pace. "I had these thoughts in my head long before I met you. I'm here tonight because I want to be."

He raised two of his hands in a show of surrender. "All right smarty-pods, how do you want to start this?"

The question made her face pucker as she thought.

He rolled his eyes. "See? Not so easy!"

"Will you shut up?" she demanded.

He sat on the far end of the couch.

She turned to face him. "Humans had a real gift for bureaucracy. They could find ways to make the simplest things very complicated. NorCons like a certain amount of bureaucracy, too. It's like they have a need for order and conformity in their lives. Tomorrow, tell what's-his-name that you need to form an advisory committee. You can say that it'll help you to find the best labor candidates. Screening out the old and the sick will make for a more efficient construction process. I'll head up the advisory group, and we'll do the recruiting."

Her plan relied on the same type of deceptions that he'd used against Grilleck and the trophy hall staff. He signaled his approval with his eyes. "I'm going to have nightmares if I don't ask one question. How can you possibly know what to look for in a Lapropod that will tell you if they are…um…you know?"

She snickered. "Junk polisher."

He bristled at the insult. "What's that all about?"

Bevf composed herself. "I'm sorry. I first heard the term as a grad student. The 'Pods who work in the trophy halls are called junk polishers because that's all they do. Well, that's all we think they do. Obviously, we…I…was wrong. I'm sorry."

He responded with a broad smile. "I'm the senior curator for my trophy hall. I supervise the 'Pods who polish the junk."

She smiled. "Point made. Look, I have family background and social skills that you don't. You're obviously better with the NorCons than you are with our own people. That's your strength. Let me use mine. My experience with college-aged 'Pods will give me an edge when it comes to spotting the militant thinkers. I have a bad feeling there won't be very many. Even so, I can do it right in front of the NorCons."

The boast made him raise one eye. "The slug buckets are more observant than you might think. It's been my experience that they expect obedience but they're always on the lookout for treachery. They expect you to do a bad job. They expect you to fail."

Bevf snorted. "That's not being observant. That's prejudice."

He lowered his gaze. "That prejudice can get you eaten."

She stood up. Her mood was darkening and she didn't want to spoil the evening by assaulting Bibix with a rant about her unfortunate past. "I need to go. You've lived with this secret longer than I have. You'll probably sleep well tonight, but I won't. I need to slow down and think. I don't want you to misinterpret my actions. We can be good for each other. I just need time to think."

"Thinking doesn't always help," he commented as he walked her to the door.

She turned to give him a light kiss on the way out. "Now that I know what NorCons taste like, I won't be so quick to fear them. You've opened my eyes to a lot of things. I want to do this again some time. Thank you, and good night."

He closed and locked the door after she'd gone. He focused his attention on the dinner dishes in an effort to calm down, washing them by hand. He'd only known her for two days, and Bevf was already having an impact on his life. She was attractive in every way that mattered to him. She understood him in a way that was both comforting and confusing.

Chapter 17

Bibix was unable to sleep with so many thoughts buzzing around in his head. He spent the night reading from his collection of political books. Several volumes on spy history proved to be enlightening. He eventually found himself engrossed in a lengthy explanation of resistance movements in Western Europe during the Second World War. The nuts and bolts of secretive, low-tech guerilla operations captured his attention and held it well past sunrise.

As he prepared for the day, his enthusiasm grew. Bevf was right. With her help, he could enlist the aid of others. He practiced what he'd say to Veknar as he made breakfast. He considered individual words again and again, repeating the ones that fit until every

374 | Bibix

phrase felt right coming out of his mouth. He talked to himself quietly during the drive to work, rehearsing responses to anything Veknar might question. He entered the trophy hall through the front door.

NorCon engineers were busy taking the building apart. Lapropods of all shapes and sizes scurried to pack the exhibits. Bibix strode through the chaos with real confidence.

He cleared his throat in the most authoritative way he could imagine. "Pack those crates like your lives depend on it! Supervisors, come see me when you've got your morning schedules on paper. Nobody gets eaten today!"

Murmurs of approval echoed from around the trophy hall. Bibix was a hard 'Pod to please, but they knew he was on their side. His loud proclamation was reassuring and it had the desired effect. As their morale improved, the staff worked faster.

The curator went to Veknar's office. He knocked before putting on a breath mask.

"Enter!" the chief administrator bellowed.

Bibix opened the door and stepped inside. "Greatness, I'd like to discuss the labor assignments."

From behind its desk, the NorCon waved an imperious mechanical claw. "You have the labor lists? That was fast."

The Lapropod closed the door and went to the only other chair in the room. "With all due respect, Greatness, I think I've got something better."

The NorCon's helmet assembly turned slowly in Bibix's direction. "I don't share my predecessor's taste for innovation. This had better be good."

Bibix opened his briefcase and handed over a single printed page that described his proposal for a labor draft advisory committee. "I wouldn't waste your time with anything else. I was reviewing what I could find relating to the last labor draft. I think we can be more efficient with our resources. All I'm asking for is a small process change…a minor alteration of the bureaucracy. If you approve this plan, I'll guarantee that we can start construction of your new trophy hall by the end of this month."

"I have not yet decided on a location," the NorCon commented as it studied the page.

Bibix took a long, filtered breath. "That doesn't matter. The last big effort resulted in thirty percent casualties. The engineers couldn't meet their deadlines because they couldn't keep their workers alive. If you allow us to select our own best laborers, we can cut casualties to just five percent. We can also keep up with your engineers. I was thinking that your master would be very impressed. Who knows? You might even get a reward."

Veknar's head tilted as it examined the succinct proposal. "Casualty rates are irrelevant. I don't care how many of you die in this effort."

"You should," Bibix prompted.

The NorCon studied its subordinate. Inside the armor, its community was divided. It suspected a trick. Lapropods disliked manual labor, and it knew that fact all too well. "Explain yourself. Don't lie to me. You are useful, but even you can be replaced."

378 | Bibix

Bibix shrugged, knowing that it was the most appropriate gesture for an actor in his position. "Greatness, you and I both know that your recent success has earned you a promotion, as well as the attention of others who would like to rob you of your gains. There must be other NorCons who will try to do what you did. Perhaps they will attack your trophy hall. If you are caught without a sufficient labor force, you could be…defeated."

Veknar thought about that. It had counseled Grilleck against the Eagle River attack because it thought the effort might use up too many martial resources. Grilleck was dead, but its plan had succeeded. The nasty little Lapropod was more insightful than it had realized. Other commanders in this region would most certainly wait for Veknar to make a mistake. If that error turned out to be something as trivial as labor depletion, it would lead to a defeat that would do more than ruin the being's career. It would be sent to wander the oceans of the home world in permanent disgrace.

The NorCon realigned its gaze. "I will consult with my master. You will go back to your duties. Expect to hear from me in one hour."

The curator walked out of the administrator's office. He shut the door and calmly peeled off the breath mask. Hanging the mask on a hook near the door, he walked away, placing one pod in front of another as if he had no worries. Both hearts raced as he went back to his office.

Bibix entered the main exhibit hall. He supervised the packing of a particularly delicate exhibit until an announcement over the public address system summoned him back to Veknars's office.

"Good job," he told the trio of Lapropods as they finished.

They watched him go to the administrator's office. Under the hard glare of a bright LED light, one of them whispered to the others, "Someday, he's going to go in there and never come out. I don't want that to happen anytime soon, but I'm ready for it."

"He will be missed," another said softly.

Bibix looked at the nearest clock as he put on a breath mask. An hour had passed. He took a long deep breath, and knocked. He entered when Veknar bellowed.

Veknar gave him a data chip. "Plug this into your personal data device. It contains your new orders and an authenticator that most NorCons will recognize. Don't lose it or you risk being eaten. My master has approved your plan. You will arrange for me to meet your advisory panel. You will do this tomorrow morning."

The curator's eyestalks rose in fear. "I'm not sure I can do it that fast."

Veknar raised and lowered both of its mechanical claws. "The snow falls in this region approximately eight weeks from now. I will choose my new building site within forty-eight hours. You will begin labor recruitment in forty-eight hours. I want to see this advisory group for myself. You know what will happen if I am disappointed."

Bibix looked at the chip in his hand. "I've never known you to be in such a hurry."

"I have better things to do with my time," the administrator snapped.

382 | Bibix

Daringly, the Lapropod asked, "What other lofty goals do you have in mind?"

The deskbound soldier opened the maw of its helmet slightly. Bibix gathered the gesture was intended as the being's equivalent of an evil grin. "Two of our deep forest patrols have gone missing in an area just west of our food processing plant in the last week. The grizzly bears that are common to this region rarely attack. We accept the loss of one deep forest patrol each year due to climate and the actions of such creatures. The loss of two patrols in such a short span of time suggests more organized activity."

Bibix thought about Carl. Then, he shook his head. "I don't know about such things, Greatness. I'm a trophy hall curator. Now you have tasked me with becoming a labor leader. I'll trust in your ability to keep my people safe."

Veknar's translator synthesized a laugh. "I don't care about your safety."

The curator bowed to show that he was groveling. "Wolves and bears of any type are a real danger to my people, Greatness. The grizzlies you mentioned can eat my people in one bite. I'm not sure how much that would slow down your construction efforts—"

"Get out!" the NorCon blustered, both clawed hands raised in a violent gesture.

Bibix left the room in a hurry. He was pleased with himself. Leaving the breath mask on its assigned hook, he hustled back to his office with a smile on his lips. Veknar's concern clearly had something to do with the humans that Bibix and Carl had set loose. The chubby Lapropod was happy to know that his efforts were getting results so quickly.

Once safely inside his office and behind a closed door, he plopped into his chair and savored the moment. In less than a full calendar year, he'd manipulated the NorCons into killing each other, he had personally killed one, and he'd unleashed a group of violent humans. As if that weren't enough, he now had a friend and confidant who understood him, and he was about to gain more allies.

He allowed his eyes to roam around the interior of his moderately lit office. In spite of his best efforts, the place was a mess. The bookshelves were cluttered. The bulletin board overflowed with notices, memos, and outdated inventory lists. In one corner, a stack of unidentified artifacts reached the ceiling. Various hand-held items littered his desk.

A fat metal cylinder caught his attention. According to the tiny lettering stamped into its bottom, it was a one-kilogram plasma-boosted thermite charge, made in China, a location Bibix understood to have been one of the humans' larger nation-states. He picked it up and looked at it with both eyes. The small bomb was rare, so unique that it had ended up on his desk. It was the only one in stock. Like everything else that cluttered his desk, he hadn't been sure what to do with it.

He put the weapon aside and reached for his briefcase. He searched for his PDD. Locating it, he put the data chip Veknar had given him into a side port. He was surprised to see the tiny golden symbol that appeared on his primary display and stayed there.

He watched the tiny NorCon glyph for several seconds. "Great. My own little symbol of collaboration. My mother would be so proud."

He put the PDD back into his briefcase. "Phone, dial Professor Bevf at the University, Department of Human Studies."

Bevf answered on the third ring. "Human Studies."

He leaned back in his chair. "Hello, this is Senior Curator Bibix at the trophy hall. We've never met. Have you got a moment?"

She turned in her chair to shut the door to her office. "Good afternoon, Senior Curator. How can I help you?"

He was pleased that she was so quick to follow his lead. "Administrator Veknar has instructed me to create an advisory panel for a large labor draft. He has a big construction project on the drawing board, and he wants to make the most of local resources. I was hoping that somebody in your department might have knowledge of human labor practices."

Bevf knew that NorCon ears might be listening in. "You want a panel of experts to work with Administrator Veknar? Hmm. That sounds dangerous."

Bibix was proud of her performance. "Actually, they'd be working for me. The administrator has given me the task of labor recruitment and work group assignment. That's why I need your help. To be efficient, I'll need to screen out the elderly and the infirm. We could speed things up if we could identify the skilled labor. You know what I mean – professional builders, mechanics, electricians, engineers, and the like."

"What are you going to build?" she carefully asked.

388 | Bibix

The curator smiled. "The administrator wants a new trophy hall. One that's bigger and better defended. The hard part will be getting it done before winter."

Bevf had no trouble acting surprised. The deadline seemed unrealistic. "Is that possible?"

Bibix tried not to stumble over his tongues. "Administrator Veknar knows what it's doing. My job is to make it happen while keeping the accidents to a minimum. We will save lives if we can beat the snow. We save more lives if we can build this new trophy hall without cutting corners. We've got a chance to do this without whips and chains. Can you help me?"

The professor pretended to think. "Okay, you've convinced me. Humans were very good at organizing. They employed several management techniques that would be very useful to you. Who will head up this panel?"

He tried not to giggle. It was just the sort of question that a ladder-climbing bureaucrat would ask. "Hmm. You are the senior 'Pod in your department. Would you like the job?"

It was her turn to smile. "Yes, I would. Thank you for offering. I assume I'll have freedom to pick the other panel members?"

Bibix choked. He should appear either ambitious or lazy. He didn't know which. "Umm. I...that is...Yes, I think that would be appropriate. I want to see you and five of your colleagues here at the trophy hall tomorrow morning at nine. You'll be introduced to Administrator Veknar, and we'll get to work."

Bevf cringed. "That's too soon. I can't—"

"Bye!" he interrupted loudly and abruptly hung up.

His stomach rolled and lurched in reaction to his sudden rudeness. He put the phone receiver down as his composure slipped. An ironic laugh burst out of him. He was filled with dread. The pacing of events was out of his control, and he didn't have the nerve to explain that over a line that might be monitored.

Bibix calmed himself. He reached for the small bomb on his desk. Grasping it with two hands, he lowered his head and bent his eyestalks to examine it closely. A wicked thought filled his mind.

He sat up and examined the layout of his office. All of the Lapropods who worked in the trophy hall assumed the NorCons who made up the administrative and security sections were spying on them.

He thought about his covert break-in at the Eagle River trophy hall. Then he took a second look at the bomb that rested comfortably in just one hand. The sinister machination that sparked and sizzled in his imagination now seemed quite possible, if he were bold.

He stood up and went to the south wall of his office. Laying a hand on a row of prefabricated panels, he closed his eyes just for a moment. Veknar might still be in its office. It was a creature of habit that disliked leaving its office for trivial matters. It would still be in there, sitting behind its desk, being arrogant.

"There's nothing in here I'm going to miss," he mumbled.

Bibix pulled the arming tape off the device and flipped the trigger tab into its upright, locked position. Giving it a full turn, he pressed the activator button and laid the charge on the floor with its rounded top facing the wall. Then he left his office at a quick walk.

The impulsive act filled his veins with adrenaline. He breezed into the main exhibit hall and headed for the front door. Both eyes swept left and right, each looking for a NorCon. Any of them would do. He needed to be seen interacting with one of the slug buckets when the bomb went off. It would be the only way to avoid suspicion.

To his left, a security officer was supervising the packaging of arctic war gear. Four busy Lapropods acted on its terse commands.

Bibix called out and approached. "Excuse me, Greatness. I need to check the lot numbers on this exhibit. Do you want these items stored with the civilian cold weather garments?"

The NorCon was consulting its personal data device just as the charge detonated. Originally designed to defeat the reactive armor of thick-skinned military vehicles, the man-made explosive went off with a huge roar. A long jet of superheated, ionized copper ripped through the administrator's office. The temperature of the air in the blast's path exceeded a thousand degrees Fahrenheit. Veknar's chair melted and its desk caught fire as the remaining office walls blew out. It perished quickly, boiling inside its armor.

The shockwave demolished glass cases and destroyed lighting fixtures. The expanding cloud of plasma set fire to the building. Halon extinguishers reacted as automated sensors melted after registering the extreme heat. Cold white clouds of gas billowed from ceiling vents. Lapropods in every part of the building screamed and fled. Most bolted for the nearest door. Others took advantage of newly created holes in the structure to make their escapes.

"Everyone out!" Bibix commanded.

394 | Bibix

The NorCon closest to him raised its weapon, looking for targets.

The terrified senior curator was too busy shooing the staff out of the crumbling trophy hall to notice a shattered roof support that trailed flaming insulation. As it fell, it struck him in the head. Bibix was knocked off his pods and plunged into an exhibit of hunting knives. Glass and fiberboard gave way as he hit the floor. Several chunks of hot, heavy debris landed on his back. Blackness closed in as his eyestalks pulled back into his head. He gasped for air and passed out.

Chapter 18

Bibix woke some time later to find himself strapped to a gurney in the back of an ambulance. He panicked when his eyes wouldn't open.

"Take it easy," a calm voice told him through his raging headache.

"I can't see," he whimpered.

The Lapropod paramedic calmly laid a hand on his shoulder. "Your stalks were burned. Your eyes have been lubricated and bandaged shut until the doctors can have a closer look. You've been hurt pretty badly. I gave you a shot – some neuro-blockers to keep you from feeling the worst of the pain. Can you tell me who you are?"

"My name is Bibix. I'm the senior curator for the trophy hall."

The medic made a sad sound. "You're one lucky 'Pod, Bibix. The trophy hall is still burning. Just relax and let me do my job. We'll be at the hospital in five minutes."

Bibix turned his head. "I can't hear a siren."

The attendant snickered. "Relax. You're not dying. They know you're coming. You'll be wheeled right into an operating room, and they'll fix you up in time for dinner."

"I can't feel the vehicle moving," Bibix grumbled through the ringing in his ears.

The experienced Lapropod sat back. "You've got enough drugs in your body to stock a small pharmacy. I'm surprised you can still talk. Settle down and enjoy the ride."

Bibix passed out. He dreamed. In a series of nightmares, giant NorCons pursued him. At various moments of heart-pounding terror, burning Lapropods cursed at him and blocked his path, no matter which direction he turned.

He woke drenched in sweat. Silence filled his ears. He lay on his back, nestled in what felt like a mattress. A cool sheet covered his body.

"I'm dead and my body is in the morgue," he thought out loud.

"No such luck," Bevf said from nearby.

He relaxed. "The last thing I remember is being in an ambulance. I think they had me strapped down. The attendant told me that my eyes had been bandaged. How long have I been unconscious?"

She sighed. "You're in the hospital recovery unit. You've been here for almost three days. You're eyes are still bandaged. How do you feel?"

He shifted slightly to see what worked, and what didn't. "I feel numb, but all of my arms work. I can't feel my fingers or my pods. Must be the drugs."

The professor sat up in her chair. "They've still got you on neuro-blockers. The doctor says you'll be in a lot of pain until things heal. They did quite a bit of work on you."

Bibix licked his dry lips. "I can't smell anything. They must have really stuck it to me. Please, tell me, what sort of 'work' did they have to do?"

Bevf hesitated. "You've had a few skin grafts. You were badly burned in places. Bibix, you lost an eye. They've already done the transplant, a full stalk-and-eye combination. The surgeons are really quite pleased with the results. I'm told that you'll never be able to tell the difference. You'll be busy with biomorphic treatments for the next week, but everyone says you'll pull through in great shape."

Bibix laid two hands on his face. Probing with careful fingers, he felt the bandages that circled his head. "Are we alone?"

Bevf shook her head. "The NorCons have placed a guard outside your room. I'm sure it can hear every word we say."

400 | Bibix

He sighed and laid all four hands on his chest. "Thanks for coming."

"I've been here off and on for the last two days," she admitted.

"My mother must be having fits," he muttered.

"She's here, down the hall. I can go get her if you want."

Bibix raised a hand. "No, don't. Please, not just yet. Can you tell me what happened?"

She stood to hold his hand in two of her own. "The NorCons have gone crazy. There was some kind of attack on the trophy hall. It's all over the news. Three NorCons are dead."

"What about the staff?" he asked.

She hesitated. "Some were hurt, like you. They got sent to the hospital. There are three that I know of. All of them are in the extreme care unit. The NorCons ate the rest. I think they did that because so many Lapropods ran away without trying to save the exhibits. I'm sorry, Bibix. I wish I could tell you more. I never did like television, and the pictures they're showing now are just too much. That's one human invention I can do without."

He held her hand tightly. The news of so many needless deaths made his eyes water inside their sockets. "Do they know how it happened?"

Bevf used a free hand to wipe at her nose. "The NorCons aren't saying. The entire city is in lockdown. Your mother and I have special passes to be here. All the shops are closed. Even the university has been affected. People are already starting to go hungry. I don't have much at home, so I've been eating here in the hospital's cafeteria."

"Sorry to hear that," he joked.

She giggled. "It's really not that bad." She paused. "I should go get your mother."

He released his grip on her warm hand. "Please, don't leave me alone with her for too long. We haven't spoken in a very long time, and I don't know how she's going to react to all of this. Give us about fifteen minutes. Then look in on me."

Bevf started for the room's open doorway. "Your mother is actually quite nice. She seems to think we've been dating."

Bibix turned his head in her direction. "What did you tell her?"

The professor peeled back the doorway curtain that provided a small degree of privacy. She glanced at the NorCon guard who stood motionless. "I told her that you're the most amazing 'Pod I've ever met. Did you know she wants you to have four podlings?"

"Bevf…" he muttered with a half-smile.

She laughed. "Relax. I told her you couldn't handle more than two."

Once he was sure she was out of the room, he laughed. Then he shifted in his bed, trying to get more comfortable.

He and Bevf really had bonded. The more he thought about that, the more he liked it. Was this the kind of thing his parents had shared for so many years? He thought so. That depth of emotion would explain his mother's prolonged grief.

404 | Bibix

He heard her in the hallway as she addressed the guard. "Excuse me, Greatness. I'm here to see my son."

For the first time in his life, her deference to a NorCon bothered him. He braced for the encounter.

"Bibsi, sweetness. I'm here. It's your mother," she whispered on entering.

"I'm not asleep," he replied in a normal voice.

She approached. "So many bandages and machines, Bibsi. Are you in pain?"

He shrugged. "The drugs make it so I can't feel anything."

The older Lapropod eased into the chair. "Does that mean you can't be mad at me?"

She was nervous. He didn't need working eyes to know that. He could hear it in her voice. "Mom, I have no reason to be mad at you. How is everyone?"

The matron fidgeted with her things. "Sweetness, your grandfather would be furious if he heard you addressing me by a human nickname." She paused. "No, that's not really true. It's your grandmother who'd pop the cork. Please, call me 'Mother.'"

He cleared his throat. "Is it going to be like that?"

She trembled. "No, Bibix, I don't want it to be like that. Sweetness, this is hard. I'm your mother. I had to come when I got the news that you'd been hurt. I love you, and nothing will ever change that. You know I can't invite you home until everyone agrees. It's our way."

406 | Bibix

"It's Grandmother, isn't it?" He wanted to hear her say it.

His mother nodded. "Yes. It's been her all along."

Bibix could feel his eye stalks strain against the bandages for just a moment. "I'm sorry. I didn't know. I always thought it was you. I assumed you took Father's death very hard. When I came to the house, Grandfather met me at the curb."

The matriarch sighed. "He told me. I'm sorry you got mixed signals."

Bibix thought about what he'd just heard. "I've been such an ass. No, wait. Please, let me finish. I've been away from home for a long time. It was my choice to go. I had, and still have, things I need to do.

"I was naïve to think I could come back whenever I wanted without any consequences. I've been so busy with NorCon stuff that I forgot about the Lapropod way of doing things. I blamed you for locking me out of the house. I didn't really stop to think that others might have had a hand or two involved in that decision."

She moved to the edge of her seat. "You have your father's patience."

"I do?" he replied with real surprise.

"You do."

The two of them sat for a moment in awkward silence.

She reached out to grasp two of his hands in two of her own. "I miss him so much. There were times when he could be so mad that it would make your eyes hide in your head. He takes after his mother in that way. But, in all the time I knew him, he never held a grudge. He never wanted to get even with anyone. He used to say that tomorrow was a new day, and that meant a new chance to try again if he failed."

Bibix used a free hand to point at his bandaged head. "Trust me. Optimism doesn't make a very good hard hat."

"I love you," she said, giving him a teary-eyed smile.

"Does that mean I can come home?" he asked.

She let go of him and sat up. With two hands, she hunted through her things for a handkerchief. She wiped her eyes and stalks. "Your grandmother says no, but I say yes. I hate family politics. I hate what they've made me do. Please, Sweetness, come home just as soon as you get out of this hospital, and bring your fiancée."

Bibix flinched. "Yeah, about that…"

His mother blew her nose. "I need some sunshine in my life. Introducing your future wife to my mother-in-law will make her be quiet for once. It'll also make me happy and bring a good feeling back into our house. Your grandmother may have some bad things to get out of her hearts, but even she will be happy for you."

Bibix licked his dry lips. "She doesn't like the fact that I work for the NorCons."

It was a dangerous statement to make. The guard standing like a statue just outside the room would certainly report the observation to its superiors.

The elderly Lapropod cast a one-eyed glance at the open door, and the guard. "Bibsi, I'm your mother. I'm not stupid. Your grandmother is set in her ways. The rest of us understand what you've done, and why. Your father was very proud of you. Did you know that?"

Bibix nodded. "Grandfather told me, the night I came to the house. He said he was proud of me, too. I think I knew that, but I don't think I ever really appreciated it."

She squeezed his hands. "We're all proud of you. Your grandmother is proud of you, too. She's just unhappy that you're in so good with the NorCons. She wishes that you'd followed in your father's footsteps."

He knew there could be more to it than that. In spite of the drugs coursing through his veins, he was sad.

Did his grandmother want him to fight back? Or did she just want him to be safe? He might never know. To keep them all safe, he could never tell any member of his family what he was doing to fight the NorCons. His grandmother would have to go on hating him, in spite of the truth.

The curator turned to face his mother. "Grandmother has some strange ideas. Don't let her get to you. We're safer when we cooperate with the NorCons."

The older pod watched the guard with both eyes. "Shush. Don't talk like that. We're not a violent species. Your grandmother is just…different. She remembers life on our home world like it was yesterday. Besides, I hear that you've become quite important."

She paused for a painfully long moment. "Bevf is quite the Lapropod. Now that I've met her, I must say that I approve in your choice. How did you manage to catch the eye of someone so smart and attractive?"

Bibix struggled to find the right words. His mother was working hard to overcome family prejudices. He spoke slowly to avoid tangling his tongues. "How did you meet Father?"

The question made her smile. She released his hands and slid back into her chair. "I met your father two years before we left. Bibsi, things were so chaotic. You have no idea. The government had just announced the results of our long-range probe effort. We were all so happy that our scientists had found another planet we could live on. The push was on to build starships for the evacuation."

"I know that history," he interrupted.

She frowned, and then decided to skip ahead. "Your father and I were still in secondary school. There was a lot of pressure on us to graduate quickly. We didn't know what we were going to find on our new home, and our leaders wanted everyone to have as much education as they could before we left."

She went on when he didn't respond. "We didn't think we would ever get the chance for college. Nobody my age did. Your father and I met when our parents hired the same preparatory tutor. Both of us were bad at math. We studied in the school's library, after classes. What else can I say? We fit together like two halves of a whole. In spite of everything else that was going on around us, your father was confident about our future. He wasn't sure how we'd survive, but he truly believed that we would. Did you know that he pulled strings to make sure that our families traveled on the same ship?"

"Grandfather told me that story when I was young."

His mother continued her happy recollection. "We graduated from school. Four months later, we left for Earth. Five minutes after we landed, your father picked up a handful of dirt and let it slip through his fingers. He said it was a good sign, and then he asked me to be his mate. I consented.

"Things were hard in the beginning. We waited to have children. You're my only child. I'm sure you know that story." She paused. "So, tell me. How did you come to meet Bevf?"

He wracked his brain for an answer that wasn't a lie. "We…I…what did she tell you?"

His mother laughed. "She told me that it was a happy accident. You had some books checked out of the university's library that she needed."

"That's just how it happened," he confirmed.

She was delighted. "I love happy coincidences. Don't you?"

"They're the best kind," he replied slowly.

His mother giggled. "Oh, Bibsi, my fierce little podling. If you could see the look on your face! I'm not trying to embarrass you. I'm happy for you. The doctors tell me you're going to make a full recovery. Would you please bring your mate to live with us?"

"Mother! I had a building fall on me. Parts of me were on fire, and I lost an eye. I've only been awake for a few minutes. Please, let me live long enough to get out of the hospital before you start trying to run my life!"

"Your grandmother will do enough of that for the both of us," his mother sniffed.

He squirmed under his bed covers. "I'm serious. You're pushing, and I don't need that right now. Bevf is…interesting…and I'm not going to mess that up just to make you happy. I wish my stalks weren't covered. I'd look you right in the eyes."

The concerned matron bristled, and then relented. "I keep forgetting how self-sufficient you really are. I'm sorry. Someday, when you have children of your own, you'll understand. Let's do this one step at a time. Come to the house after the doctors are finished. Introduce the family to Bevf. Please warn her about Grandmother, but be sure to bring her along. The rest can be worked out later on, if you want it."

"Thank you," he sighed.

She stood up. "The doctor said I shouldn't stay too long, but there is one more thing. I know this isn't the best time or place to be asking you about this, but there is a rumor…"

He was suddenly grateful for the drugs that kept him numb. "Go on."

The Lapropod clutched at her things. "Bibsi, there's a rumor going around about a labor draft. Something about a big construction project, the kind of thing they did years ago. I wouldn't ask, but your name is involved and I am your mother. Is it true?"

He rested all four hands on his chest. "Yes, Mother, it's true. Administrator Veknar ordered me to draw up the assignment lists. It wants to build a new trophy hall."

418 | Bibix

The news shocked his mother. Of all the things that could be true about her son, she didn't believe that he would be involved in something that any sane Lapropod would hate and fear. Stories about the first NorCon labor gangs were still used to scare children. It was one of the few nightmares from their collective past that could still compete with the human terror.

She looked at her son with both eyes. "Bibix, how could you do such a thing? They'll kill us by the thousands! What happens if we're forced to work outdoors after the snow falls?"

Bibix could hear the anger and fear in her rising voice. He struggled to focus his thoughts. "Administrator Veknar has given me special authority to decide who works and who doesn't."

"Administrator Veknar is dead."

"Are you sure?"

His mother shuffled on her pods. "It's all they talk about on the TV, Bibix. Don't you know what happened?"

"No," he lied.

She came over to clutch at him. "I'm sorry! You must be out of your mind on the drugs. Bibsi, there was a really big fire at the trophy hall. Most of it was destroyed. Your administrator was one of the casualties. Does that mean there won't be a labor draft?"

"I don't know," he hedged.

There was hope in her voice. "Bibsi, the NorCon labor battalions are evil! They put a chain around your neck. No, don't hush me. I don't care if there is a NorCon outside this room. I'd rather be eaten. You can't let them put us through that again! Please, tell me you'll try to stop it!"

He felt an urge to pull off his bandages. Both stalks wiggled in their sockets. Her plea caused both of his hearts to skip a beat. He felt her warm tears land on his face. His perception of her fear was magnified by his inability to see.

He kept a steady grip on her hands. "Mother, I promise, I'll do what I can. I may still be able to keep the old and the sick off the lists. Who knows? The NorCons may decide they don't need another trophy hall. I'll tell you, just as soon as I know more."

Chapter 19

A great deal of medical knowledge had been lost when the Lapropods migrated to Earth. Much of their surgical know-how and technical expertise hadn't survived the human conflicts. Human tools had long since been adapted to serve the aliens' needs. Decades of rediscovery and reinvention, combined with the innovations made possible through captured human research, equipped modern doctors with more than enough resources to repair Bibix and make him whole.

Twelve days of advanced therapy in a series of environments encouraged the many small skin grafts he had received to merge with his body. The transplanted eyestalk began to respond to growth regimens by the end of the sixth day. The doctors and technicians who saw to his every need were optimistic about his chances for a full recovery.

Bibix grew stronger. He was able to think more clearly about what he'd done. According to the gossip Bevf and his mother brought to him, the NorCons were paranoid, outraged, and spoiling for a fight. Dozens of Lapropods across the city had been eaten since he had been admitted to the hospital. The smallest infractions were being punished with lethal force. During periods of long sedation, he dreamed of being arrested for his crimes. In each bloody nightmare, a gigantic, angry NorCon ate him.

He still couldn't find the thing inside him that had prompted the sudden use of the bomb. As the days passed, he began to doubt his ability to continue on his covert quest to liberate his people.

Bevf somehow guessed what was on his mind. "You should relax. The doctor will be here in a few minutes to take off your eye coverings."

He sat on a raised platform in the cold examination room and glanced in her direction. "Now I know what it's like to be blind. Thanks for being here. I really appreciate it. Where is my mother? I thought she'd want to be around for this."

The professor stayed in her chair. She smiled. Bibix looked pale and thin under the white fluorescent light that shone down from the ceiling. "It's not a problem. I'm not here all day. I come after work."

He waved a pair of hands in front of his face. "I've lost track of time. If you're here at night, it must mean that my mother is here during the day."

Bevf nodded. "That's right. She's not here tonight because…um. Well, it's…"

"It's my grandmother. The old fossil is meddling again." He sighed.

She shook her heard. "No, it's not like that. It is family related, but it's not that."

"Tell me," he insisted.

It was her turn to draw a deep breath. "Your mother seems to think I'm going to be your mate. According to your grandmother, it's inappropriate for the mother to interfere in things that the wife does. By the way, neither of them likes the word 'wife.' It's too human. The 'old fossil' was kind enough to call on the phone to say that."

Bibix laughed. "Sorry. I can't do anything about them. Is there a guard outside?"

Bevf leaned over to look through the white curtain that covered the doorway. "Actually, no, there isn't. That's been happening a lot lately. They must not think you're worth watching anymore. Congratulations."

He shivered. "I'm going to freeze. Where is that doctor?"

She relaxed. "You're not going to die from hypothermia for at least another fifteen minutes. You know how it is with doctors. If they had five hands, they'd wish for six."

"Gee, thanks," the curator replied sarcastically.

She made a polite gesture. "It's what any good wife would do."

He tried to get comfortable. "Okay. We know what my mother thinks. We even know what my grandmother thinks. What do your parents think about…us?"

"I don't know. I haven't asked them."

"Are you embarrassed?" he asked.

She blinked, then wiped at her glasses with a clean cloth. "I think my family is bound to be more accepting than yours is. None of them are living. My parents would've liked you. I, on the other hand, am still trying to make up my own mind about you. We met by accident. Do you remember that?"

Bibix lightly knocked on the side of his head with one fist. "Yeah, I think the memory is still in here."

"I'm still scared," she confessed with a dry mouth.

He folded his hands across his middle. "I can feel my chest. I really have lost weight. Look, I know we have a lot to sort out. When I get out of here, we can talk about that thing we want to do. We can try dating, if you want."

She glanced at the door. "That's a very human thing to do. Are you sure you can take the heat from your family?"

Bibix smirked. "I can take the heat from a burning building. I can handle them."

Bevf enjoyed the moment. "Actually, no, you couldn't take the heat from a burning building. That's why you're in this hospital, waiting for a doctor who may have gone to dinner without telling us."

Bibix pointed at himself with all four index fingers. "I'm a survivor. Isn't that good enough for you?"

She didn't have to think about it. "Yes, it is. From now on, we'll throw caution to the wind and do whatever is good for us, you and me. Now, if you'll excuse me, I'm going to go find that doctor. You're starting to turn blue."

As predicted, the doctor had gone to dinner. The bandages came off two hours later. Bibix grunted at the mild pain as his eyestalks rose from their sockets.

Doctor Kedrix examined each stalk with a lighted magnifier. "Excellent. Proper fluid pressures and healthy tissues. Blink for me."

Bibix complied. The sterile room and its contents came into focus.

"I'm feeling a little dizzy," he observed.

The physician put down the instrument. "That's normal. Your ears rely on the same fluid that fills your stalks. Your inner ear chambers are reacting to the slight change in fluid thickness that occurs when it moves. You'll get used to that in just a few hours. Tell the night nurse if the dizziness continues past midnight. One of them can give you a sedative. Most patients are fully recovered after a night of sleep."

Bibix looked for Bevf.

She smiled and waved from the far side of the room. "Hey there, Two Eyes."

430 | Bibix

He couldn't prevent the smile that warmed his face. "I can't feel anything different. Both of my eyes work."

"I noticed." She winked.

The doctor stood up. "Before I go, there is just one thing."

Bibix prepared himself for bad news.

The doctor glanced at the open doorway. "I heard there was going to be a labor draft."

The curator sighed. "Yes, I've heard the same thing."

Kedrix stepped in close to Bibix. He kept one eye on the door. "This is a hospital. None of us can help the sick and injured if we're out digging in the mud. I'm sure that a 'Pod in your position knows that. I'm not that much older than you are. I'd like to think that means we can see things the same way. I'd like to make a deal with you."

"I understand your problem," Bibix mumbled, looking at Bevf.

"Just hear him out," she whispered.

The healer regarded her with new interest. "I see. I should have known. I've heard stories about the last labor leader. Edix had spies everywhere, and bodyguards. You must be here to make sure nothing bad happens to Bibix."

"Something like that," she replied cryptically.

Kedrix kept an eye on each of them. "The NorCon supervisor who oversees this facility doesn't have to know that we talked. I've spoken to several of the department heads. We're all prepared to make it worth your while to exempt us from the draft. We can make you a very rich 'Pod, if you'll agree."

Bibix looked at Bevf, then at the open door.

She cleared her throat. "The labor leader will need some time to consider your offer. It's going to look very strange if he exempts everyone in this building from work. Some of you may be required to perform light duties. Others may even be fortunate enough to get indoor assignments."

The doctor hadn't thought about that. "Naturally, we'd be open to some negotiation. As long as the doctors, nurses, and technicians are exempt, you can do what you like with the rest of the staff. Name your price and we'll pay it."

"Mm," Bibix rumbled, reluctant to commit to anything.

Bevf pointed at the door. "That'll be all, Doctor. You can go now."

Kedrix bowed his head and retreated. "Thank you, Greatness. I'll get a nurse and a wheelchair to take you back to your room. You can be on your way first thing in the morning."

"Did he just call me 'Greatness?'" Bibix blurted out after the doctor had gone.

The professor giggled. "How did it feel?"

The labor leader stuck out one of his tongues. "Nasty."

She got up and went to him. "You don't have much experience with bribery, do you?"

He shook his head. "Bribery, the kind you mean, is strictly forbidden in the trophy hall. We trade favors.

We never trade food, money, sex, or drugs. Anyone who tries, dies."

Bevf reached out to touch him. "I'm sorry, I didn't know. I've never heard much about what goes on in that place. They don't encourage visitors, you know?"

He did. "Administrator Grilleck joked about charging admission to the exhibits just a few days before he died in battle."

She raised a skeptical eye. "A NorCon told you a joke?"

He nodded. "Their humor isn't 'ha-ha' funny. It's 'laugh-or-I'll-hurt-you' funny."

She squeezed his hand as a nurse came in with a wheelchair. "I'll walk with you back to your room, and then I'll go home."

"When will I see you again?" he asked.

Bevf waited for the nurse to seat him in the wheelchair. "How about that thing you wanted to do?"

He glanced at the nurse with one eye. "Okay…"

The professor rolled her eyes. "I mean the other non-violent thing you wanted to do."

A date. He flinched. "Yes! Let's do that. Bring food, and I'll cook."

The nurse favored them both with a one-eyed stare.

Bevf laid a hand on Bibix's arm and said to the nurse, "Excuse us. He's been through a lot. Sometimes he doesn't know where he is, or what he's saying. Let's get him back to bed."

Bibix remained silent as the nurse took him back to his room and tucked him into bed. Bevf went to the open doorway and peeked down the hall, first left, then right.

She went back to his bed with a smile. "There's no guard."

"Lucky me," he fretted.

The dim light helped Bevf to relax. She leaned on the safety rail of the bed. "Everybody knows your name. Everybody knows you have the NorCons' blessings. They're afraid of you. I'd be willing to bet that most of the NorCons think that's really funny. They don't need to watch you. If you do anything out of line, you could be killed by your own people."

He grasped the sheet with all four hands. "I can see why my mother likes you. You're such an optimist."

She bent over to speak quietly. "Can I ask you a serious question?"

He scanned the room with both eyes. "Now?"

"Yes," she nodded.

He let go of the sheet and tried to relax. "I'm sorry. They've still got me drugged. Please, go ahead. Ask me anything."

She enjoyed his trust. "Did you blow up the trophy hall?"

He could feel his eyes wobble at the ends of their stalks. "Yes. Yes, I did. I don't know what came over me. It was an impulsive act. I was talking with you on the phone, and there was this…thing…on my desk. It was like being somebody else, just for a few minutes. After we finished talking, I just did it. Boom."

She reached out to hold one of his hands. "You don't know it, but you made a lot of friends when you did that. Some of the 'Pods in my department thought it was you. Even I thought you did it."

"You did?" He cringed.

Bevf glanced at the dark doorway. "Relax. It's okay. The drugs will be out of your system by the time you have breakfast. The NorCons don't suspect you. If they did, we wouldn't be having this conversation."

He wasn't comforted. "I was hoping that nobody would guess it was me."

The professor stroked his hand. "Bibix, being under the NorCon boot doesn't mean we're stupid. A lot of our people hate those trophy halls. They're symbols of oppression. They remind us of things we'd rather forget. What you did was both therapeutic and inspirational. It's just the sort of thing that I've come to expect from you."

Bibix basked in her appreciation. "I need to find a less painful way to impress you."

She touched one of her eyestalks. "I hate glasses, and I have a rare condition that means the transplant thing doesn't work for me. You might think about setting off smaller explosions in the future. We can't be mated or have sex if you're dead."

He laughed. "You really think it's going to come to that?"

Bevf let go of his hand and stood back. "Ask me again tomorrow night."

He sat up. "You're putting me off. Why?"

She blinked. "I wish I could say more. Please, trust me."

He could plainly see that she was conflicted. "I'll see you tomorrow night for dinner. Could you do just one small thing for me? Don't bring salmon. I may never be able to eat that fish again without thinking about the NorCons."

Chapter 20

The NorCon forces occupying Earth had been frustrated by the Lapropods ever since their arrival. The NorCon species thrived on conflict. War, in particular, was their preferred state of existence.

Their need for conflict was both mental and physical. Individuals were incapable of emotional stability. Separation from the group resulted in feelings of loss, insecurity, and depression, often leading to psychosis or suicide. The species name, "NorCon," was itself the result of a group decision.

The NorCons felt happier, safer, and more aggressive when they congregated in large numbers. This harmonious condition resulted from the commingling of hormones, pheromones, and other bodily secretions that saturated their natural liquid environment. Other sentient species would consider their dependency on this cooperative chemical exposure an addiction.

NorCons had prowled the stars in search of conflict for so long that they'd lost track of their own origins. It would've been more truthful to say that they'd deliberately chosen to forget the truth of their humble aquatic beginnings.

Theirs was a rapacious culture that did not respect docility or surrender. As predators, they took what they wanted, used what they found, and made do when there was nothing new to fight over. Earth was considered a hardship posting only because there was so little conflict that the imbalance caused three percent of the occupation force to suffer mental anguish that often resulted in deranged behavior.

The chain of command had taken steps to alleviate the problem. Earth's total garrison had been reduced to an absolute minimum because there was nothing left to do except harvest local delicacies for export to the various far-flung outposts and combat zones. The terrible truth was that pacified worlds were not good for any NorCons who were encased in the modified armor that had once belonged to members of a defeated and now-extinct species.

The population of each suit thought of itself as one individual. Sensory technologies, adapted from yet another defeated species, allowed every member of the individual communities to play some role in daily life. Audio and visual inputs were translated and redesigned for chemical transmission into the pressurized, nitrogen-rich, illuminated fluid medium that sustained their lives.

They'd never felt the need to develop artificial inputs for touch or smell during their centuries old rampage across the stars. Taste occurred during digestion, which was achieved through a process of mechanical mastication and dissolving of dismembered beings. The community would eat when their fluid environment was rich with proteins and useful fats. Waste would be discharged and fluid levels would be adjusted using a method that was totally unknown to the Lapropods.

Wireless telecom chatter between the community organisms was frequent. This created an unintended form of isolation that made the NorCons unaware and unconcerned about many of the things the Lapropods did. Out of sight was literally out of mind.

Bibix's people were the only species they'd ever encountered that didn't fight back with any degree of efficiency or conviction. For the first time in their violent history, the NorCons were an occupying force. No amount of brutality on their part had ever sparked a Lapropod uprising. In spite of their efforts to study such a baffling species, the NorCon chain of command was unable to explain the inner workings of such complete pacifism.

Genocide had been discussed at the highest levels. The policy had been rejected due to the estimated costs associated with such a large-scale extermination. The Lapropods wouldn't be eradicated because the process would be too inconvenient.

Thirty years of supervising a passive population did have its rewards. Lapropods were not technically sophisticated by NorCon standards, but they were comfortable in Earth's low-pressure atmosphere.

They complained very little and were quite industrious when properly motivated by the right amount of fear.

Recent developments in the Alaska sector suggested to the chain of command that some form of armed resistance was beginning. Opinions varied as to the source of this mischief. As unlikely as it seemed, the region's commanders had to entertain the possibility that Lapropods were responsible for the attack on the food processing plant. A minority point of view suggested that humans were to blame for that assault, as well as the attack on the Anchorage trophy hall.

It was acceptable that some of Earth's non-sentient indigenous lifeforms killed a few NorCons each year. Military analysts suggested that the recent trend in larger than average losses might be the result of a growing insurgency. Formation leaders at all levels became frustrated and agitated when no obvious opponent could be identified.

A few of the most politically astute groups suggested that the stress of ongoing non-combat operations might be taking its toll on the mental health of the most aggressive NorCons in the region. It was the closest thing to a determination of low morale that any clinicians of their species had ever made. The observation was not widely shared.

The garrison requirements for Earth were reduced further. The restless, bored aggressors wanted to fight, but they had no targets worthy of their might. News of Grilleck's successful campaign to take a rival's trophy hall did little to salve the many smoldering egos that yearned to be on other worlds, locked in bloody combat.

448 | Bibix

Veknar's demise and the verifiable details leading up to its diabolical death reignited old hopes that Earth might still hold a few surprises worth even a short war. NorCons around the world waited with interest and impatience for reports of a growing guerilla movement in the Arctic region.

Humans had once lived on every landmass of this hot, toxic world. They'd possessed the technology to overcome or adapt to every climate on every continent. It was secretly hoped that after thirty long years, they might have regrouped and be willing to fight.

Bibix was not at all surprised when a pair of NorCons came for him on the morning of his scheduled release from the hospital. He'd spent the night trapped in nightmares about being interrogated by unseen forces that nipped at him with cold metal jaws.

He was physically clean and well fed when he stepped out into the autumn sun. Minutes later, he found himself deep the bowels of a nameless government office building. He didn't see any Lapropods during his trek through five secured checkpoints.

He was ordered to put on a breath mask. Then, he was ushered into a dark chamber adorned with dozens of large plasma screen monitors and a hundred small displays of a similar type. He was introduced to a NorCon identified as Sector Commander Sheerz.

Bibix quickly noticed that this conqueror didn't look like most NorCons.

"Labor Leader Bibix," it said from high upon a central dais.

"Yes, Greatness," he groveled.

The commander dismissed the Lapropod's guardians. Its translator broadcast with a high degree of clarity. "Take a look around. There is nothing here you should not see. Questions are permitted."

"Thank you, Greatness." Bibix genuflected.

With one eye on the commander, he scanned the room. "I've never seen so many NorCons in one place at the same time. I don't understand all of what I see. Twenty NorCons. Lots of workstations. The images on most of the screens I can see are of this enclave and the surrounding countryside. May I assume that this is some kind of monitoring facility?"

The Lapropod took note of the commander's armor and accessories. Subtle design differences from the gear used by the other bucketheads in the area stood out. That scared him. Sheerz's overall appearance showed no sign of hardship or combat damage. This very unusual detail made Bibix shudder.

The NorCon walked around an instrument panel to look down on its trembling subject. "Your fear is justified. The loss of our trophy hall means that you have no job. No purpose. No reason to remain living."

The observation made Bibix break out in a sweat. His newly transplanted eye twitched. He looked up at his tormentor. "With all due respect, Greatness, I don't think you allowed me to use up a lot of medicine and doctor time just so you could eat me for a late breakfast. I'm a senior curator. I've been around long enough to know that…um…I just know you're not going to eat me right now. What do you really want?"

452 | Bibix

The NorCon's translator did a superior job of rendering a laugh. "You are everything that Administrator Veknar said you were. Your overall record of service has been superior. Do you know that?"

"I did not," Bibix lied with all the humility he could show.

"I have served on the staff of the Hemisphere Command. You will find that I am not so easily lied to. Come up here."

The senior curator noted that Sheerz was unarmed. It didn't appear to have a pump attached to its armor. With both eyes forward, the Lapropod shuffled up onto the dais. His fear was slowly replaced by caution as he walked around a pair of readouts to stand at a respectful distance from the high-ranking NorCon.

The commander waved one of its mechanical claws over a computer interface. "The Anchorage trophy hall is a total loss. The only portion to survive was the cryogenic vault. Refrigeration systems in and around that part of the structure prevented the fires from doing any real damage to the human storage containers."

Bibix examined video images of the ruins as they appeared on the screens nearby. "I don't know what to say. I feel like this was my fault. I spent so many years in the building that I miss it. An acquaintance told me that there were very few survivors."

"There were no survivors," Sheerz said flatly.

Bibix waited for the displays to go dark. "I was told that there were at least two members of my staff in the hospital. Shall I presume that they've been eaten?"

454 | Bibix

The NorCon's helmet pivoted. Its serrated visor and jaw assembly parted slightly in what Bibix thought might be a cruel grin. The soldier seemed to enjoy the moment. "I ate them myself. You should also be aware that none of the NorCon supervisory team or security detail survived their exposure to the extreme heat. All have since died from their injuries."

Bibix was surprised by the news. He tried not to squirm. "I'm sorry, Greatness. I regret your losses. I had no idea that your people were vulnerable to heat. Then again, my own people are somewhat flammable under the wrong circumstances. Why was it necessary to eat the last two surviving members of my staff?"

Sheerz took a moment to examine the fidgeting Lapropod with its enhanced imaging systems. Bibix was a good liar. He showed very few of the biological symptoms that were so common to Lapropods in moments of obfuscation and high stress. "Your own wounds were quite extensive. The chain of command does not believe that you were responsible for the sabotage. No rational being would burn and maim itself to evade suspicion. Your colleagues were not hurt to the same degree. There was some doubt about their innocence. They were eaten as a preventative measure. I have no doubt you are familiar with this cautious policy."

The Lapropod was horrified. He struggled to hold his composure. "As you say, Greatness, I am familiar with the policy. Why have you spared me?"

The NorCon took one step closer to emphasize its words. "You are direct. Good. I will get to the point. I am the new controlling authority for this region. For the next twelve months, I will be using all of the labor that you can organize. This enclave will be fortified against attack before the snow falls. In the spring, defensive improvements will be made to the food processing plant. By the middle of next year, a new and improved trophy hall will be built to centralize all of the holdings for this area. The contents of both surviving installations will be moved under one roof."

Bibix felt as if he'd just been kicked. He kept one eye on Sheerz while observing the NorCons around him with the other. "Greatness, I'm not an engineer. A trophy hall is one thing. I've worked in one for a long time, so I have some degree of understanding about its structure. The rest of what you're asking for is beyond me. I have no experience with military matters. Why is all of this necessary?"

The commander reached out to another console. It seemed to be searching for something. "You are an exhibit handler with above average comprehension and a knack for organization. You are not needed for any other reason. Like the members of all conquered species, your people will work harder if they believe one of their own has some say in their assignments."

The curator felt his mouth go dry. "In the short run, I will provide them with a false sense of hope that will improve their morale. In the long run, I will be the one they hate the most. If they're focused on me, they aren't thinking about you."

"I am glad we understand each other," Sheerz said without any overt hint of emotion. Internally, the NorCon was pleased. Its estimation of the Lapropod had been correct.

Bibix could feel his new eye twitch. His stomach lurched. He was standing in the presence of a greater threat than any he'd ever known.

The commander pointed to a monitor. "This is why we need to upgrade our defenses."

458 | Bibix

"Agh!" Bibix screamed when a close-up view of Carl Tippet appeared on the screen.

The hairy human reached out to the camera with a dirty hand. His palm smothered the lens. The full-color image tilted to one side, and then went blank as the camera was disconnected.

"There is more," Sheerz warned.

The Lapropod watched in stunned silence as three more recordings were played for him. In each case, Carl could be seen sneaking up to a remote camera before deactivating it. He was dressed in a mismatch of civilian and military clothing.

Sheerz turned off the video feed. "I admire this human's ability to get so close to our cameras before he is detected. Some have been lost without recording his image at all. We surmise that he is brave and skilled."

Bibix was appalled. What was Carl thinking? Didn't he know he was being photographed? Did the commander know more than he was telling?

He struggled to speak through tangled tongues. "I just don't know what to say, Greatness. If this is a joke, it's not funny."

The senior NorCon was satisfied. The Lapropod's reaction was most appropriate. "The historical record is clear. Your people have many reasons to fear humans. I think you will agree that this threat should motivate your people to work hard, for the sake of their own home defense."

The labor leader was speechless. Once again, he'd lost control of his future. Events of his own making had done more harm than good. His hearts began to sink. He summoned his courage. "Two steps forward, and one step back."

"What does that mean?" Sheerz demanded.

Bibix rubbed his face with a pair of nervous hands. "It's just an expression."

The aggressive leader tapped the blank monitor next to Bibix. "Even if this man is alone, his presence represents an opportunity that will be good for both of us. If you fail to make the most of it, you will be eaten. I will have the pleasure and the glory of this hunt, no matter what you do. Do you understand?"

"Yes, Greatness," Bibix replied, hanging his head.

Sheerz summoned a guard without talking its gaze off the sweaty Lapropod. "You will have forty-eight hours to implement the advisory panel that you suggested to Administrator Veknar. You should requisition new housing. If the first draft lists are not on my desk in five days, you will be found and dealt with."

The curator raised his head and both eyes. "I'll need supervision authority. Monetary disbursement power, too. Before his passing, Administrator Veknar had given me an add-on for my PDD. I don't suppose you might have another one? Something to show as proof that I'm allowed to be so bossy?"

The request was valid. Bibix's personal effects hadn't been retrieved when he was rescued. The NorCon turned to its nearest computer interface. "Adjustments have already been made to your work history, personal profile, and credit account. I will assign a member of my staff to be your liaison. Take whatever you want from whomever you want. Failure to meet any deadline will result in your immediate punishment, which may include death or dismemberment. If you need to have anyone arrested, interrogated, or eaten, submit that request directly to me."

Bibix went numb. The machinations of a single NorCon had derailed his conspiracy. He was now a collaborator of the worst kind. What else could go wrong?

Chapter 21

Bibix went home. Placing his thumb on the coded lock to open the door, he entered his apartment slowly, wandered into the living room without any enthusiasm. The door eased shut. Curtains kept most of the morning sunlight from coming through the modest window.

He surveyed his gloomy surroundings. All of the gear and gadgets that he'd stolen from the trophy hall were gone. Several shelves that had held his favorite books were empty. The dining room table had been cluttered. It now sat bare, except for a small piece of paper. He went to the table and picked up the note. <u>You have not been robbed. The building manager let</u>

464 | Bibix

<u>me in to pick up some things for you. I borrowed a few things, too. Regards, Bevf.</u>

He looked at the door to his home. "That explains why I wasn't arrested," he thought. "When did you do this? It must've been right after I went into the hospital."

Bibix went into the kitchen and turned on a light. His living space had been closed up for nearly three weeks. He tapped the calendar on the wall with one finger while his nose sampled the stale air. His rendezvous with Carl wasn't far off.

He held his breath and opened the refrigerator. He was rewarded with a clean interior. Both eyes swiveled on their stalks as he searched for hazardous leftovers. He saw neither expired condiments nor food items.

He breathed in some of the cold air flowing from the appliance. "I may have nothing to eat, but at least I'm not in danger of being poisoned."

Bibix closed the refrigerator and went back to his couch. He flopped down on it with a reckless, irrational thrill. He was mentally disturbed and emotionally drained. He wiggled his pods and tried to get comfortable. His mind raced, and then wandered.

His relaxation was interrupted by a knock on the door. He stood with a groan, then walked to the door and opened it. He saw Bevf and smiled.

She raised a finger to his lips to indicate silence. With another hand, she held up a note written in blue ink. He read it with one eye. <u>Your apartment is bugged. They can hear everything you say. Come with me.</u>

"How do you know?" he whispered.

She reached past him and closed the door. She took him by the hand and led him out of the building through the rear entrance.

He stepped into some nearby shade to avoid the sun's glare.

She urged him to keep going. "The building has video monitors in and around the entrances. There's a small park two blocks from here. Let's walk."

They started in the direction she'd indicated. "The NorCons bug the offices at the university two or three times a year. I knew they'd be smart enough to search your home after the fire at the trophy hall. I got some help, and we took all of the human stuff out of your place."

Bibix nodded as they crossed a quiet street. "I've had their devices in my apartment before. Four years ago, it was a microphone."

Bevf slowed her walk as they neared several storefronts. "My colleagues and I think they only spy on five percent of the population at any given time. Their technique isn't very good, and they're random about it. Even so, they are persistent."

The observation made Bibix stop in his tracks. "We'd be dead if they had anything on us. How did you get into my apartment?"

She smiled nervously. "I told the building manager that I was your mate."

Bibix stopped to sit on a concrete bench. He waited for a casually strolling Lapropod to pass them by before speaking. "I know that my mother likes you, but—"

She rushed to sit next to him. "I'm sorry! I know how that must have sounded. I'm not trying to take advantage of you. There was no time to do anything else. We had to act."

"Who's 'we'?" he asked.

She passed to gather her thoughts. "Unlike you, I have friends. I trust my friends. We talked, and we decided that you would be eaten if the NorCons found all that stuff in your apartment. It's a crime to possess weapons. You had human weapons. What else was I supposed to do?"

His eyestalks drooped. He pointed. "I used to spend a lot of time in that park over there. I like the fountain. It's a great place to sit and think."

They stood and walked. Bibix crossed the street and led her to a wooden bench.

Bevf looked around. "I can see why you like it here."

He pointed at the gurgling fountain. Water flowed from a trio of ornate ports into a pool that rippled. "I watched a group of 'Pods build that. I came out here every day after work. It's a combination of granite and quartz. It took them a week to finish it."

The professor adjusted her glasses to study the water sculpture. "It's one of ours, all right. Very peaceful. You don't see that from anything the humans left behind. Okay, some of their stuff is good, but this is…you know."

He relaxed. "Did you ever look at the video on that PDD?"

"Yes."

After a painful pause, he asked, "What did you think?"

Bevf looked around. They appeared to be alone. She moved closer and said quietly, "I wet myself. I had nightmares. I'm not the same person I used to be."

Bibix allowed her to embrace him. He kept one eye on her and the other on his surroundings. "From the day we're born until the day we die, we'll fear being eaten. Most of us can stay alive if we let the NorCons have their way. I can't do it. I just can't stand by and let them have their way any more."

She kissed him. "You're not alone. We're all doing this for the first time."

He enjoyed her embrace. "I'd like to meet this 'we' you keep talking about."

The university lecturer sat up. "There are some things we need to do first."

"Of course," he mumbled.

She broke away and stood up. "I can still keep my promise. You'll know everything by tonight. Please, trust me a little while longer."

The moment was awkward and unreal in a way he'd never experienced before. "I remember what you said in the hospital. I want to trust you. I really do. I guess it's just hard to break old habits. A 'Pod who gives up freedom in exchange for safety isn't really free or safe."

She checked the time on her PDD. "I need to go. I told them I was taking a long lunch."

Bibix took one last look at the fountain. "So peaceful. I really should get out here more often. Let me drive you back to the campus. As long as I'm the big, bad, scary labor leader, I might as well start acting like it."

"What are you going to do?" she asked as they moved.

He shuffled along, keeping his voice low. "The first thing I'm going to do, after I drop you off, is visit the library and check out everything they have on Edix. I need to know what he did right and what he did wrong. It'll be safer than looking it up on the cybernet."

Bevf waited for a pack of pedestrians to pass. "You're right about that. The NorCons don't care about hard copy books. That seems to be a cultural bias. If it's not in electronic form, they don't read it. I'll check the department's file storage. We encourage the undergrads to research and write about our ancestors. I'm sure somebody has done something on Edix."

They crossed the street in silence. He pointed to an expensive shop front as they passed. "Everything I remember about him comes from grade school. He was hated. He walked around with gold chains and other symbols of wealth around his neck. I need to avoid that mistake. Have you read Machiavelli?"

"It's better to be feared than loved," she paraphrased.

Bibix looked at his reflection in a large carbon-polymer window. "That's a human for you: violence before compromise. I'm not a human, and

I'm certainly not a NorCon. How can I possibly know what the right amount of fear should be?"

Bevf shook her head as they crossed another street. "Edix has been dead for almost thirty years. His legend has grown. Our own people have seen to that. According to historical accounts, he was responsible for labor relations all around the world. The NorCons are only tasking you with activity in this region."

"What are you saying?" he asked as they neared his apartment building.

She swung her arms thoughtfully. "Times have changed. We need to stop looking to the past for solutions to our problems. As you say, we're not humans, and we aren't NorCons. We're Lapropods. We need to figure out what's good for us and do that."

"I don't want to be hated," he mused.

"Do you want to be loved?"

He stopped moving. "I want to be…I don't know. Why are you asking me questions like this? I thought you liked me."

She touched him lightly on one shoulder. "I do."

He started walking towards the parking lot, and his lev. "Okay, then; that's what I want. I want to be liked. I want—"

"You're babbling," she warned as they approached his vehicle.

The drive to the university was quiet and uneventful. Midday traffic was always light. Bibix noted with inward apprehension that he'd only seen one NorCon on patrol. Was it possible that the city was policed by only a very small number of NorCons? As unlikely as that seemed, he couldn't get the thought out of his mind.

He stopped to let Bevf out near her office. She got out and closed the door. He waved, and then drove on.

* * *

Bibix found a dozen books about Edix at the school's vast print media archive. The librarians were eager to cooperate with his requests, after putting in a word for themselves and their families regarding the upcoming labor draft.

Bibix then drove to an isolated part of the city where he could see the cool, rolling waters of the Cook Inlet. The sun reached its highest point in the sky for the day while he thumbed through some of the volumes he'd checked out.

He paid close attention to the photos included in each of the dusty books, while reclining in the driver's seat.

Bibix dwelled on what Bevf had said as he flipped pages. <u>We're not humans and we aren't NorCons. We're Lapropods. We need to figure out what's good for us and do that.</u>

"What is good for us?" he muttered to himself. The question was aggravating.

Edix seemed to glare at the camera in each of his official photos, as if he, too, were frustrated by the complexities of his situation. Bibix laid a finger on one image, taken just days before the 'Pod's violent end.

"How many choices did you really have? What can I do that you couldn't?"

He drummed his fingers on the steering column. The ocean view was mesmerizing. Both of his eyestalks undulated slightly as he followed the motion of the surf. The harmony of the moment was almost enough to make him forget about the NorCon menace and the many perils associated with renegade humans.

He looked back at the books. Serenity fled from his consciousness. His hearts raced as he compared the photos in several volumes. Most of the images presented in each history, biography, or academic policy dissection showed Edix in the presence of at least one NorCon. More than half of the books Bibix had checked out contained the same photo sets. He counted seventy-six out of an estimated one hundred images that rendered Edix in close physical proximity to one or more of his NorCon superiors.

"Were you brave, or just stupid?" he wondered out loud.

The question gnawed at him as the sunshine caused the temperature inside his car to start rising. Nobody in his right mind would stand close to a NorCon, and certainly not within reach of those powerful mechanical arms.

He picked up another book and began flipping through its pages. "Things were different back them. The NorCons were new. Recently arrived."

The argument was too flimsy. It made no sense to him. Edix must have known what would happen to him if he failed.

Bibix stopped turning pages when he found a photo that was different. Taken in bad light, the infamous labor leader appeared to be standing next to a cornerstone. He squinted at the poor image.

"You're looking at that cornerstone with both eyes."

The big block of granite was inscribed with a five-digit number. Lapropods numbered each structure they built. The building's number was almost always etched onto the foundation stone used to begin construction. Bibix found his stylus and writing box. He made a note of the identifier and went back to his reading.

Random sampling in each book suggested that Edix was more than a hated villain from the past. He was given credit for exempting millions of 'Pods from the hated labor battalions. He played a crucial role in the development of the laws and education system the Lapropods still used. According to the official record, he and his underlings argued legal cases before several NorCon tribunals. Twenty-nine of his subordinates were eaten after they lost their legal battles.

Bibix thought about Bevf and her colleagues at the university. "That's why she has so many friends willing to help me. They know more about Edix than I do. Do they look at me and see him? I hope not."

He turned his attention to the 'Pods who had worked with Edix. Many were listed in the vast indices that he found at the end of each book. Few were discussed at length or in any detail. His left eye twitched when he read Bevf's name. He ignored the coincidence until he'd found her name in three of the fat volumes.

According to the historical record, 'Bevf' had been a professor of propulsion physics. She was born on the home world forty years before the exodus. He skipped the lengthy list of her awards and accolades.

482 | Bibix

The notations went on to say that she'd been on the design team for the faster-than-light drive that had been used in the escape ships. She was also credited with saving many lives during the first winter after arrival.

Bibix was impressed. This Bevf had been mated to a 'Pod named Breder at some point, though there was no date given for the event. She had been appointed to chair the first Physics Department at the first Lapropod university, which had been established in a place called Tampa, Florida.

A single birth to the pair was noted. Bevf had her mother's face, as well as her name. There was some doubt about the fate of Breder. Some historians claimed he'd been killed resisting the NorCon invasion. Others claimed he'd been eaten for some professional failure.

Bibix stopped reading to search for a photo. He found just one. The caption under the full color plate was historically ambiguous. <u>Prof. Bevf consults with Edix and a NorCon delegation.</u>

He studied the image carefully. The professor was looking directly at the camera. She'd been standing in front of a human-style chalkboard. All four of her hands were busy. Two held pointers. The other two held sheets of paper that appeared to contain charts and graphs. Edix appeared to be hanging on her every word. Two NorCons had their backs to the photographer.

Bibix nodded when his new eye twitched, again. "Don't worry, I see it. Her daughter looks just like her, down to the eyes."

According to the photo tag, the picture was now more than forty years old. The wise female who'd been staring at the camera had the same large gray eyes he'd come to appreciate on the Bevf that he knew.

He shook his head. "That face…that chin…those eyes…those brains! You are truly your mother's child. Your family must've pushed you in school. That's why you ended up with glasses. I'm starting to think our first meeting was no accident."

Bibix forced himself to keep reading. His hearts fluttered when he read what was on the next page. "'Bevf was eaten after she failed to win a civil rights case which she argued before the NorCon regional law tribunal. All records of the proceedings were destroyed, as per NorCon decree.'"

The stunned Lapropod closed the book and stared at its dusty cover. "She didn't meet me by accident. She knew what she was doing from the start. She's been leading me on. No. Wait. That can't be right.

Maybe she wants revenge for what happened to her parents? Does she want to help me or use me?"

He sat up and carefully put all of the books in the back seat. The sun was going down and he needed to think. "I'm jumping to conclusions. It's not like she hid the truth from me. I haven't really ever asked about her parents or her past."

He looked at himself in a side mirror. "I really should stop talking to myself."

Bibix guided his lev back to his apartment's parking lot. He was surprised when Bevf stepped out of the shadows. He exited the vehicle and locked the doors.

"Are you a mind reader?"

She approached and took his hand. The glare from a street lamp reflected off her glasses. "I'm just a little

486 | Bibix

freaked out right now. I took a phone call from a high-ranking NorCon this afternoon, and I'm still trying to get over it. I had to see you."

Bibix lead her to the sidewalk and they began to stroll in the fading dusk. "Your scare is my fault. I had a run-in with Commander Sheerz today, and I mentioned your name."

She cringed. "You saw that slug bucket face-to-face?"

"I did," he replied in an apologetic tone.

The worried female slowed down as they turned a corner to go around the block. "I keep forgetting how brave you are. It's hard to keep quiet about all the things you've told me."

Bibix summoned his nerve. "I was under the impression that you've been talking to your most trusted friends about me."

The professor stopped. "I have, but it's not like that. I don't gossip like a human."

"Why not?" he jabbed.

She looked hurt. "You wouldn't understand."

The curator thought about the books in his lev. He chose his words carefully. "I know what our problem is. Well, that's not true. I know what my problem is. I haven't gotten it through my thick head that a lot of us hate the NorCons. We've all got our own reasons for wanting to be rid of them."

She started crying. "Why is this so hard?"

488 | Bibix

Bibix didn't know what to do. He felt helpless in the presence of her tears. There was no one else on the street. He held her close with all four arms. "I think we're doing it. We're finding each other and sharing our problems. It's happening too fast, but we're doing it."

"What should we do now?" she asked, sniffling.

He looked up at the darkening night sky as she embraced him. "We'll calm down and have dinner. Since my apartment's bugged, we'll go out. We'll talk. I have some things to tell you and a few favors to ask. When we're done, you'll go home and try to get a good night's sleep. Tomorrow morning, I'm going to act like a leader and make some very large demands. Then you and your friends are going to help me do something very scary."

Chapter 22

Bibix was particularly demanding over the course of the next two days. He assaulted every Lapropod in a position of high authority with big budget requests and hard questions. With Bevf's help, he made his case for building space, office equipment, and 'Pods to work for him in every extravagant capacity that the two of them could think of. He negotiated aggressively with any NorCon who showed signs of resistance.

The entire settlement was on edge. Bevf's carefully planted rumors fed the evening news broadcasts. Every 'Pod in the region was made painfully aware of who Bibix was and what he looked like. Program directors scrambled to find and run old video clips of

490 | Bibix

Edix. In their drive to learn more about the terror in their midst, media researchers contacted the university's Department of Human Studies.

On the morning of the second day, Professor Bevf was ready to take their calls. "Please don't make me go on TV. It's the one human invention I really don't like. Yes, it's true that Labor Leader Bibix has appointed me to be his Chief of Staff. If you log into the cybernet, you'll find a complete media packet that should answer all of your questions. This is a new era, and Bibix is a different kind of 'Pod."

Bibix made a spectacle of himself, tearfully pleading for NorCon protection. He played his role with all the energy, cowardice, and self-pity he could muster. His behavior was intended to mislead Commander Sheerz. The persistent 'Pod belted out his lines with all the falsely fearful anxiety of any human actor. "Please, Greatness! They hate me in ways you can't imagine. I don't want to be killed by my own people! One guard, that's all I ask. Just one. Please?"

Sheerz enjoyed denying his request. It had Bibix thrown out onto the street three times before it lost interest. "Don't come back unless I specifically send for you. You will give me the labor assignments, and you will do it within twenty-four hours. If you fail, you will be eaten. I will bring in extra troops to eat your entire family and any 'Pod who works for you."

The hapless labor boss fled to his new offices. He rode a private elevator to the top floor, where Bevf and a small coterie of new advisors met him.

They clapped as he caught his breath. "I think I had TV news reporters following me."

She hung a thick gold chain on him and smiled. "Spectacular!"

His eyes wobbled at the ends of their stalks when the cold weight of the chain slapped his chest. "This thing looks silly. Um. Hello to everyone. I'm sorry we don't have more time to get acquainted. Would you all please come with me?"

The gossiping group followed their new figurehead into a large conference room. Bevf ushered the breathless, sweaty labor leader to his chair at the head of the long table.

"I need a drink," he croaked.

She narrowed her gaze, inspecting his appearance. "Talk now, drink later."

He folded his hands in a common gesture of patience while his audience took their seats.

"Say it just like we planned," Bevf whispered.

"Just like we planned," he mumbled through parched lips.

Bevf smoothed the hairs on his head and rapped her knuckles on the hardwood table. "Attention, please! Attention! For the time being, we need to act with some secrecy. It's better if Bibix doesn't know your names. We've all been reading the human books on espionage, so let's use what we've learned. Eyes front and ears open."

Bibix examined the room while he waited for somebody at the far end of the table to close the door. He gazed at the fifteen Lapropods who stared back at him.

Bevf stepped away from the labor leader. "With all due respect…Greatness…I'd like to present the faculty members from my department. It won't be hard for the NorCons to figure out who we are if things go wrong. We can drop the pretenses once we've carried out the special mission you have planned for us."

The nervous 'Pod searched his things for a handkerchief. His transplanted eye twitched as he wiped his damp face. "Yes, we should get started. Does anybody have questions?"

The professor scowled. "There isn't a memo for this. Speak from your hearts."

He put away the wet cloth. "I think we all want the same thing. In one way or another, in one form or another, we've all been prisoners on this planet for the last sixty years. We blame our captivity on the humans and the NorCons. Mostly the NorCons."

Expressions changed. Heads nodded.

He continued, "It's time for us to blame ourselves. We're still in this mess because we choose to stay in captivity. We sacrifice all of our freedom for a few crumbs of security. As long as we don't make trouble, the bucketheads won't eat very many of us. That's the deal we think we made. That's the lie we tell ourselves every day. That's the falsehood we teach our children. From now on, no matter how much it hurts, we've got to embrace the truth and learn how to live with it."

Bevf smiled with affection and pride. Bibix was rambling, but he was making sense. He was getting through to the group, and they were agreeing with every word he said. Would they follow his instructions out of fear, or would they be genuinely inspired? For the first time in her adult life, she wasn't afraid. She experienced love and hope at the same time.

Bibix tried not to lick his lips. "Bevf has told you that I'm planning a rebellion. You're all here today because you can keep a secret. I need your help. I also need your patience and your silence. It's not enough to kill the NorCons. We've got to make them go away. With your help, I'm prepared to do what it takes to make that happen."

An elderly 'Pod at the far end of the table raised a hand. "All I'm hearing right now is a prepared speech. All I've heard for the last few weeks is a long-winded argument and some rather biased claims about your unverifiable exploits. You're not the first Lapropod to plot and scheme, and I don't think you'll be the last. Professor Bevf is proof of that."

Bibix sat up and put all of his hands on the table. He pulled his eyes close together. "I'm well aware of my limitations. I'm aware of yours, too. All of you. We're not an aggressive species. We didn't know what it was to be prey until we came to Earth. The truth is that we can't change our pacifist ways without some kind of outside help. We need an interactive example we can learn from."

A 'Pod seated near Bibix rolled his eyes. "Is this going to be about human religion?"

The labor leader shook his head. "No book, blog, television show, movie, or video game can give us the kind of help we need. I brought you all here today to announce that I've made contact with the human resistance."

Every 'Pod at the table went silent. All eyes jerked, and then focused on Bibix. Somebody coughed.

The nervous conspirator sighed with his genuine relief. "Phew. That's a lot harder to say than it sounds. Please, don't look at me like that. I don't expect you to just take my word for any of this. I brought proof."

The elder 'Pod cleared his throat. "I'd like to see this proof before we go any further."

Many heads nodded as Bevf handed Bibix an old PDD. He turned on the device's holographic projector and set it for wide screen display. The large image sparkled to life near the center of the table. Computer software adjusted the light level in the picture. The view wobbled as Bibix tugged at his camouflage coat. He looked right the camera. He spoke slowly.

His classroom English was a bit stiff. "Hello, my name is Bibix. I am a Lapropod. I'm here in this lovely underground hideout with a human named Carl Tippet. He is my friend. We are about to go and rescue a lot of humans."

The academics assembled around the conference table gasped at Bibix's appearance. He looked so fierce. They didn't know what to say.

"Here's the good part," he assured them.

The image changed to reveal a hairy human dressed in dirty winter clothes. He sat with his legs crossed. Candlelight from somewhere in the room painted him with a sinister glow.

The man scratched his beard with a thoughtful expression. English passed his lips with fluid ease. "Hi. I'm Carl Tippet, on loan from the Alaska National Guard. If you're watching this, I'm probably dead. The fat guy with the goofy eyeballs is called Bibix. He really is here to help you. Pay attention to what he says, and follow his advice."

500 | Bibix

Bibix turned off the display and gave the device to Bevf. "As you can see, I'm trusted. I was in close proximity to that human, and he didn't hurt me. With more careful diplomacy, I'm confident that we can make friends with them."

The oldest academic stood up from his chair. "You're asking us to believe a lot. I'm willing to consider the notion that there might be small tribes hiding in the mountains. They might still be dangerous to Lapropods, but there's no way contemporary humans can be a threat to the NorCons. Their cities have been sacked. Their technological base has been destroyed. They have no armies. Even if every word you say is true, they can't help us. They wouldn't."

Bevf stepped up to the table. "With all due respect, you're making an assumption that relies on an incomplete picture of the situation. The NorCons are not invincible. They never have been. We'd all know that if we weren't so busy trying to stay alive and unhurt."

The white-haired 'Pod rubbed his chin. "Prove it and I'll sit down and be quiet."

"Go ahead," Bibix told her.

She aimed the device at the table. "What you're about to see is video taken during battle. Bibix had a PDD clipped on, and it captured what he did when the fighting was over. I'm warning you now, this is pretty graphic."

Nobody spoke. She hit the 'play' button. The camera's perspective swam up and down for several seconds. Lapropodian hands could be seen gripping a plasma gun. Carl Tippet, armed and wearing camouflage, came in and out of view several times. Bibix could be heard swearing under his breath as he

502 | Bibix

approached a fallen NorCon. Steam rose from several large holes in its mechanized armor. Auto-focus kept the image sharp as Bibix reached into the slushy interior to grab one of the community creatures. The lump in his hand turned green.

The audience gasped and shrieked when Bibix's arm moved past the camera to jam the squirming creature into his mouth. Sounds of rapid chewing made the viewers nauseous. They cringed when the noise of his hard swallow reached their ears.

Tippet's menacing figure came back into view. "I guess you showed them."

The camera recorded Bibix's sticky hand. "I won't be afraid of NorCons any more."

"How was it?" Carl asked from off-camera.

Bibix flicked some of the goo off his fingers. "Exotic. Reminds me of fish. Something like the red salmon that are common to this region, without the bones."

Tippet became serious. "I'm really glad for you, Bibs, but we gotta go."

Bevf turned off the recording. "The NorCons are aquatic community organisms. They're not that much different from some of the creatures on our home world."

The old 'Pod was shocked. "We're being kept subjugated by food?"

The labor leader got out of his chair. "Don't let the comparison fool you! These aren't krellum. These are ruthless, war-loving conquerors who have laid waste to everything in their path. I know exactly what you're feeling right now. I still have the same prejudices."

The scholars began to argue.

Bibix slapped the table. "Shut up and sit down! That's an order!"

Everyone sat in shocked silence.

Bevf remained near Bibix. "I told you this was a special gathering. The NorCon construction project puts us all at risk. They're going to make us work through the winter. Thousands will die. Human intervention is our best option. Bibix can arrange that, but he's going to need your help."

The disturbed 'Pods looked away.

Bibix paced up and down the length of the room to keep his audience off-guard. "With your help, I was able to complete the first labor lists. I turned them in last night. I still feel dirty. Commander Sheerz thoroughly enjoyed my misery."

He stopped next to a small refreshment table to pour a glass of water. "We can save some lives by screening out the sick and the old, but that's just not good enough. I didn't want this job, and I don't want even a single Lapropod's death on my conscience. I'm sorry to drag you into this. If there was another way, I'd find it."

The nearest 'Pod lowered her eyes. "You're embarrassing us."

Bibix wet his lips. "Good. You'll need a dose of shame to be properly motivated. I'm not asking you to save your own spongy hides. I'm asking you to help me save our people."

506 | Bibix

"How can we possibly do that?" somebody hissed.

The reluctant leader pounced on the remark. "You're not fighters, but you are thinkers. When you leave here today, you'll go with truth and proof. Everybody gets a copy of my files. All you need to do is help me run this labor draft. No, really. I'm not kidding. The bucketheads aren't worried about a new trophy hall. They want to fortify this settlement. Do the job, keep a few secrets, and give me time to work with the humans."

He stopped next to the oldest professor. "You've all read Sun Tzu. 'The enemy of my enemy is my friend.' Humans are scarier than NorCons, but we Lapropods aren't eating humans for breakfast, lunch, dinner, and snacks. I've already convinced…some humans…to work with us. I need time to build on what I started."

The senior academic looked at him while keeping one eye on the crowd. "Some 'Pods still practice a form of passive resistance that involves working very slowly. Is that what you want us to do?"

Bibix gestured with his water glass. "Every rebellion has to start somewhere. Build a bureaucracy that'll make their motorized heads spin. Break tools. Mess things up when you can. Force them to put more guards on every work detail. I'll make sure the humans attack before the NorCons can be ready."

"Why would we want to do that?" somebody shot back.

The elder 'Pod made a disapproving noise. "All of you were born on this planet. None of you are old enough to remember what it was like during the first few years of NorCon occupation. Bibix is right. If we force them to watch us closely, the NorCons will stop patrolling the hills and mountains. I seem to remember that humans were very good at sneaking up on Lapropods. We all know the nursery rhymes. No need to repeat them."

Bibix was relieved. He put a hand on the wise 'Pod's shoulder. "Bevf will chair this committee. You will be her primary hands."

The elderly professor puffed with pride. He swung his gaze around the room. Some of the advisors looked away.

Bevf took a deep breath. "I expect good things from all of you."

Bibix drank his water. "Everyone, please get comfortable. I've arranged for dinner to be brought in. We have a lot to discuss, and I know you'll have questions."

"Can't we do this tomorrow?" begged a tired 'Pod.

Bevf tapped her PDD. "Time is blood. From now on, we spend it wisely."

Bibix went for his briefcase. "I've got some handouts. We'll start with the basics of labor management; then we'll move on to covert cell recruitment and personal intelligence gathering methods. I have notes on NorCon patrol patterns. Can we get coffee in here? It's going to be a long night."

Chapter 23

Bibix watched the sunrise from the rooftop of his newly commandeered administration building. It glowed with a soft brightness that fell on the settlement through high clouds. He leaned on the safety rail that skirted the observation platform. Chilly wind battered his cheeks. His eyes turned on their stalks to look at the Chugach Mountains.

Bevf came out to meet him, carrying more coffee.

He waved off the mug. "My guts will fall out if I drink any more of that."

She joined him in admiring the view. "I didn't know that meeting was going to take all night. I'm sorry for that. You must be terribly frustrated."

Bibix rapped on the wooden rail with two sets of knuckles. "We asked them to believe a lot in a short amount of time. I can't blame them for being skeptical. I lied a lot, and I think some of them knew it. Especially that contrary fossil."

Bevf giggled. "That 'contrary fossil' and I go way back. He knew my parents before I was born. He's much more militant than you know."

The tired Lapropod turned both eyes on her. "You've never mentioned your parents before. Tell me about them."

The teacher blushed. "It's not important."

He folded two of his hands together. "My parents are important to me. Why would you say something like that?"

She took a deep breath, obviously gathering her nerve. "It's complicated."

Bibix gestured at the sprawling city. "We just started a conspiracy by lying to some of the smartest 'Pods in this region. There is nothing you can tell me that would be more complicated than that."

"Do you know who my parents are?"

His left eye twitched. "I've read a few things."

Bevf fidgeted with the hot cup in her hands. "My mother was responsible for some of the technology that got us to Earth. My father was a very passionate 'Pod. He was involved in government. Both of them did things during the exodus and arrival that made them famous. They fought the NorCons. My father was killed. My mother was eaten."

Bibix trembled at the agony in her words. "All of that happened when you were a baby."

Her bloodshot eyes blinked behind smudged glasses. "NorCons went out of their way to eat the children of Lapropods who fought back. They enacted a specific military law just for that purpose. It may still be in effect."

That thought sobered him. "Let's go inside."

She followed him into the top floor lounge. "My grandparents raised me. They didn't hide me, not like humans would. They just kept quiet about my parents. I didn't find out I was adopted until I was fifteen."

514 | Bibix

Bibix found a chair and sat. "I can't imagine what that must've been like."

Bevf put down her cups and paced. "I was fine until I went to college. Then I started to run into faculty who had known my parents. They had expectations. They wanted me to do what my parents did. When I didn't run out and start fire-bombing the town, they lost faith in me. Until you came along, I thought they were right."

"It's okay."

She turned away. "No, it's not. It hasn't been 'okay' with me for a long time. The permanent records from that period are all either sealed or destroyed. I've been told a lot of things about my parents that I can't confirm. Some of it sounds good. Some of it sounds very bad. I don't know fact from fiction and it makes me indecisive."

Bibix nodded. Then he shook his head. "You're not indecisive. You're feeling lost without the approval of your parents. You're afraid that believing the good stories about them means you've also got to accept and believe all of the bad stories, too."

"I've heard all this from my therapist."

Bibix stood up. "I'm not a therapist, but I know what it's like to live with that fear. I turned my back on my family to save them from the consequences of my actions. I became antisocial to keep the 'Pods I work with from being hurt. I know what they all say about me. Some is good. Some is bad. To be honest, a lot of it is bad. That doesn't stop me from doing what I know is right."

"Why?" she asked through her tears.

516 | Bibix

He forced the words out. "No matter what happens, I know that my family loves me. My mother's visit to the hospital proved that in ways that still hurt. Even though I haven't lived up to their expectations, they still love me."

Bevf mopped her face with a handkerchief. "From what your mother said, your family is very impressed with you just now."

He took a step closer. "Your parents would be impressed with you, too."

Her eyes turned on their stalks to look right at him. "Some of the old stories about my parents are very unkind. I have a hard time believing that anyone who could love me would do those things. I don't really think Lapropods ate humans, but it hurts me to hear the stories."

Bibix thought about the tales of Lapropod barbarism he'd heard from Carl. "Bevf, we can't change the past. We can change the future. We're both doing things that feel wrong because they run counter to everything we've ever experienced or been taught to believe."

"Do you love me?" she asked quietly, turning towards him.

He reached out to hold one of her hands. "Love and respect."

She smiled and put away her handkerchief. "If this were a human movie, we'd go back to my place and make babies."

He shook his head. "We had four thousand films on file in the trophy hall. I've seen most of them. I'm pretty sure the ritual calls for sex right here on the floor. If we were both human, I'd be all for it. Since we're not humans, I'm going to suggest we each go home and get a few hours of sleep. We gave the committee enough work to keep them busy for a week, but I've still got things to do before my great disappearing act."

She hugged him. "Everything you asked for is in your lev. It's parked in the back, next to the loading ramp. For the record, I don't like this part of the plan."

He led her towards a bank of elevators. "I may not have your credentials, but I'm still a student of history. I'll be killed if I stay, either by scheming NorCons or angry Lapropods. The NorCons will underestimate you and the Lapropods will worship me as a martyr out of guilt and remorse for the chance at freedom they've lost if everyone thinks I'm dead."

Bevf stepped into the elevator car with him when the doors opened. "And we're all surprised when you come back in the spring with an army of human troops."

"Yes." He nodded with more certainty than he felt.

"Have you seen all the stuff on that PDD?" she asked.

Bibix pushed the 'lobby' button. "No," he admitted

She laughed as the elevator door closed and descended. "Your bloodthirsty friend was quite busy with his diary and video. We showed the committee less than half of what he wrote and recorded. That's all I had time to look at. Very scary. Are you sure you can trust him? He looks and sounds like the stereotype of a 'Pod-killing human."

520 | Bibix

Bibix shrugged. "Remember what I told you about his origins. His war never ended. Ours is just getting started. I'll likely be just as nutty, if I can live long enough to get back here."

She followed him out of the elevator when it stopped. "Speaking of nuts, are you ready to deceive your family? I reached your mother by phone last night during the dinner break. She thinks we're coming over tonight for the big intro. Your grandmother was in the background, barking off a long list of demands for the occasion. I'm supposed to have my luggage delivered to the house before we get there, so she can inspect my personal effects before we move in."

"I hope you said yes," he replied through a yawn.

Bevf raised a challenging finger. "If you weren't about to fake your own death, I'd hurt you. That frosty old

'Pod makes me mad. I'm all for tradition, but she goes too far."

Bibix took off his gold chain and put it around her neck. "One word from you, and…"

"I wouldn't!" she protested.

"I would," he muttered.

She pulled him close with playful fury. "I'm an only child, and I didn't enjoy the experience. When you get back, I want four podlings. Not two. Not three. Four. Anything less, and I'll make you wish we'd never met."

Bibix gave her a long, full-throated kiss, using both tongues. "I'm going to bring back a friendly human army that doesn't exist. If I can do that, I'll give you as many pouchmarks as your body can stand. We'll start with four and see what happens."

She followed him to the back of the building. "The committee was very impressed with all the artifacts I took from your apartment. I don't think they're going to miss the weapons and gear you had me put aside. I do have just one question."

He opened the driver's side door of his lev and slid in. "The explosives?"

"The jacket. Why do you have human camouflage?"

He waggled his eyestalks. "Do you like it?"

She paused to check the alley for bystanders. "It's different, in a heart-stopping way."

Bibix reached into the back seat for the military jacket Carl had made for him.

He tossed it to her. "That thing you have there, Professor, is going to be a great conversation starter. Keep it. I'll get another one."

Bevf held up the four-sleeved garment. "I see. Scavenged and modified for Lapropod use. Intimidating design. Does this concealment pattern work?"

"Yes," he lied.

She rolled up the coat and stuffed it under one arm. "Better not let the NorCons see that."

Bibix looked up and down the alley. "Have you ever noticed that they're not consistent about the way they place surveillance cameras?"

Bevf nodded. "Years ago, I heard a theory that they rely on Lapropods to build new camera systems. It seems to me that they break down a lot. Do you want me to look into that after you make your flashy exit?"

He thought about that. "Don't waste your time. If our people are breaking cameras faster than they can be replaced, it means we're not alone in our efforts. Start mapping the city. Try to work out the camera coverage. The gaps in surveillance might be big enough to let you sneak around without being caught."

She watched him close up the lev. "I still wish there was more time for us."

He powered down his driver's side window. "You want to quit and run away together?"

Bevf smiled and went back into the building. Bibix watched her go, and then drove to his apartment. He parked and made his way inside with a large duffle bag. He let himself in with mixed emotions, dropping the bag on the dining room table and entering the bathroom. A long, hot shower helped to relax his body and clear his mind.

He ate a slow breakfast. Time passed before he unpacked the duffle and placed the contents on the floor. A dozen containers of industrial compounds and cleaning products stood like fat plastic sentries waiting for his next command.

He walked slowly through the apartment to collect the things that mattered most to him. Family photos, diplomas, and a few keepsakes were tucked into the bag.

He glanced at the nearest clock. "Not much to show for fifteen years."

526 | Bibix

He flopped on to the couch and reached for the phone. His request to speak with Sector Commander Sheerz was denied.

He left a recorded message. "Good morning, Greatness. This is Labor Leader Bibix. It's just after eight a.m. The next round of labor assignments will be delivered to your office by ten o'clock. You should expect those 'Pods to begin reporting to their project leaders within the next day. They don't like it, but they will obey."

He hung up, feeling smug. Knowing that his apartment might have new listening devices hidden in it, he went quietly to the kitchen. He searched for a lighter, a candle, and a small bowl.

"Time to get ready for work," he said for the benefit of the hidden microphones.

He opened all of the containers and filled the dish with a flammable liquid. He placed the lit candle in it. Then, he reached for his bag.

"I love my job!" he stated with too much pride before leaving the apartment.

The charade was a calculated risk. The NorCons wouldn't believe that he'd been killed in the rather obvious fire, but his neighbors might. The controversy would stir conflicting gossip among the Lapropods, which would work to his advantage.

Bibix drove his lev to his mother's house. The neighborhood was quiet. The family would still be waking up. Breakfast was still an hour away. He left his duffle bag in the empty driveway. Bibix heard the sound of distant fire engines as he took the most indirect route out of town.

He talked to himself as he steered. "You bucketheads will know I'm not dead, but you won't dare say it. You'll stop underestimating us, too. You'll be so paranoid. You'll overreact and send troops into the city. You'll do things that my people will hate. A few choice words from Bevf and, poof, no more labor draft, because the city is in total chaos."

Chapter 24

Three decades of sedentary and uneventful occupation had taken its toll on the NorCon garrisons. Never before in the history of the species had it taken so many compliant prisoners. Administrators overseeing all Earth sectors agreed that Lapropod usefulness was at an all-time high. Harvesting of food and other natural resources proceeded at an unheard of pace. Genocide was unnecessary.

The NorCon masters approved. No conquest had ever yielded such rich returns. The stratified layers of NorCon society had always been led by scavengers. Technological innovation had occurred through assimilation of captured components and whole electro-mechanical systems.

530 | Bibix

The most intelligent and resourceful groupings rose to power in the chain of command through their ability to identify and use the spoils of interplanetary war. The culture that had provided them with the motorized battle suits, which moved and preserved their communities in hostile non-aquatic environments, had ceased to exist. The facts of that glorious campaign were lost to the ravages of time and countless planet-wrecking wars.

The NorCon perception of Lapropod society was limited by technology-driven audio and visual sensory inputs. The community organisms inhabiting millions of powered suits lacked empathy. They experienced emotions within the confines of their liquid enclosures. Audio translators adapted from the spoils of several successful campaigns attempted to read the moods of each group of users, passing on digital interpretations which Bibix and his fellow Lapropods had become skilled at deconstructing and comprehending.

From the start, NorCon occupation policy had been dictated by circumstance. For thirty years, rule by fear and intimidation had gotten the aquatic beings whatever they'd wanted. Casual study of human military systems had enlightened the masters to new facets of surveillance policy and patrol doctrine, which they implemented inconsistently. Thirty years of administration without a single instance of outright rebellion had fostered the assumption at all levels that there was nothing more to learn from either the humans or the docile Lapropods.

Terrestrial predators had been responsible for every known NorCon casualty until Bibix and Carl attacked the food processing plant near the ruins of Wasilla. On its own initiative, Sector Commander Sheerz had investigated the aftermath of that attack. The evidence it found was unsettling. The post-combat release of humans who'd been classified as 'subversive' could never have happened by accident. The attack on the facility had been deliberate.

The threat potential of a human insurgency blinded Sheerz and its subordinates to the growing Lapropod threat in their midst. The loss of cameras in remote areas, when combined with the monitored exploits of Carl Tippet, reinforced the expectation that the humans were at last going to mount some form of resistance. Sheerz cleansed reports and hid the truth from its superiors, including its master, in an effort to save the promotion potential for itself and its loyal underlings.

Surveillance cameras were taken from the Lapropod settlement to replace losses in the field. Equipment failures due to sabotage and mechanical wear deprived NorCon observers of the chance to catch

Bibix in the act of destroying the highly prized trophy hall. The senior curator's extended hospital stay was ignored. NorCons assigned to watch Bibix during his recovery reported that the labor leader complained about anything and everything.

In its drive to prepare for battle, the sector leader relied on recommendations made by two deceased administrators once under its command. Grilleck and Veknar had both possessed exemplary service records. The temptation to push the hated Lapropods into forced labor to upgrade local defense was too great.

Sheerz noted in its own report logs that Bibix was too preoccupied with personal safety. It recommended that the whining Lapropod be replaced at the first sign of failure.

534 | Bibix

The staged apartment fire was reported to local command as an out-of-control blaze. Lapropod firefighters battled the roaring inferno without NorCon supervision for nearly fifty minutes. Bevf watched the scene unfold on TV from the comfort of her own apartment. She was terrified when NorCons from sector command pounded on her door an hour later.

Sheerz was suspicious of what the local news anchors were calling a tragedy. He raged at the professor when she was brought in for interrogation. "I do not believe that Labor Leader Bibix was killed in that fire. His personal transport is missing and our investigators have found no body. Did that coward run away?"

The instructor was careful to get a good look at her surroundings. "Honestly, Greatness, I don't know what you're talking about. We put in a long night. I can provide you with a dozen witnesses. I saw him get into his lev. He said he was going home."

The NorCon walked to the far end of the interrogation room. It stood next to a rack of human tools. "Every vehicle in this vicinity is tracked. His lev is no longer in the area. If he fled, he will be found. You would be wise to cooperate. I know from experience that your species has a low pain threshold. Tell me what I want to know, or you will be eaten."

Bevf shuddered with anger. Family gossip hinted that her mother had been tortured after lengthy questioning, before she was eaten. Then the fear set in. The wily conspirator looked down at the restraints binding her hands. "Greatness, I can't tell you what I don't know."

Sheerz watched the Lapropod squirm in her chair. "Your mother said the same thing."

536 | Bibix

"Excuse me?" Bevf squeaked.

The commander reached for a hacksaw. It held the tool in one claw. "Your gene scan was taken as soon as you entered the building."

She cringed. "You can do that?"

The NorCon enjoyed her obvious discomfort. "Blood does not lie. We have confirmed that you are the offspring of two registered dissenters. Your mother was executed for a long list of crimes twenty-eight years ago. Your father was killed in battle. You were arrested as a matter of procedure. Now that I know—"

As a child, Bevf had often dreamed about the fate of her parents. Their last moments played out in vivid nightmares that left her trembling, half-awake, in cold sweat. Night after night, her overactive imagination conjured screams that weren't real. Those banished recollections came back to her as the sadistic NorCon approached.

"Where is Bibix?" Sheerz demanded.

Bevf's trained mind sprang to life. Each of her eyes searched the interrogation room. Her hands grasped the gold chain that crossed her chest.

Inspiration made her hearts leap. "All right, Greatness. You want the truth?"

The commander threatened her with the saw. "You are the offspring of dissidents. You are expected to lie. Choose your next words carefully."

The schemer took a deep breath. Sheerz wanted to hear something, anything, that wasn't a denial. She'd have to lie if she wanted to live. How did Bibix do this without getting caught?

Bevf narrowed her gaze in a show of fierce determination. "I killed him," she hissed with hate she didn't really feel.

The answer was unexpected. The group consciousness that was Sheerz debated.

Bevf watched the silent NorCon lower the fine-toothed cutting tool into a nonlethal position. Her mind raced to create the rest of her fiction.

"Explain," Sheerz ordered as it stepped back.

The professor regained her poise. She raised a fistful of gold chain. "I killed him because I wanted his job. He was weak and indecisive, and I was tired of doing his work for him. I don't expect you to understand. You have rank and power. I…well…I…you know."

The NorCon was still suspicious. "Your motive is clear, but your actions are not. Where is the body of Bibix?"

She fought the urge to shrug. "I took his body out of the city and buried it."

The NorCon looked at her closely. "Where? Name the location."

Bevf remained outwardly calm. "I don't know. Ten or fifteen kilometers outside the settlement. It was dark, and I got lost. If you find his lev, you'll be within walking distance of his grave. I didn't dig very deep. You can't miss it."

Sheerz hesitated. Her explanation was too convenient. "Lapropods desire personal transportation. Why did you abandon the vehicle?"

The nervous 'Pod shook her head. "I'm not good at killing. There was a lot of blood. It was all over the place. I wanted the lev for myself, but I couldn't take the chance that somebody would notice the mess."

The administrator understood. Lapropods did not condone killing for the sake of professional advancement. Most NorCons abided by similar laws. Every collective, regardless of rank, feared treachery.

The NorCon assumed a threatening pose. "Lapropods are not capable of long marches. You did not walk back into the city."

Bevf wiggled her pods. "Lapropods are built for walking. I had wanted the lev because it's a status symbol. I'm not lazy. I have expensive tastes."

"You are lying," it insisted.

She regarded him with the same authoritative stare she used to gain the upper hand with difficult students. "Nobody liked Bibix. I, on the other hand, am respected in my field and liked by everyone who knows me. I saw the news report. You can pretend he was killed in a needless apartment fire. Chalk it up to poor construction or bad wiring. Maybe it was an accident in the kitchen. Eat somebody to discourage deeper investigations, if that'll make you feel better."

The NorCon assumed a neutral posture. Tiny motors opened its jagged helmet visor slightly. The gesture was intended to communicate disgust.

"You have no honor," it judged.

Bevf jostled her cuffed hands. It was the opening she had hoped for. "I learn from my mistakes. I also learn from the mistakes made by others. That includes Bibix and my parents. Success for you is success for me."

"What do you know about the human threat?" Sheerz asked.

The experienced teacher looked around the room with one eye. "The human threat is whatever you say it is. I'd keep it a secret if it's real."

Sheerz considered its options. This female was more assertive than Bibix had been. Lapropods had an irrational fear of humans that might still be exploited.

It dropped the hacksaw to the floor. "I will approve your appointment to the post of labor leader. You will not be given any protection. If you fail in any way, you will be eaten."

Bevf took another deep breath to hold back the tears. She imagined that her mother wouldn't have cried under these conditions. "I'll get my own guards. As long as you provide me with good supervision, good instructions, and good materials, I'll have my people build anything you want. This is your show."

The ambitious NorCon thought of its master. The Lapropod was more prescient than it knew. Success would result in promotions for itself and its most loyal subordinates. Failure would result in any number of terrible punishments. The prospect of being spilled out of its armored container to die in Earth's low-pressure atmosphere sent the Sheerz collective into a fearful frenzy.

544 | Bibix

The observant academician wrinkled her nose at the scent of sulfur that suddenly suffused the room. She allowed one eye to scan the fluorescent-lit ceiling while she waited for the military leader to speak.

Sheerz made its decision. "Bibix has died in a fire. You will say nothing about the human threat. I will make that announcement when it serves my purpose. I will keep your secret. You will keep mine."

Bevf looked at him with both eyes. "Bibix was right about one thing. You are smart. I won't do anything that could jeopardize your promotion. I promise."

Chapter 25

Bibix worried when he couldn't immediately find Carl's hiding place. The wind blew yellow leaves from the trees growing wild in the ruins of Anchorage. The alert Lapropod drove slowly, using one eye to look for familiar landmarks.

He brought his lev to a stop in a cluttered intersection. The high clouds were getting denser by the minute. He drummed his fingers on the dashboard. A flash of light caught his attention. He focused both eyes on the gleam as it repeated itself.

"Thank you," he mumbled.

546 | Bibix

Bibix drove around a ruined home to park in the overgrown back yard. Tall grass and wild rose bushes sprang up after the lev passed to hide it from casual view. He switched off the power, put on a translator band, and got out.

"Show me some hands!" Carl shouted from a concealed spot.

The Lapropod's left eye twitched. He stood up straight and raised his hands.

"Turn around," the human commanded.

"I came alone!" Bibix protested, turning in place.

Tippet moved closer. "You're not alone, Bibs. I saw an infantry carrier drop off six NorCons ten minutes ago. They're working in pairs, going house to house. There are no cameras this far out from the settlement, which means they're guessing, or you've been bugged."

Bibix shot a frightened look at where the human's voice came from. He lowered two hands to search through his personal effects.

The human stayed in hiding. "Go slow. Look for anything unusual. Check your wallet."

The Lapropod smiled nervously. "The NorCons aren't that sophisticated. They don't plant bugs on us. They usually threaten other 'Pods to do their dirty work for them. They don't bug us to follow us, but they do put listening devices in our phones and homes."

Carl wasn't satisfied. "Do they put trackers in your cars?"

548 | Bibix

Bibix regarded his lev with one eye while using the other to finish looking at his personal belongings. "Location trackers in our levs? Are you serious?"

The human's laugh made Bibix queasy.

"I'm glad you think this is funny," he responded in a hurt tone.

The gruff man didn't speak for several seconds. "I'd like to make you squirm a little more, but company's coming. They'll work fast. You need to unload and go. The bad guys will be here in thirty minutes or less, and I'm sure you'll be missed if you stay out too long."

The Lapropod coughed. "Yes, about that. I'm now a fugitive. I can't go back."

Carl stood up a mere ten meters away. Dressed in dirty, mismatched clothes, he held a rusty knife in one powerful hand. A filthy translator band curved snugly around his bony wrist. "Lie and die. I mean that. Talk fast."

Bibix composed himself as the man approached. "The NorCons put me in charge of an unpopular project. I was afraid for my life. If I had stayed, my own people would have killed me. It really is a long story. Can we go now?"

Tippet stopped just two meters away. "Bibs, your eye is twitching. When humans do that, it means they're lying. I know you little freaks are wired differently, so I'm going to give you five seconds to explain."

The Lapropod kept one eye on the knife and the other on his questioner. "I blew up the trophy hall. It was a spur-of-the-moment thing. I'm still not sure what made me do it. I was injured. I lost an eye. The doctors gave me a transplant. The new one is a little odd."

Carl took a closer looker. "Yeah. I see that now. The left is slightly bigger than the right. The color's a little off, too."

"It is not!" Bibix protested.

The human put away his knife and moved in for a closer look. "You had major eye surgery? A whole eye transplant in just a few days?"

"Stalk and eye."

Tippet shook his head and backed away. "Wow. I heard stories about doctors who could do that sort of thing, but I never met any of them. Lapropod medicine must be pretty good."

Bibix went to the rear of his lev to open the hatch. "We lost a lot of our knowledge and tools when we came to Earth. We lost more to the NorCons. We've been able to reinvent some of what we lost. The rest has come from building on what the NorCons accidentally give us and what the humans left behind."

Carl tapped on the roof of the lev. "This didn't come from us, and it's too small for the NorCons to ride in."

Bibix paused to stroke the vehicle's metal skin. "Most of the original levs we brought to Earth are gone. This one is reconstructed. At least half the parts came from our home world, which makes it a real prize. I think your term for it is 'sentimental value.' It brings back many good memories or happy thoughts."

Tippet leaned into have a look at the cargo. "The only happy thought I want to have right now is the one that gets us out of here. I was hoping you'd have more loot."

The 'Pod flexed his muscles and reached for two heavy bags. "I was hoping you'd have more humans to help us carry all of these things."

Carl reached in for a bag. "Yeah, well, I've got my own stories to tell."

Bibix closed the hatch and followed his shabby guide through a tangle of wreckage into the ruined basement. Two candles provided light. He gagged on an unpleasant smell. "What have you been doing in here?"

The human dropped his bags. "Come and see."

The cautious Lapropod followed Tippet to a corner of the basement.

Chapter 25 | 553

The man lit two more candles with a salvaged lighter. He pulled a dusty tarp off the carcass of a NorCon. Bibix extended his stalks for a better look.

Carl pointed and lectured. "Relax. This isn't a recent kill. This pump they wear is definitely meant to charge the liquid they swim in with pressurized nitrogen. It's not protected. See? No armored casing. It's held in place by a threaded socket. Look here. This socket is kept in place by some kind of weld that I'm not familiar with."

Bibix shrugged. "I have trouble with can openers."

Tippet reached for a candle. "Look at the other arm. This is where the particle weapon hooks up. The weld is different. Check this out. The trigger for the gun is inside the suit. No wonder I couldn't make it work."

554 | Bibix

Bibix watched as Carl put his hand inside the segmented appendage to make the claw do his bidding.

"There are a dozen switches. They start at the elbow and run all the way down to the end. The power cell in the gun provides energy for the entire suit. I don't know what most of the controls do, but I can fire the gun."

The news was encouraging. Bibix eyed the weapon. "Does it have an aiming device?"

Carl pulled his arm free with a wet sucking noise. "These guys do everything inside their suits. I assume they aim and shoot using some kind of interface. I still haven't figured out how they see or hear."

"How many have you killed?"

Tippet dragged the mechanical arm into the center of the underground room. "Six or eight since I've been out of cryo. You can't sneak up on them. Their heads are always moving. Sometimes they turn all the way around. You've got to hide and wait for them to walk by when they're on patrol. I think that means they don't have infrared. They don't do well against snipers. That's how I get 'em: wait and shoot."

The anxious Lapropod waited for the human to gather his things. The man filled a small rucksack and picked up the NorCon limb.

Carl slipped his left hand in it and strapped it in place with a length of cord. "Take two of the bags. I'll get the other one. We'll leave the car and go on foot. If anything happens to me, you keep walking. Stay off the roads and follow the setting sun."

556 | Bibix

Bibix waited for the man to blow out the candles. Then he followed him outside.

Tippet pointed at the lev. "Watch this!"

"No!" The 'Pod shrieked as Carl fired the particle gun.

The projected plasma tore through the vehicle. Metal and plastic ran like water, setting the grass on fire. Bibix chased after Carl as they fled.

"I was hoping to come back for that in the spring!" he protested.

The human slowed down. "You and I are going to talk about priorities."

Bibix cast a forlorn eye back in the direction of the burning lev as he jogged. "I suppose it will make a good distraction. The NorCons will certainly come to see what's on fire."

Carl stopped behind a fallen tree when Bibix fell behind. "We need to keep moving. I left a surprise in the house across the street from our hiding place. It'll go off any time now."

"Where did you find explosives?" the 'Pod wheezed.

Tippet pulled a cracked wristwatch out of his pocket. "It's not an explosive."

"What it is it?" Bibix asked while catching his breath.

Carl snickered. "It's a bear. I lured him in with the guts from a moose that I shot two days ago. Do you know how long it takes a grizzly to eat his fill from an open buffet? About thirty minutes."

The Lapropod started to shuffle forward. "How long has it been eating?"

558 | Bibix

Tippet put away his watch. "Just on half an hour. He'll move when he smells smoke from the fire. This is his territory and he'll defend it. If the NorCons really don't have infrared sighting gear, they'll be in trouble. One good swipe from a bear's claw and off comes the helmet or the pump."

The sweaty 'Pod stopped. "Did you have any luck with those humans we rescued?"

Carl looked at the sky to get his bearings. "Yes and no."

"What does that mean?" Bibix queried as they resume their march.

Tippet swung the NorCon appendage like it was a toy. "It's hard for me to find the right words. I feel like the guy who doesn't know he's the butt of a joke. I keep expecting things to get better, but they don't."

"You're not making any sense," Bibix commented as they slowed to a stroll.

The man struggled with his load and kept walking. "They hid from me. Every time I got close, they moved away. One was killed by a bear. Two more died from exposure. I found their bodies. I don't know if they understood a single word I said."

"How many are left?" the 'Pod asked delicately.

Carl spit. "There's a woman who keeps watching me. I've seen her peeking at me through the trees. She runs if I look directly at her or try to talk. I leave clothes and food in the woods and she takes them. I keep hoping the others will come back for some of that loot, but they never have. They're probably all either dead or long gone by now."

560 | Bibix

Bibix remained silent for the next hour. His pods hurt, but he kept walking. Using all four hands to grip the heavy bags of gear, he stayed just a few steps behind Tippet.

The troubled man stopped when they reached the edge of a long, rectangular field of tall grass. He pointed. "We're about twenty miles from your settlement. This marks the outer edge of the NorCon patrol radius in this area. I've never been able to figure out why they don't keep watch beyond this point."

The depressed 'Pod allowed his eyes to roam. "I think you're mistaken. The patrol radius is twenty-five miles. My people aren't known for their desire to be out in the wilderness. We have too many bad memories of the cold and starvation."

"How are you holding up?" Tippet asked, not making eye contact.

Bibix put his bags down. "I faked my own death today. I burned my apartment as part of the plan, and now I miss it. I left a very nice female to come out here. I was hoping to convince those humans we rescued to help me. Now I'm cold, hungry, and facing the wilderness like my parents did. I feel terrible."

Carl looked around. "I honestly can't remember what it was like to have hot and cold running water. I remember sinks, showers, bathtubs, and washing machines. I can even remember what clean clothes smelled like, but I can't remember the taste or feel of water from the tap."

Bibix picked up his bags. "Trust me, hot water is very nice."

562 | Bibix

They crossed the field and followed the gentle slope of rising foothills until the afternoon sun began to turn red. Tippet guided Bibix to a campsite surrounded on four sides by dense, black spruce trees.

The exhausted 'Pod dropped his load next to a brown nylon tent. "Where do you pee?"

"Pick a tree," the human replied, waving his arm in an expansive gesture.

Bibix returned from his ablutions to find Tippet unpacked and sitting on the ground. The human was building a fire. The 'Pod stood quietly as the man nursed a small pile of tinder into a rising blaze. The process fascinated him.

Carl signaled him to come closer. "You should learn how to do this. There are several different ways to start fires. Save your lighters for rainy days and your matches for the winter. Use dry sticks and wood shavings to get the embers going whenever you have the time. Focus bright sunlight through the lenses of old glasses to light shavings or dry moss."

The 'Pod slowly absorbed the lesson. "Rubbing sticks together to create friction. The wood shavings catch fire and you get to live another day. What happens if you don't have tinder or tree moss?"

The survivor reached into his pockets. He showed off handfuls of bark, spruce needles, and moss. "The joke is, 'Never leave home without it.' I don't know why that's funny, but it's what people used to say. Fire keeps you warm and it lets you boil water so you can drink it. You can survive being hungry. You'll only freeze to death once."

564 | Bibix

Bibix fed more sticks into the fire. "I promised a lot of 'Pods that I'd be coming back in the spring with friendly humans."

Tippet reached into his tent for cooking supplies. "I haven't seen any friendly humans."

The 'Pod watched Carl fill a small, tarnished pot with water from a glass jar and ease it closer to the fire.

"I don't know what to say, Bibs."

After a long silence, the sullen 'Pod muttered, "It's going to be a long winter."

Carl put some dirty fern bulbs into the warming water. "It's not going to be that bad. I've got meat stored nearby. I found a usable cabin, and I've been chopping wood. Trust me, when the snow falls, any man, woman, or child, who can see our smoke will come to us. Frostbite can make anyone cooperative."

Bibix sat down close to the fire. "I once heard a NorCon say that ten percent of the human population was never accounted for after their invasion. I was hoping we might find some of those people and reason with them."

Tippet scratched a bug out of his beard and tossed it into the fire. "Every time I look at you, I see the only thing I've ever really hated. It's affected my judgment. It still does. I don't blame the people we rescued for attacking me. I don't blame them for running away. In their place, I might have done much worse. The 'reasonable' humans you're looking for don't exist."

The Lapropod leaned over to put more fuel on the fire. "We're being watched."

"Don't look." Carl commanded.

Bibix reined in his roaming eye. "Sorry. I didn't realize I was doing that. Lapropods try to watch everything all the time. It must be a defense mechanism."

The agitated man nodded. "If I had eyes like yours, I'd use 'em. Where is she?"

"Behind you," Bibix whispered.

"What does she look like?"

The 'Pod shook his head. "Too many shadows. She's tall. I think she's looking at me."

Tippet laughed. "I'll bet she is. I guess nobody sleeps tonight."

Bibix cringed. "Would she really kill me?"

Carl unbuttoned his shirt to cool off. "She might not know what you are."

A gust of wind blew leaves and tree branches in and around the campsite.

Bibix weighed his options. "She's not running. I know she sees me."

Tippet turned around to stare. "What do you suppose she's thinking?"

Bibix inspected the lurker with both eyes. "I'm not an expert in human studies, but I know somebody who is. I think she's afraid, but she's also curious. Carl, I don't think she knows what I am. What should I do?"

The man got to his feet. He waved to the shadow. "If she had a gun, we'd both be dead."

568 | Bibix

Bibix stood up and repeated Carl's gesture. "Did you give her one?"

Tippet waved again. "Absolutely not."

The 'Pod was relieved. He took a few steps away from the fire.

"We have food!" Carl shouted.

The woman vanished.

Bibix looked at the items in the boiling pot. "I don't blame her."

Tippet sat down. "She frustrates me."

The hungry Lapropod reevaluated his dinner. "I've heard stories about the first winter my people spent on this planet. Millions died."

Carl took out a bent fork and stabbed one of the fern bulbs. He handed the dripping utensil to Bibix. The rebel 'Pod pulled his eyes inside his head and ate the bitter food.

* * *

Two days later, Tippet showed Bibix into the log cabin he'd found. "The door is barred from the inside, which means we can both sleep at the same time."

The Lapropod dropped his things and collapsed on to the nearest bed. "My pods hurt. I have dirt in my teeth, and I think I hate green, leafy vegetables."

Carl sat in a wooden chair. "That mattress is stuffed with cut grass. Don't roll around too much or you'll get itchy."

570 | Bibix

Bibix fell asleep immediately. When he woke, the cabin was dark and smoky. A fire popped and crackled in a stone hearth on the far side of the large, open room. Carl sat in a chair, holding a lit candle while reading a moldy old book.

The human looked up. "Hey, Bibs. Do you read English?"

"Of course," the 'Pod replied, rising from the bed.

Tippet closed the book and tossed it on to Bibix's bed. "Have a look. I found that in this cabin. It's got pictures and descriptions of plants and animals in Alaska that are safe to eat. It's got a few maps in it, too."

Bibix and Carl foraged far and wide as they prepared for the onset of a harsh winter. They salvaged several useful items from an airplane crash site while continuing to gather both food and firewood.

Bibix marveled at the stacks of chopped wood. "Is there some reason they have to be so close to the house?" he asked.

Tippet pointed to the snow-capped mountains. "When that gets down here, it'll be pretty deep. Going outside will be dangerous. Also, if we get attacked, the wood will stop most bullets."

Bibix tried not to think about being assaulted by marauding humans. He adapted some of the recovered cold weather clothing to meet his needs with some help from Carl. Cooperation brought dialogue, which helped the two understand each other. The constant hard manual labor helped Bibix to shed a few pounds of fat in return for new muscle.

The first heavy snowfall came four weeks later, taking the Lapropod by surprise. "I had no idea the snow would be this deep! How will anyone find us now?"

Carl put another log on the fire. "From now on, we sleep in shifts. Somebody needs to be awake at all times. I'll put some spruce needles on the fire during daylight hours to make extra smoke. Cold and hungry people will fight their way through almost anything for a chance at shelter and the possibility of food."

Bibix thought about the woman who had shadowed them a month earlier. "I haven't seen very many humans with good manners."

Tippet stepped back from the fireplace and picked up a gauss carbine. "They might come asking for help. On the other hand, they might come to just take what they want. No matter how badly you've got to go, don't go outside without a weapon. We have the upper hand as long as we don't get stupid."

Bibix and Carl took turns shoveling snow away from the door. The exercise lessened the daily boredom that gnawed at both beings.

"It's called cabin fever," Tippet said bluntly when Bibix asked about the increasing agitation they were both starting to feel. "The constant darkness and snow can eat your brain. You'll do almost anything to keep from being bored. I've seen—"

"I don't want to know!" Bibix protested.

Two days later, Carl was plodding back from the outhouse when he noticed movement on the far side of the snowfield. He rushed into the cabin to grab a damaged rifle scope.

574 | Bibix

Both of them watched the approaching figure with growing anticipation. Bibix gripped the cabin's door and struggled with an old pair of binoculars.

"I can't tell if it's male or female," Tippet said as he watched the person through the salvaged optics.

"Looks like the same kind of clothes you wear," the 'Pod observed.

Carl put down his scope and went for his gun. "He or she might not be alone. I'm going outside to look around. If you hear shooting, bar the door."

The stranger continued approaching slowly. Bibix watched the figure stumble through snow that was waist-deep in places. Tippet ran breathlessly into the cabin several minutes later.

He closed the door. "Our visitor is being followed by a wolf pack. I counted four, but you know there have to be more. They're kind of scruffy looking, which means they're hungry."

Bibix opened the door slightly to peer out. "There was a bulletin, several years ago. Many of the wolves in this region are infected with rabies."

The anxious man peeled off his coat and slapped a stocking hat on his head. "They'll hang around this cabin for the rest of the winter once they get our scent."

"What do you want me to do?" Bibix asked.

Tippet picked up a rusty hunting rifle with a working scope. "I'll climb the woodpile and get on the roof. I've got sixteen rounds for this thing. I should be able to get 'em all before they attack."

576 | Bibix

Bibix understood. The wolves wouldn't give up their prey without a fight. He picked up his own weapon and zipped up his coat. He followed Carl outside into the fading daylight.

The nimble man scrambled up to the roof while Bibix kept an eye on the approaching human. He raised his binoculars with two hands while keeping a steady grip on his carbine with the others.

The stranger fell and didn't rise for several minutes. When Bibix caught sight of the pursuing wolves, he licked his lips. The distance was just over two hundred meters. He raised his weapon and activated the sight. He looked up with one eye to see Carl perched on the roof.

The anonymous refugee slowly stood and waved at the cabin. Bibix waved back.

"Come on!" Carl shouted.

The figure began to trot towards safety. The wolves attacked. Their long, sinewy bodies surged through the snow to reach their prey as it spent valuable energy in a desperate thrashing sprint. Carl checked his footing on the roof, took aim, and fired.

Two animals fell to the first shots. An old cartridge jammed inside the rifle's firing mechanism on the third. Bibix dropped his binoculars and used all four hands to steady his weapon. Both eyestalks retracted as he pressed his face up to the sight.

"They're so fast," he worried out loud.

The howling pack bounded through the snow directly behind the fleeing human. Carl bounded off the roof to land near Bibix. He rolled to one knee. "Stay calm, and keep the crosshairs on the woman. When she falls down, take your shot."

The 'Pod shifted his aim. "How do you know it's a woman?"

The runner's partially covered face leapt into the Lapropod's field of vision, its evident femininity answering his question, as her legs gave out. He fired. The old gauss weapon made his ears ring each time he pressed the trigger. Three wolves fell to five rapid shots.

Carl ran out to help the woman. Bibix kept watch as they entered the cabin. He paced back and forth in an ever-widening circle near the front door in an attempt to stay warm.

Tippet came out fifteen minutes later with a metal bowl to gather snow. His assessment was grim. "I can't tell if it's the same person who spied on us last fall. I don't recognize any of the clothes she's wearing. Her coat was torn, and there were bite marks on her legs. She's gonna lose a few toes to frostbite. She's got scars on her face and hands that are consistent with exposure. I really don't think she's one of the people we rescued."

"Can she talk?" Bibix fretted.

Tippet shook his head as he scooped up the snow. "She wasn't making any sense before she passed out."

The Lapropod looked at his carbine. "What should I do now?"

Carl turned to look back at the distant tree line. "The next few days are going to be real hard. You'll hear a lot of screaming and see a lot of blood. I'll have to get those toes off while she's still out of it. Then we wait and see about the rabies."

"I don't know the first thing about human medicine," Bibix protested.

Tippet continued to scan the distant forest. "I need your eyes more than I need your hands. We only got five wolves. According to that book I found, howlers in these parts run six to twelve per pack. I need you to stay on guard when the sun is up. Shoot 'em when you see them. I'll be too busy to help you. You'll have to do it on your own."

"Any other advice?"

Carl held the bowl in one hand. He picked up his jammed rifle with a free hand and went back into the cabin. "Don't touch those carcasses. Bury them in the snow, right where they are. Use some of the firewood to make a shelter so you can be near the door and still stay out of the wind. Come inside at random intervals to get warm. When it gets dark, come in and stay in until it's light."

Bibix slung his carbine and went to find a shovel. "It really is going to be a long winter," he grumbled.

Chapter 26

Bibix buried the wolf carcasses and built his windbreak. He then paced around the cabin. Two layers of insulated synthetic clothing and mittens on all four hands kept him warm.

"It's so strange to have my pods covered," he complained to himself. "Feels like I'm wearing a diaper."

Carl emerged from the smoke-filled cabin as the sun was beginning to set. "You've been pretty quiet out here," he observed, wiping blood off his hands.

The 'Pod yawned. "I heard screaming."

Tippet leaned on the nearest woodpile. Sweat rolled down his face. "I wasn't kidding about those toes. They had to come off or she'd have died from the infection and blood poisoning. I've seen it before. I can think of better ways to go."

Bibix adjusted his rifle sling. "I'm sorry."

The man searched his pockets, offering Bibix a fistful of smoked meat. "I know you must be hungry. Thanks for giving me room to work. I almost forgot what it was like to have other people around. You should come inside."

The Lapropod took the offered snack. He talked as he ate. "I think the expression is 'out of sight, out of mind.' I'm glad you have a human friend."

Carl picked at his beard and chuckled. "You've been making a lot of sense to me over the last few weeks.

584 | Bibix

We really don't have any choice. We've got to work together. It's that or die in hiding. I've been thinking about that a lot since our guest arrived. I spent nearly half my life hiding from you little freaks."

"Don't—"

Tippet shook his head. "When I was a kid, the old folks used to shine me on about winning the war and taking back what was ours. When I was older, I told the same lies to the next generation of roaming refugees and landfill scavengers. The truth is that we were merely fighting to stay alive for just one more day."

Bibix thought about the wolves. "'One more day' doesn't seem quite so bad."

The man kicked snow off his boots. "You were right about one thing. Somewhere, somehow, we lost our way. I don't know how we can come back from the edge of extinction, but I know we've got to try. That woman in there didn't say much, but she convinced me of that."

"Really?"

Carl raised a hand to shield his eyes. He scanned the tree line. "She's not one of the people we rescued. She's not very well fed – all skin and bones. She had stuff in her pockets that you'd find on any human who was used to living from the land. She never once said a word about you, not even when she was helping me get rid of those bad toes."

"She helped you?" Bibix choked.

Tippet shook his head with a smile. "She doesn't know what you are. Trust me. If she did, you'd know it. She seemed to think you were my dog."

586 | Bibix

The Lapropod rolled his eyes at the ends of their stalks. "Dog? As in 'arf-arf?'"

Carl nodded. "Dog."

Bibix finished the last of his food. "We ate most of the dogs when we arrived," he said thoughtfully. "The NorCons helped themselves to the rest. We didn't even have dog-related artifacts in the trophy hall." He paused. "How can she possibly think I'm a dog?"

Tippet looked inside the cabin to make sure his patient was still asleep. "I've eaten more than my fair share of dog. Look at me. You're missing the larger point. She's not afraid of you. She might not hate you. If she can lead us to other humans who don't know what you little freaks are, we might have a chance to find those 'friendly people' you told your girlfriend about."

Bibix peeked into the cabin. "All I can see is a lump of blankets. Is she on my bed?"

"She was afraid to sleep in mine," Carl said under his breath.

The 'Pod looked at him with one eye. "I'm really not surprised."

Tippet pulled some snow off the roof and stuck it in his mouth to quench his growing thirst. "Relax. She's already into the first stage of a fever. I'll have to stay close for the next few days to make sure she doesn't hurt herself."

"Let me help," Bibix insisted.

Carl realized he was being possessive. "Sure. It'll give you a chance to get used to each other. If she lives, we can give her a translator band."

The Lapropod looked at his human counterpart carefully. "I'm not going to hurt your female."

Tippet blushed. "She's not my property!"

"She thinks I'm a domesticated animal, and you still call me names. When you're not referring to me as if I were a child, you're calling me a little freak. Sometimes, I think you appreciate me. Sometimes, like now, I think you're just putting up with me because I'm necessary. If I can't deal with you, I won't have any chance to live peacefully with her!"

Carl backed away. "Ease up."

The angry 'Pod took one step forward. "No! I won't let you get away with this any more! I'm way past the point of compromise. I appreciate what you can do for me, but I'm not going to take your crap anymore! Humans might be the solution to the NorCon problem, but none of your violent impulses will amount to anything without a lot help from 'Pods like me."

Tippet stared at Bibix for a moment, speechless. He rocked back on his worn heels. "Lots of help, eh?"

Bibix folded his arms over his chest, which was now firmer than it used to be. "You're using every piece of stolen equipment I could bring. I have a resistance network waiting for me back at the settlement. What do you have? So far, all I see is one broken woman and a bad attitude."

Carl looked at the cabin and then at the surrounding hills. "Okay, B-b-b...okay."

"Say my name!" the angry 'Pod demanded.

The embarrassed man swayed. "Okay, Bibix, you win. Just don't hurt the girl."

590 | Bibix

The insurgent checked his translator. "I don't understand."

Tippet went inside the cabin. "It's what the hero used to say in old movies when he was giving into the heavy. It means you won't get any more trouble from me."

Bibix followed the man inside and began warming himself by the fireplace. "Am I supposed to be the hero or the villain?"

Carl knelt by the sleeping woman and pulled the blankets away from her face. "This time, Bi…Bibix, I think you get to be the hero."

The 'Pod came closer. "If she lives, I think we both get to be heroes."

Long brown hair that had never seen scissors framed a wind-burned face that started with a scarred forehead and ended with a small chin.

"What's her name?" Bibix asked.

Tippet moved to the end of the bed to check her bandaged feet. "Hope. She said her name was Hope. Either that, or she's a hallucinating optimist. Come here and look at this."

Bibix shuffled over to look at the woman's mutilated feet.

The human talked while he worked. "We have to change these dressings every time they soak through. Always look at the entire foot. The skin can be pale, pink, or even a little red. Dark red, blue, or green is bad. If we see any blue, the rest of the foot will have to come off. If you see a red line or stripe going up the back of either leg, it means she has blood poisoning that'll affect the rest of her body. That goes right to the brain. You die within a week."

The grim diagnosis made Bibix cringe. "For her sake, I hope she's an optimist."

Carl shook his head. "She had enough toe jam in her boots to make a sandwich. I'm guessing she's been lost and on her own for a while now. It's a good thing she found us when she did. Frostbite kills."

Bibix put his gun aside. He took off his gloves and jacket and then lit a pair of candles.

Carl peeled off the bloody bandages. "She might wake up while I'm doing this."

The 'Pod went to stand where she might see him. "What should I say?"

Tippet reached for a metal bowl full of water. "Be diplomatic. Non-threatening. We have all winter to talk. The food will run out faster with three of us eating, but you know what? For the first time in my life, I don't mind."

Bibix became nervous when the injured woman's eyes opened. They were green. She watched him without moving her head.

"Hello," he said in clear English.

Her cracked lips formed a smile. "Good doggie."

Chapter 27

Time passed slowly for Bevf. Alaska's harsh winter conditions invaded her nightmares as she attempted to keep a tight grip on her duties as both labor leader and conspirator. With help from her handpicked inner circle of like-minded academics, she worked ceaselessly to sabotage NorCon efforts while nurturing a revolt that refused to ignite.

Lapropods in and around the settlement cursed her name as their NorCon overseers forced them to work in subzero conditions. Some 'Pods took the drastic step of putting on winter clothing, when they could get it. Frostbite took a terrible toll on the workforce, causing the hospitals to be filled beyond normal capacity.

Commander Sheerz was forced to call a halt to defense planning when outdoor conditions became too severe. Lapropods everywhere gossiped intensely when it was learned that two of the hated NorCons had frozen to death while standing guard duty. Bevf's conspirators used the incident to their own advantage. They circulated rumors that Bibix wasn't really dead. They insinuated that he was somehow responsible for every recent NorCon death.

Bevf was pleased to discover that many of the patients in the various hospitals were eager to embrace the rumor of Bibix's rise from the dead. Each care unit proved to be fertile ground for wild speculation. She encouraged the notion that Bibix himself had started the fire that destroyed the trophy hall.

Despite her success, Bevf still had nightmares. She soon found herself addicted to sleeping pills. They had become necessary to stop the bad dreams that often drove her to fits of insomnia. If and when she slept, her imagination would conjure Bibix. In some of her dreams, he froze to death. In others, he'd be torn apart by wild animals and left to die in the snow. The narcotics, which she took every other day, allowed her to sleep. Her appetite faltered and she began to lose weight.

Bitter cold and deep snow did more than force an end to NorCon construction. The labor assignments were halted, allowing the surviving Lapropods to stay indoors. They resumed their lives and careers with mixed emotions. Renewed hatred for the NorCons inspired many to venerate Bibix even as they reviled Bevf.

The calendar year ended with six more mysterious NorCon deaths. Lapropods around the settlement observed the local human tradition of giving thanks for what they had while hoping for a better year.

At the turn of the year, a few 'Pods began discovering data disks in strange places. Some were found in mailboxes. Others were found on shelves in stores. A few were found in books at the university's central library. Each disk contained a random portion of the video taken by Bibix during his attack on the NorCon food processing facility.

Those who dared to watch the video found some of Carl Tippet's journal entries and a few of the more chilling still photos he'd taken while evading the NorCons. The evidence offended and terrified those who came in to contact with it. Most of the disks were destroyed by fearful 'Pods who worried for the safety of their families. A precious few were secretly passed from one household to the next.

598 | Bibix

A spineless informer turned in a single scratched disk to the NorCons. Commander Sheerz was surprised and outraged. It summoned Bevf and other high-ranking Lapropods for questioning.

"What are you talking about?" Bevf protested.

"Someone is attempting to start a rebellion!" the administrator bellowed.

The professor tried to ignore the fact that she was strapped into an interrogation chair. "How is that possible? A thousand Lapropods have died from exposure to the cold in the last three months. Another two thousand of us are in hospitals, being treated for frostbite and a long list of work-related injuries. With all due respect, Greatness, that's not a rebellion. That is a medical emergency."

The NorCon leader paced from one end of the brightly lit room to the other. Servomotors whined as it stomped. "Even if this video record is false, it is still an act of sedition. I must be certain that you're not lying. Talk now and your death will be quick!"

Bevf trembled. Images of Bibix and Carl were frozen on a dozen wall-mounted displays. "Are you sure this is real? According to the time and date stamp on the video, these images are at least six months old. Those things happened last summer, long before I met Bibix. That…human…is not my problem."

Sheerz stepped back in to her field of view. "You are an expert in human studies. What can you tell me about this man?"

Her eyes roamed independently, from one image to the next. "He's large. That could mean that he's one of the more successful examples of his species.

600 | Bibix

Humans are known to be exceptional predators. Facial expressions and body language suggest that he's uncomfortable, as if he's in a place that he doesn't like. Where was this video taken? What location is that?"

The community that was Sheerz debated. It chose a softer line of questioning and pointed to the nearest digital image of Bibix. "We found the burned out remains of his lev, but we did not find his body. Our patrols encountered a grizzly bear in the area, which may have eaten his remains. Until I see his body, I shall assume that Bibix is still alive."

Bevf tossed her head in a show of sarcasm and bitterness. "Please, Greatness. Give me some credit. I killed that fat, lazy 'Pod with my own hands. He can't still be alive."

Chapter 27 | 601

Sheerz turned to face his captive. It opened its mechanical maw slightly to menace her. "Your sincerity is not genuine. Even so, I have kept your secret. Now I want your assistance to evaluate the human threat."

The teacher lowered her eyes. "I can't help you if I'm always kept in the dark."

The agitated NorCon stood up straight. "Do you agree that this human could be a danger to your people?"

"Yes."

"Explain."

Bevf studied the NorCon. One of her eyes fixated on his pump as the other sized up the human. She wanted to smash the device and suffocate him.

602 | Bibix

"Single humans were known to have erratic travel patterns. This one has been malnourished in the past, but seems to be in good health in these images. We are, of course, assuming that he is still alive."

Sheerz thought about that. "Somebody has secretly planted this data in the settlement. It is clearly meant to agitate your people. We have unconfirmed reports that there are other disks containing more data. This activity suggests that the human in these pictures is still alive."

Bevf jostled her restraints. "I can't help you if I'm tied up."

The commander picked up a sharp cutting blade. "Administrator Grilleck noted in his reports many times that Bibix was much more useful than the average Lapropod. I find myself making similar observations about you."

"I don't understand." She fidgeted.

He pointed the knife at her. "You are the child of known troublemakers. You may be tempted to be like your parents."

She rolled both of her bespectacled eyes. "Where am I going to go? The temperature outside is thirty degrees below zero on the Fahrenheit scale, even without the wind. My own people don't like me. Humans would take turns killing me. That leaves me no choice. I have to work with you."

Sheerz laid the knife on a stainless steel tray. "The Human Studies department at your university will prepare a threat assessment. Our experts will examine that report for new insights. We will prepare a defense plan for this settlement."

She blinked. "You want us to evaluate a single human?"

The NorCon's translator approximated a sigh. "I want data for a threat assessment. Do you know what that is?"

"No," she lied.

Sheerz reminded itself that Lapropods had no military tradition. "Ambition and aggression are not the same things."

Bevf looked at the NorCon. Her stomach lurched. "With all due respect, Greatness, I don't know what you're talking about. Would you like me to try and find out where these data disks are coming from?"

The commander interpreted Bevf's cooperation as meaning that she wanted to keep her job. "What would you need to conduct such an investigation?"

The instructor licked her suddenly dry lips. She'd spoken too quickly. Now she was obligated. "You could bring this matter to the attention of our police officers, but that might cause a panic. Nobody would like the idea of humans sneaking around inside our city. Everyone would stay home and lock their doors. Nobody would go to work."

Sheerz now realized that it had been a mistake to question the settlement's high-ranking officials. They couldn't help him. Eventually, the human threat would be common knowledge to the Lapropods and, as Bevf had observed, the entire population would be paralyzed with fear.

606 | Bibix

He dismissed the agitated Lapropod and cancelled the remaining interrogations. Merchants, politicians, bureaucrats, and academics were all sent home without explanations. Bevf reported the incident to her fellow conspirators.

"There's human activity outside the city," she explained. "They think our activities are related."

Her advisors were pleasantly surprised by this turn of events. They quietly distributed more disks containing a complete record of Bibix's actions at the NorCon food processing plant.

Those who enjoyed dishing ripe rumors didn't hesitate to pass on what they learned to others who were more reticent. Public opinion quickly became divided. The alleged existence of armed humans caused many Lapropods to dismiss the whole thing as a cruel hoax. They argued that no Lapropod in his right mind would seek the cooperation of any human.

* * *

Weeks passed. The frequency of NorCon patrols inside the settlement increased. Several dramatic raids resulted in the capture of nervous Lapropods who surrendered their copies of the inflammatory media before they were eaten on live television. Rebel leaders released all of the information they'd collected from Bibix immediately after these killings.

Lapropods from all walks of life gathered secretly to be amazed and terrified by the adventures of Bibix. Propaganda materials, skillfully created and carefully inserted by Bevf, proudly proclaimed that Bibix really was responsible for the fire that destroyed the much-hated NorCon trophy hall. Carefully chosen words and images fostered the notion that the very scary Carl Tippet worked for Bibix. They allegedly worked well together, as equals.

Carl's video testimony and graphic journal entries were presented without edits or translation. His personal account of Lapropodian invasion and atrocities set off many debates. A few of the oldest 'Pods shamefully admitted that some of Tippet's incredible stories had a grain of truth to them. Desperate Lapropods had indeed once eaten humans. Defeated Lapropods had ignored or enjoyed the enslavement of humanity in their desire to forget those acts.

Universal shock set in when it was learned that Bibix had eaten NorCon flesh. The barbarity of the act, followed by Carl's profound statement, made this the most popular and controversial piece of video being examined by the insecure insurgents.

The angry human's comments made many stop and think. "'Bad situations can drive us to do bad things. That's how some of us justify staying alive. Nobody deserves to be eaten. Take their lives before they take yours, but don't eat them. Cannibalism is a mindfreak that nobody comes back from.'"

The apparent success of the raid on the food processing plant suggested to many that Bibix might be onto something. The revelation that NorCons might be similar to a very tasty fish inspired a bitter prejudice in every Lapropod who regarded the exploits of Bibix as authentic. Understanding and hate were tempered by the need for self-preservation. Those privy to the new truth were still too scared to act.

Could Bibix really find an army of marauding, bloodthirsty humans who would be willing to save them? Could these legendary nightmares actually defeat the NorCons? Would they hold a grudge against the Lapropods? What terrible price would the Lapropods have to pay for their freedom? Would it be worth the effort?

Bevf was thrilled to learn that 'Pods in and around the settlement were meeting secretly to debate the moral and ethical value of their liberation from the NorCons. Some argued that the elimination of the NorCons would leave the Lapropods at the mercy of the humans. Others feared that a rebellion would fail, leaving them worse off than they had been before.

The most paranoid 'Pods contended that this whole thing was a grand deception, intended to root out and destroy aggressive Lapropods. They insisted that there was no such thing as a cooperative human. Either Bibix was lying or the whole thing was a NorCon scam.

Sector Commander Sheerz continued to monitor the situation. It took every military precaution at its disposal. Its entire chain of command was on alert, ready for the first sign of a human attack. A reserve element was placed on standby to counter any assault. The quirky behavior of the settlement's population was baffling to NorCons that studied it.

Bevf overcame her fears long enough to give new orders. "The bucketheads are looking for a threat outside the city. See how they ignore us? We need to make their fear work for us."

Her followers went into action with greater confidence. Lapropodian informers began to disappear. Their bodies were found outside the city. A few were bound with rope and left to freeze. Others showed signs of physical trauma, as if they'd been in fights. Half of the frozen corpses were discovered by NorCon patrols after hungry wolves had mutilated them.

612 | Bibix

The escalation in violence took its toll on Bevf. Her nerves were shot. "So many secrets. So many lies. I hate being the labor leader."

She appointed 'Pods she could trust to new positions of leadership. "From now on, you'll need to operate as separate groups. Each cell will act on its own. We need to decentralize our efforts so that we don't all get caught."

She checked herself into a hospital just six weeks before the spring thaw. Sleeping pills no longer kept her fears locked away. Sympathetic medical doctors and social psychologists recommended isolation and drug reduction therapy.

Time passed slowly. She refused to have any visitors for fear that they might bring unpleasant news. The conspirators carried on without her. Surveillance cameras were smashed in non-vital areas of the city. Two NorCons went missing.

Bevf ate, slept, or read her favorite books in a windowless room when she wasn't in therapy. Seven days of intensive detoxification restored her appetite. Two weeks of controlled exercise and physiotherapy allowed her to start gaining weight. Three more weeks passed before she was able to manage a normal nine-hour sleep schedule.

The spring thaw began. She was reading late into the night when the sound of a distant explosion got her attention. The blast was followed by a series of unfamiliar noises that reminded her of busy woodpeckers in search of bugs. She put her book down. The rat-tat-tat noise came again. She put on her glasses.

614 | Bibix

Another explosion felt like it came from the hospital's basement. Her teeth rattled as the lights went. She flinched at the sudden darkness.

"What's happening?" she wondered out loud.

Bibix slipped in to her room undetected. "Do you always talk to yourself?"

She fumbled through the darkness to reach him. "You'd better not be a figment of my imagination!"

He switched on a small LED illuminator attached to his vest.

The professor stopped in midshuffle. The smile vanished from her face. The dim blue light emanating from the device on Bibix's muscular chest accented the clothes and equipment he wore, making him look fierce and predatory.

He moved quickly to embrace her with four lean arms and calloused hands. "I missed you, too. Get your things. The sun is coming up. We have to go."

Bevf was hurt when he pushed her away. "Bibix, I was afraid you were dead."

Chaos in the hallways caused him to move towards the door. "We didn't blow the backup generator. It's only a matter of time until somebody turns it on. I wish I had time to say more, but we need to go. We can talk once we're out of the city."

She stuffed her personal effects in to a shoulder bag. "Are the humans attacking?"

Bibix reached out to hold the doorknob with one hand. "Yes. They're here. I said I'd come back for you. I meant it."

616 | Bibix

Bevf followed him out the door. "I wasn't expecting you until the spring."

He pushed his way past roaming patients and hurrying nurses. "The days are getting longer. Spring is here."

He waited for her to catch up. "This way. Turn right and take the stairs. I found the humans. They're going to help us. This attack was their idea. I'm just taking advantage of the moment to save you."

She moved down the stairs after him. "What exactly does that mean?"

"Which part?" he asked as they made their way down to the ground floor.

"Humans," she gasped as she tried to keep up.

Chapter 27

Bibix slowed his pace so that Bevf could follow safely. "It's complicated. I didn't really find them; they found me. Lapropods don't mean much to this group of humans. They don't hate us. They don't particularly like us, either."

Bevf lurched to a wheezing stop as they reached the bottom of the stairs. "Bibix! That makes no sense. Why don't they like us? What have you done?"

He tugged on a sling hook, which released a short gauss carbine in to his waiting hands. "The people I found have been hunting NorCons since the bucketheads landed. We haven't heard of them because they stay away from Lapropod settlements. They agreed to attack this enclave because I convinced them that the 'Pods here would revolt."

A doctor rushed by. "Please go back to your room."

618 | Bibix

Bibix cleared his throat. The 'Pod fled.

Bevf laid a hand on Bibix's warm shoulder. "We are revolting."

He shrugged. "I know. Follow me and stay close."

She watched him handle the gun. "You're not listening to me!"

He sighed. "Yes, I am."

Bevf's eyes wobbled on their stalks. "I'm sorry. I haven't been myself lately."

He raised his gun with two hands. "It's been hard on everyone. This isn't the kind of thing you can put on your scheduler."

She followed him down a long dark corridor. "I tried! I really did!"

Bibix pointed at a nearby fire exit and steadied his gun. "I've been in town for two days. Heard a few things. Seen a few, too. Your parents would be proud. You've done a great job."

Bevf adjusted her glasses as they left the building. "What a choice, liberation or extinction. I wish I'd done more while you were gone."

He sloshed through a puddle of melting snow. "I think you did enough."

She followed him to the end of the alley. Sunrise cast a bright orange glow that made her blink. "I wish I had your confidence."

Bibix grinned and took her by the hand. "See for yourself."

620 | Bibix

Bevf allowed herself to be guided out to the sidewalk. A NorCon was being attacked by a dozen angry 'Pods in the middle of an empty intersection. The sentry was on its knees. Green foam spewed from its open helmet. Pieces of its shattered pressure pump lay scattered on the wet pavement, mingled with the corpses of six eviscerated Lapropods.

Bevf watched in stunned amazement as the mob spilled the contents of the suit onto the street. Dozens of white squirming, scaly orbs turned green as they choked on the cold, dry air.

She turned away. "I can't watch."

Bibix took her hand. "You're going to see a lot worse before this is over."

She allowed him to take her away. "I'm not sure that's possible."

He laughed. "Don't say that until you've met the humans. They have a taste for violence that you've got to see before you'll believe it."

She squeezed his hand. "No matter how this turns out, I'm with you."

Chapter 28

Activity increased inside the NorCon operations center. Sector Commander Sheerz was excited. It relished what it was seeing on a dozen monitors. Heavily armed humans in cold weather gear were infiltrating the city in small groups. Security cameras around the city winked out as troops made hard contact with the enemy.

Sunrise gleamed off high-rise towers while Sheerz listened to NorCon message traffic on its wireless network. All the communities were swimming furiously inside their powered armor. Battle against the legendary humans had at last been joined.

Real-time feeds from the remaining cameras were exhilarating. Humans were working in teams of three, six, or eight to attack NorCons with a wide variety of weapons. Their masked and hooded faces flickered through faltering links as they were projected on flat plasma screens around the room.

The hormone balance in Sheerz's onboard liquid supply changed. The community slowed its frenzied movements. Every NorCon in the area of operations underwent the same transformation.

Sheerz composed itself as its predatory instincts heightened. It gave orders only when they were needed. "Notify regional command that we have engaged hostile human forces. Units outside this region may enter our A.O. to get a taste of this glory only after they've transferred five percent of their trophy hall inventories to our control."

624 | Bibix

The demand was unusual. NorCon units traditionally engaged their foes based on a time-honored formula of battle honors and deployment seniority. Sheerz's demand for tribute had actually been its master's idea. The practice of buying entry into a combat zone hadn't been observed in two centuries. The five percent fee was modest when compared to the percentages that had once been paid for the privilege of doing battle with stubborn resisters.

Sheerz couldn't bear to redirect its optical receptors away from the displays. It watched the invaders closely, appreciating their flexibility and coordination. Automatic slug throwers, gauss repeaters, and energy weapons clutched in gloved hands took a grim toll on his battalion.

"Glorious!"

Standard operating procedure called for the garrison's behavioral analysts to watch enemy activity for signs of predictability. They quickly reported that the humans were directing their fire against NorCons in an inefficient manner.

Sheerz studied a trio of live feeds in an effort to understand. "They are acting to destroy our pressure pumps," it realized.

Every community in the area burst in to sudden rants over a dozen wireless frequencies. Arrogance and outrage fueled their chatter. Every NorCon that could see a human demanded swift and decisive action.

Sheerz resorted to using its digital voice to shout for calm. It knew from first-hand combat experience that a resurgence of enemy forces was always possible. Traffic remained frantic on the wireless networks while it issued new orders.

626 | Bibix

"Primary power grid is down," an underling announced.

"Auxiliary power is out at the hospital," another called out.

The commander refused to be distracted. "All patrols must report to their static defense points. All units are cleared to fire at will. Neutralize any resistance. Target the humans or the Lapropods, as needed."

A subordinate signaled for attention on the far side of the dimly lit room. "New reports. Lapropods are attacking. Some are smashing our cameras. Others are doing things that don't make any sense. Incomplete traffic suggests they are…killing us."

Sheerz experienced a moment of revulsion as it watched a Lapropod, who suddenly appeared with a piece of lumber in hand, make a rude gesture with two hands as it wrecked the video device. The remote camera feed went dark.

There was no doubt in the commander's collective mind that it had been taken by surprise. The humans were obviously striking on their own initiative, which suggested a complex plan of action. Their decision to target sensitive equipment suggested a superior knowledge of NorCon physiology.

Were the Lapropods merely imitating what they saw? Recent discovery of anti-NorCon propaganda made that notion seem absurd. No. The humans had somehow gotten to the Lapropods. There was only one way that could happen.

"Find labor leader Bevf and bring her to me," it demanded.

"We must call for reinforcements," a planner urged.

628 | Bibix

The senior NorCon turned slowly. "We are the first to fight human forces. That's an honor I won't share unless it is purchased. We will rally this battalion and halt their advance. Then we will counterattack with the units who have met our price to join this battle."

"The chain of command will not like that," a logistician warned.

Sheerz raised one claw. "It is the will of our master. Look at those humans and their equipment. Fresh warrior meat. Weapons, radios, and personal effects. Think of those rewards, and your collective. For the moment, we are the chain of command!"

* * *

Bevf allowed Bibix to lead her through the chaos until they reached a public telephone. She pulled hard to make him stop.

"You know it's monitored," he snapped.

She flinched at his behavior. "You're not the only 'Pod with a plan."

"Be quick."

Bibix shuffled to the curb while Bevf made her call. He looked up and down the empty slush-filled street. Lapropods were good at becoming scarce when violence was at hand. His current frustration made him wonder about the 'Pods he'd seen outside the hospital. Were they really fighting back? It was hard to think of what he'd seen as anything else other than revolt.

Bevf made her call as fast as she could.

"Hello?" a mild voice answered.

630 | Bibix

Bevf kept one eye on Bibix. "No names. Do you know who this is?"

"Yes," the 'Pod admitted slowly.

"Do you hear what's going on outside?"

"Yes," the conspirator answered more certainly.

Bevf shivered against the morning chill. "Use your phone list. Start at the top and go all the way down, one call at a time."

"What do I say?"

"Tell them Bibix is back in town." Bevf smiled and hung up, feeling a sense of accomplishment. She pulled the phone cord from the handset and tossed it on to the ice-covered sidewalk.

"My first destructive act," she proclaimed.

"Let's go kill some bucketheads." Bibix replied in an effort to capitalize on her mood.

* * *

Bevf's fellow conspirators had been busy. Her absence had prompted them to act with greater freedom. Some had taken it upon themselves to silence informers. Others had gone after NorCons. The majority contented themselves with minor acts of sedition and sabotage. The aggregate effect of their endeavors was now being felt.

Anxious 'Pods began to receive anonymous phone calls as human infiltrators brought heavy weapons to bear against isolated NorCon patrols. Fear motivated most of the 'Pods who carried out their secret missions. They worked in clumsy cells or as awkward individuals to bollix computer networks and transit systems.

NorCon officers were dismayed when their troops got stuck in traffic. They listened in on human radio traffic that was being sent in the clear as firefights unfolded around the city.

Bibix ran to his rally point, with Bevf huffing and puffing just to keep up.

"Slow down," she gasped.

He slipped into a small space between two parked levs. "Over there," he said, pointing.

She squeezed in behind him, as the sounds of battle got closer. "I smell salt water. Are we close to Kincaid Park?"

"They've been calling it Victory Park," he scoffed.

Bevf cast a furtive glance in the direction of the coast. "I have some influence. Remind me to speak with someone when this is over. I'll have them rename the place, just for you."

"Just don't let them name it after me," he muttered while sniffing the air.

She wrinkled her nose. "Oh, I'd have to insist on it. 'Bibix Memorial Park.' There will be a tall, gaudy monument. What is that horrible smell?"

The 'Pod let the reek fill his nostrils. "Smoke and something rotten. Fish?"

"NorCons."

The reminder caused Bibix to focus. "Watch both ends of the street."

634 | Bibix

She let one eye roam while watching his every move with the other.

Bibix opened a belt pouch and began to assemble the parts for an improvised radio. "Both eyes," he insisted.

"What are you doing?"

He slid a battery into the ad hoc system and clipped it to his right ear. "Short-range radio. I have to announce myself. You can't just walk into a human camp. Carl says it's called 'being trigger happy.'"

Bevf folded two arms and nodded sagely. "I know the term. It's an unrestrained urge to kill, which might actually be considered a form of bad behavior. It's not to be confused with psychosis, which is—'

Her lecture was cut short by the sudden arrival of a NorCon patrol. Two powered suits appeared fifty meters away, near an entrance to the park.

Bibix laughed.

"What's funny?" Bevf hissed as the conquerors paused in the middle of the road.

Bibix touched his radio while whispering in slow deliberate English. "Check, check. This is Eight Ball, on your eastern approach. How copy?"

Bevf strained to hear the tiny voice that crackled in her paramour's ear.

Bibix rose slightly to keep an eye on his prey. "Roger that. I'm looking at two bucketheads near the coastal trail. They're in my way. What? No. No, I can't just 'handle it.' That's why I'm calling you!"

636 | Bibix

Bevf studied the NorCons while she thought about her father and the decisions he'd been forced to make. She put a hand on Bibix.

He looked sideways at her.

"We can do this."

"I won't get you killed," he replied gruffly.

"Are you being sexist?" she bristled.

Bibix looked at the hostile sentries, then back at the outraged 'Pod. "These humans have a saying. 'Die so that others may live, but only if it's necessary.' We don't have to fight these guys. We can go around."

Bevf eyed the devices on his vest. "Bibix, you've got the tools to do this. We could let the humans do most of it, but we shouldn't. It's no good to win the war if we lose the peace. Let's earn some respect for our people by showing the humans that we can fight, too. It's the only way we can make them deal with us fairly after the shooting stops."

He slouched and sighed. "First and foremost, I am not being sexist. Do you see what's lurking over there?"

"I do," she affirmed, nodding seriously.

He allowed himself another peek. "Hm. All we have to do is go around. What's come over you, anyway?"

Bevf leaned on two pods. "Look at them. They have to know we're here. It makes me feel shame. My father would've done something."

Bibix moved in to get a closer look at her. "Oh, no you don't. I miss my father, too. They were good

'Pods, but they're not here right now. We are. You've got to snap out of this!"

"We need to be fighters!" she persisted.

He could see that she was anguished. "Okay. Look at me."

Clouds parted overhead to unleash early morning glare on the placid waters of the nearby ocean. She blinked to hold back her tears.

He ripped open a Velcro holster and took out a pistol. "I can't remember how many of these I took from the trophy hall."

"Fifty-three," Bevf confirmed in a soft voice.

Bibix checked the clip and worked the slide before handing the firearm to her. "Were you able to practice with one, like I asked?"

She lowered her eyes. "No. There's been so much to do, and then I got sick."

He struggled to remain calm. "Did you practice with anything?"

"Hand grenades," she admitted softly.

"I've got just what you need." He smiled.

Bibix put away his gun and peeled off a section of his black nylon load-bearing gear. It held six hand grenades. Bevf hugged him when he bent over to put it on her.

"Where's my jacket?" he asked in an effort to keep her talking.

She wiggled inside the snug fit of the combat webbing. "I'm not sure. I gave it to somebody to be copied, and I haven't seen it since."

640 | Bibix

He slid back half a meter to examine her. "Fragmentation grenades. Flick those tabs with your thumbs to open the carrier. They fall right in to your hand. Pull the pin. Five second fuses. Two of those at once will be enough to knock down a NorCon. Any questions?"

Bevf looked at the devices on her chest. "No. I think I've got this. It's kind of like bowling. Pods apart and elbows in, with an underhand toss. Let's get 'em."

Bibix turned an eye to survey his enemies. "They're headed toward the park. Let's go!"

The Lapropods went from one piece of cover to the next – levs, utility boxes, and mounds of piled snow.

Bibix checked his repeater while using his radio. "CP, this is Eight Ball. You've got bad company coming in, just ahead of me. A little cover fire would be nice."

The NorCons halted when a spray of heavy machinegun bullets stitched the path in front of them. Their helmet-mounted sensors probed the cold brush for the source of the attack.

Bibix darted out into the open and fired as one of the NorCons looked right at him. Aging servomotors in the suit whined as it raised its arm-mounted particle weapon.

A dozen nickel slugs from the Lapropod's gauss carbine bounced off the enemy's upper torso assembly. Three of those errant rounds penetrated the articulated helmet visor. Warning lights flashed inside the suit, alerting the community to the threat of oxygen invasion.

Bevf moved from one obstacle to the next. She judged her distance to be fifteen meters. She pulled three grenades, released their pins, and threw them with all her might.

Bibix forced himself to keep moving. He skidded on the ice as a sudden blast of hot lighting sliced through the air less than two centimeters to his right. The heat blistered his skin. There was no turning back.

Bevf's grenades soared through the air in a slow, high arc.

"Low and slow," she rebuked herself as Bibix fled for cover.

The second NorCon lined up on Bibix and shot.

Bevf winced when she saw Bibix catch fire and fall to the ground. Her grenades bounced on the frozen pavement between the nearest enemy's legs. She broke from cover as they went off.

The close detonation of all three explosives ruptured a series of very old jointed seals in the NorCon's armor. Chaos reigned inside the confines of the armor as hot shrapnel rang off ceramic plates and the mechanized armor fell apart. Arms and legs separated before the protective gear hit the ground. Dark, foaming water gushed from every hole, casting frightened NorCons out into the frosty morning air. The community choked to death as the intact suit of its cohort fell to the ground nearby.

Bevf turned toward Bibix. She hesitated when he waved her off. The remaining NorCon started to rise. Her enemy was just fifteen meters away. She charged.

Bibix thrust himself upright as his angry companion forced herself to a gallop. The NorCon's particle beam had come close enough to set his clothing on fire. A quick stop, drop, and roll in the slush put out the flames. Tiny bits of sand and rock tore at his flesh Blood ran down his back. He fought his way through the pain just in time to see the muddy NorCon face off against Bevf.

Chapter 29

Bevf adjusted her glasses and charged.

Sunlight gleamed off the NorCon's open maw. Its helmet assembly turned from left to right as it attempted to assess its situation. Long-range machinegun fire from the park tore through the nearby vegetation and pinged off its armor. It reported its position and asked for reinforcements. Then it turned on its closest attacker.

Bibix fought through his pain to roll over and lay on his chest as Bevf loped in with a grenade in two hands. Bullets ricocheted off the NorCon's back as it raised its weapon against her. The former curator moved his eyestalks low and close together to better focus his vision. He levered his weapon into place and searched for his enemy's pressure pump.

Bevf hurdled through puddles of cold slush as the NorCon discharged its particle beam. The white-hot flash passed between her left arms. Searing pain caused her to shriek in agony. The jolt was enough to loosen her grip on one of the precious grenades. Fear of the little bombs made her toss it without hesitation as Bibix began peppering his target with probing fire.

The wounded Lapropod was galvanized by his anger. He was mad at himself because he couldn't see where the NorCon had placed its pressure pump. There was only one thing to do. He stood up and changed clips as Bevf pitched her grenade. The flick of her wrist put the ordnance on a trajectory that lobbed it into the NorCon's open helmet visor with an audible plop.

Bevf and Bibix both gasped when the motorized armor came apart with a mighty boom that showered them with droplets of boiling water and pieces of steaming fish. Exoskeleton segments flew in all directions. A cheer went up from somewhere in the park.

Bibix watched in amazement as the hated enemy's helmet hit the ground and rolled to a stop in front of him. He picked it up and approached Bevf, who was trembling.

"I think this is yours," he grinned.

"I pulled the pin," she whined.

Bibix looked at the grenade she was holding with steady three hands.

"I don't know what to do." Tears filled her eyes.

648 | Bibix

He put down the helmet and rummaged through his pockets. "You'd think the humans would've designed these with greater safety in mind."

"Since when is safety a top priority for humans?" Bevf countered with one eye on Bibix.

"Here we go," he said, holding up a small piece of curved, shiny metal.

She cringed. "That's not a grenade pin. It's a paper clip!"

"Same principle."

"Stay back!" she shouted.

Bibix looked over her shoulder. "The humans are coming. You'd better let me take care of that now."

"I'm sorry I ever doubted you."

He parted her fingers just enough to slip the paper clip in to the grenade's trigger. "I was afraid I'd lost you."

"I was afraid I'd lost you, too," she said, her voice quavering.

Bibix felt a great deal of sympathy for her. He knew exactly how she felt at this moment. Then he remembered something that Carl told him about morale, dignity, and the recovery of shattered nerves. He took the grenade from her and hung it on his own vest.

"You did good."

She took his hand as a band of men in improvised camouflage came out of the tree line. "It's really happening," she breathed.

He picked up the NorCon helmet and handed it to her. "Humans like war trophies, so you'd better take this while you still can."

"You should have it."

He blushed. "I've already got four."

Bevf tucked the warm, dripping headgear under one arm. "Okay then. Let's go make history."

Bibix approached the humans, conscious of the fact that he was bleeding from several open wounds. "Hello!" he said clearly waving widely with all four hands.

Carl Tippet burst through the crowd of uncertain men and women. "I saw the whole thing!" he shouted, brandishing a video camera in one hand.

Bibix eyed Carl with veiled suspicion. The human's hair and beard were trimmed. His clothing matched. He was being…friendly.

Bevf edged in closer to Bibix. "Male bonding. Insult him, or he'll think you're weak."

The renegade Lapropod scanned the growing crowd. Men and women were openly gossiping about his people in an unkind way.

Bibix cleared his throat and summoned his best English. "Carl's a great watcher, but he's not so good with the doing."

Anxious glances fell on Carl, who halted in his tracks. He turned slowly to survey the murmuring throng. "I told you these 'Poddies would fight!"

652 | Bibix

Half-hearted applause went up from the gathering. Some of the humans came closer.

Carl maneuvered into their path. "Easy now. Let's take this one step at a time. We'll start the introductions after I've had a minute to debrief these two."

The humans dispersed. A sudden surge in the distant sounds of combat caused many to run back to their posts. Carl got down on one knee and motioned for Bibix to come closer. "Who's your friend?"

"I'm his wife," Bevf pronounced carefully as she approached.

The gaunt man searched his pockets. "I can see that," he chuckled.

Bibix kept one eye on Bevf and the other on Carl. "Why are you in such a good mood?"

The officer pulled a first aid kit from one of his cargo pockets and started to wipe blood from Bibix's dirty face. "This was just supposed to be a raid. In and out. Your intell said the city was crawling with bucketheads. One on every street corner, et cetera, et cetera. We outnumber them, and we're killin' 'em, Bibs!"

"Please don't call him that!" Bevf demanded as she drew near.

Carl stopped what he was doing. "I don't mean anything by it."

She dropped her shoulder bag and war trophy. "Yes, you do. Your remark is a clear and deliberate diminution. I've heard all about you, Mister Tippet. Big, scary, blockheaded human!"

"Stop!" Bibix shouted.

Carl tossed away a piece of bloody cotton. "I don't have to take that!"

"Yes, you do!" Bevf insisted, taking a step closer.

"You're provoking him!" Bibix warned.

Carl looked Bevf in the eyes. "I know all about him. What's your claim to fame?"

The Lapropod straightened her glasses and raised a fist at the angry man. "How dare you question my credentials? I'm the chair for the university's Human Studies department, and I'm also the one who's been organizing local resistance to the NorCons!"

Bibix began to sweat. Humans and Lapropods had a long way to go before they could put aside past grievances. Carl and Bevf needed time to get used to each other. That process of reconciliation might go faster, if they had a referee to curb their baser instincts. He grabbed Carl by his shirt collar. "Shut up or I'll let her take your head off!" he roared.

Carl flinched.

Bevf was stunned in to silence by the sudden show of aggression.

The conflicted 'Pod took a deep breath. "We're not your enemy, but we could be if you don't stop this bad behavior. Work with me. What's causing the battle to go so well?"

656 | Bibix

The soldier glared at both Bibix and Bevf, and then rose to his feet. "Looks like there were a few holes in your story."

Bibix pivoted to face Bevf. "You stay quiet until he's done!"

Carl and Bevf looked at each other. She gestured with her hand, politely indicating that he should continue.

The human dropped his medical supplies. "It's not a raid any more. It's a full-on attack. I was at the command post when you radioed in for help. We face hundreds, maybe a thousand, but no more. There aren't as many NorCons here as you suggested. We seem to have them outmanned and outgunned. Reinforcements have been called. The decision has already been made to try and take the city."

Bevf turned when a distant explosion threw smoke and debris high in to the sky.

"It sounds almost too good to be true," she whispered.

Bibix examined Carl for any hint of subterfuge. "The NorCons will send their own reinforcements. Let's assume that we really do outnumber them. That means we can win this battle. How do we win the larger war?"

"That's a good question," Bevf muttered.

Bibix folded his arms, in spite of the pain. "I remember reading something about the 'export of revolution.' We need support from Lapropods against NorCons around the world."

Carl laughed. "He sounds like this has only just now occurred to him."

Bevf moved next to Bibix. "That's okay, because it already occurred to me. My people had instructions to start spreading the word immediately after I made a certain phone call."

Bibix hugged her. "Bevf, you are fantastic! Carl? We've got to get back in to the city! There are 'Pods waiting for us to direct them."

"When did you manage that?" Carl asked.

Bibix tugged on his combat webbing with pride. "I didn't tell you everything. I asked Bevf and the 'Pods she could trust to form the core of an insurgency."

"How did you manage that?"

Bevf was surprised when she blushed. "I… That is… My family…Which is to say… Yes. Yes I did. I started it. I did that."

"Where are they?" Carl pressed.

A massive detonation on the far side of the park shook the ground.

"What are your people doing?" Bibix asked demandingly.

The tall man scratched his beard. "Not sure. That might've been the NorCon's battalion barracks. How do we get your 'Poddies to fight?"

Bibix looked at Bevf.

She nodded.

"We'll have to lead them," he admitted, his stomach knotting.

Carl scrambled for his first aid kit. "Let me help you with those wounds."

660 | Bibix

"No," Bevf insisted.

"What?" Bibix blanched.

She touched him to get some blood on her fingers. "You'll live. These are minor wounds. Even so, our people need to see that a Lapropod can bleed. We should be prepared to bleed if we really want our freedom."

Carl handed over his radio. "Here, Bibs. Take it. Use my call sign, and coordinate with the CP when you've got some troops to command. We ought to have this wrapped in two days, three at the most."

Bibix took the communicator and clipped it on to his head.

Bevf hurried to pick up her things. "Let's go save the world," she joked.

* * *

The battle lasted for eighteen days. Human forces met stubborn resistance from increasing numbers of battle-hungry NorCons. Lapropods formed into small groups, ambushing their oppressors whenever they had the opportunity, and the nerve, to do so. Casualties on all sides were very high.

The NorCon masters in charge of the region found themselves at a distinct disadvantage. For the first time in their living memory, they lacked the resources needed to end an insurrection. The thought of engaging tough human forces was at times intoxicating, though the temptation was reduced by the knowledge that this foe was on its home world, while NorCon reinforcements were light years away.

662 | Bibix

Earth had already yielded treasure beyond any reasonable expectation. There was no perceived need to spend additional resources on what had already been the most successful campaign in the history of the species. This conservative sentiment was reinforced when new regional revolts broke out around that accursed world.

Two decades of long, bitter battles on Earth convinced NorCon rulers at the highest levels that the far away planet should be abandoned. Vast riches and many useful technologies were already theirs. Many lessons had been learned. Why should they waste any more assets on a world that wouldn't produce new bounties?

The NorCon departure was timed to coincide with a series of brutal bombardments from low orbit intended to cripple human and Lapropod recovery for the next three generations. Dozens of antique starships left that system loaded with NorCon collectives encased in aging powered armor, bound for new unsuspecting targets of opportunity.

Epilogue

Time passed, and new societies began to emerge from the chaos.

"That's pretty much how it happened," Carl said as he stroked his gray beard.

Six podlings, females ranging in ages from six to ten, looked up at him with rapt expressions. The heavy gold chain that had once been the symbol of a labor leader lay on the carpet between then.

Bevf walked into the room slowly. A crown of braided silver hair rode high on her head. Age spots covered half her body. She showed off a tray of snacks. "Your uncle is a bit loose with his facts. Time has played tricks on his memory. Don't believe all of what he told you. Some of it is actually true, but the rest is just for fun."

"Well, that was twenty years ago," the oldest podling pronounced skeptically.

The elderly human scratched his left knee, and then rapped his knuckles on the wooden shin that formed the base of his prosthetic. "I hope you don't think I made this up, too?"

"Why did it take you so long to have kids?" the youngest innocently asked.

"We were very busy, and we only had enough parts to make one." He sighed dramatically.

The children laughed. Golden rays from the setting sun spilled in through an open window. Aromas

666 | Bibix

blowing in on a salty breeze promised something delicious from the hissing barbecue grill out on the deck.

Bevf handed the tray to her expectant brood and went to the window. "Carl? Would you please go make sure your wife doesn't set my house on fire?"

The middle-aged man hauled himself to a standing position and shuffled outside.

Hope smiled at him from her place behind the hot grill. "Sorry about the smoke. Did she send you?"

"Certainly not," Carl lied, stealing a kiss.

She brushed him aside while turning a dozen beefsteaks. "Out of my way, you old marauder!"

"Where's our one and only son?" he asked as he tried for another kiss.

Epilogue

She pointed with a large aluminum spatula. "He's down there, with Bibix."

Carl grunted and shuffled to the nearest handrail. "He goes down to those rocks almost every time we visit."

Hope giggled. "He's got a lot on his mind, unlike somebody I know."

He looked down at the dark gravel. "Are we talking about Bibix or our boy?"

Footprints and a long, dimpled trail of pod impressions marked the passage of a small human and a Lapropod from the rocks down to the tidal barrier.

The woman shook her head. "Isn't it enough that they get along?"

668 | Bibix

He squinted to see through the glare. "What can Bibix possibly tell him that he won't hear from me?"

She lowered the lid on the grill. "Kids don't need to be talked to. They need somebody to listen. You'd know that if you bothered to sit still for five minutes."

Carl fumed. His failing eyes couldn't quite see the pair. In the distance, on the far end of the jagged spit, two figures sat.

* * *

Carl Jr. was mad at the world. "I hate being seven," he confided, his voice filled with spite.

Bibix picked a mussel off the nearest rock and ate it, even though the arthritis made his fingers hurt. His gold-rimmed glasses gleamed in the fading daylight. "Seven's not so bad," he mumbled.

Epilogue

Young Carl wiggled his bare feet. "My dad's telling the war story again. Are you famous? Did you really do all those things?"

Bibix cast an eye back toward the house. He could feel Carl's gaze. "Do I look famous?"

His answer made the boy laugh. "Why do you come down here so much?"

"Can you keep a secret?" Bibix asked pointedly.

"Yes!" The young human nodded emphatically.

Bibix chuckled. "I come down here every time your dad starts to tell that story."

About the Author

Justin Oldham is a legally blind writer who lives in Anchorage, Alaska. He holds bachelor's degrees in political science and history from the University of Alaska. A long-time Alaskan resident and self-described "reformed bureaucrat," Justin's many interests include collecting rare books related to the Cold War and 20th Century science fiction, reading, writing, playing strategy games, and working on his numerous home improvement projects. Justin's other works include the novel The Fisk Conspiracy, the short story collection Tales from the Kodiak Starport, How to Write Conspiracy Fiction, and Being Legally Blind: Observations for Parents of Visually Impaired Children.

For more information about Justin and his projects, visit us at http://www.shadowfusionbooks.com or Justin's website at http://www.justin-oldham.com.

CPSIA information can be obtained
at www.ICGtesting.com
Printed in the USA
BVHW010729151122
651748BV00039B/598